BEHOLD, I COME QUICKLY

The Revelation of Jesus Christ

A Verse-By-Verse Study

RON WILLARD

Behold, I Come Quickly
ISBN: 978-0-692-36777-3

Copyright © 2015 by Ron Willard

Cover Photo Credit © *Ig0rzh | Dreamstime.com - Armageddon Photo*

TwinklingOfAnEyePublishers@yahoo.com

All scripture has been quoted from the King James Version unless otherwise noted.

DEDICATION

To:

The Lord Jesus Christ and the Holy Spirit for they are the real authors and teachers of the TRUTHS revealed in God's precious Word.

To:

My wife, Cheryl, who has untiringly given of herself and encouraged me to write, and has spent countless hours in research throughout our ministry. This volume is respectfully and lovingly dedicated to her. Without her help this writing would not have been possible.

To:

My four children: Sherri, Ronda, Michael, and Michelle. They have been a continual encouragement for me to finish writing this book.

CONTENTS

ABOUT THE AUTHOR

Ron Willard became a Christian during his teens. He attended one year at the University of Idaho studying Engineering and one year at Multnomah School of the Bible in Portland, Oregon. A growing family forced him to seek employment that would support his wife and four children.

A pursuit of a career led him into heavy construction, beginning with building construction, and then leading into bridge construction. He became a project manager, bridge division manager, and estimator. Being a manager and estimator requires one to look at details, have an open mind, and approach problems and schedules with a logical mind. These attributes have helped him tremendously in his study of the Word of God.

In order to rightly divide the Word of God one must first look at the details, then keep an open mind and be able to look outside of the box, and then everything must fit together logically.

Ron has been a Sunday school teacher for over fifty years, teaching over one half of the Old Testament books and all but two of the New Testament books—some of them several times.

His interests have always gravitated to the books on eschatology; however, in order to rightly divide the truth one must look at the entire Word of God.

In his early years of teaching the book of Revelation he taught the traditional interpretation, even though sometimes it did not make sense. Over the years he realized there must be some other interpretation and sought the Lord for wisdom. Eventually, he came to the conclusion that we were looking at portions of the book of Revelation incorrectly. After he taught the book with the new interpretation in mind, his students remarked that the book made sense for the first time.

Ron determined to take on the enormous task of writing a verse-by-verse study for his children so they would understand what was in store for them in the near future, and in the end time.

They, in turn, insisted that the book should be published so all those who read the book would know that the time is short until the world will be judged. They have all cooperated together to accomplish the task of publishing this book.

Ron and his wife of fifty-eight years, Cheryl, are retired and live on *the farm* overlooking a beautiful lake where they entertain their children and friends most every week for a Bible study, followed by dinner and fellowship.

PREFACE

He hath made the earth by his power; he hath established the world by his wisdom, and hath stretched out the heavens by his discretion. When he uttereth his voice, there is a multitude of waters in the heavens, and he causeth the vapors to ascend from the ends of the earth; he maketh lightnings with the rain, and bringeth forth the wind out of his treasures. Every man is brutish in his knowledge; every founder is confounded by his graven image; for his molten image is falsehood, and there is no breath in them.

Jeremiah 10:12-14

Over 2500 years ago God revealed to Daniel what was going to come to pass concerning the "Times of the Gentiles" (Gentile rule over the affairs of the world). Many of those prophesies have came to pass just as he declared, right down to the minutest detail, only because the one revealing the prophesies had infinite wisdom and knew the beginning to the end. The remaining unfulfilled prophecies will also come to pass just as he has declared. Neither Daniel nor the world could understand all of the original prophecies when they were written; however, as God unveils the mysteries through history, mankind can begin to piece together the meaning of the writing. Complete understanding will only be revealed as we come to the last days as world events unfold and begin to unveil the knowledge that God had from the beginning.

But thou, O Daniel, shut up the words, and seal the book, even to the time of the end; many shall run to and fro, and knowledge shall be increased.

Daniel 12: 4

Again, 2000 years ago God revealed to John the conditions that will exist in the world during the church age, the period of Gentile rule at the time of the end, the tribulation period, the thousand year reign of Christ, and during the eternal kingdom as he wrote The Revelation of Jesus Christ. This could only be accomplished because God, the author, in his infinite wisdom knew the beginning and the end. For hundreds of years, man in his *brutish knowledge* has attempted to unravel and decipher what God in his infinite wisdom has known from the beginning concerning eschatology (things to come). Many documents have been written, most of which have been excellent, to reveal truths according to man's knowledge at the time. Just as in the time of Daniel, many of the hidden truths are not going to be understood until history and world events reveal to us what God wants us to know. Many prophesies will not be fully understood until after the fact and we will look back on them and wonder why we were so blind.

As the world has gone from the horse and buggy days to man in space, so our understanding has gone from spiritualizing the meanings of many of the prophesies to an understanding that prophesy can have a literal interpretation. This was largely due to the limited knowledge of man and the lack of understanding that the described events could possibly come to pass as described. Each generation needs to reevaluate their interpretations of eschatology as they experience world events that will have an effect on the outcome of unfulfilled prophecy. Since the beginning of the 20th century there has been very little reevaluation of future events, even though the world has changed dramatically. The writing of this book is an endeavor to incorporate some of the many changes in world events that have occurred in recent years that should reveal to us that there may be a different outcome in the events leading to the end of this age.

The experience of writing a commentary on any book of prophesy is very humbling and is only overshadowed by the fact that it has many rewards in helping others to understand God's precious word. May this be a blessing to all of those who try to rightly divide the word of truth.

Ron Willard

INTRODUCTION

Excitement and anticipation have reached a crescendo. Everyone involved in the upcoming ceremony has given of himself or herself to the point of exhaustion. The invitations have been sent out. Several dresses for the wedding have been fabricated with explicit instructions. Fresh flower arrangements have been meticulously constructed, and all of the many details have been completed in anticipation of this special day.

The final day has arrived in its entire splendor. The bridegroom arrives at the entrance of the ceremony and proceeds down to the front of the invited guests. Excitement is in the air and the place is electrified in anticipation of the appearance of the bride. The music begins and the bride in all of her glory begins her procession to meet the groom at his side in front of the congregation. Whispers are heard throughout the assembly. Doesn't he look handsome in his tuxedo? The flower arrangements are gorgeous! Have you ever seen her so beautiful? What a spectacular wedding dress, it is so becoming on such a beautiful woman!

Where is the excitement? Where is the electrification? Where is the clamor and chatter? One of the greatest events in human history is about to unfold and there is almost total silence. The Son of Man is about to reappear for his bride and take her as his wife. The invitations have not been sent out. No guests have been invited. Little time and effort has been spent in preparing the bride's attire and making arrangements for this momentous occasion.

The Revelation of Jesus Christ, in chapter 1, gives us one of the most comprehensive descriptions of the bridegroom in all of the scriptures. Chapters 2 and 3 likewise give us a picture of how the bride is conducting herself while the bridegroom is away preparing a place for her. The groom is immutable in his character, so his description remains constant throughout the book. It is a drastically different story for the bride. She is portrayed in diverse ways in the letters to the seven churches. In Ephesus she has lost her first love. In Smyrna she is suffering. In Pergamos she is compromising. In Thyatira she tolerates apostasy. In Sardis she is without life. In Philadelphia she is faithful. And finally in Laodicea she has no needs and is indifferent. Is there any wonder that there is no excitement or anticipation for the appearing of the bridegroom when there is such indifference and lack of commitment on the part of the bride?

Between chapters 3 and 4 there is the implication that the bridegroom has taken his bride to present her to his Father in anticipation of the wedding feast. At the beginning of chapter 4 we see a door opened in heaven where John views all subsequent visions and sees all future events from this vantage point. There is the appearance of one sitting on a throne with the living creatures, the twenty-four elders and multitudes around about the throne. Chapter 5 reveals the Lamb worthy to open the seals and advance the narrative.

From this point forward a slightly different approach will be taken concerning the interpretation on how future events will unfold. The traditional interpretation beginning with chapter 6 reveals the rise of the antichrist in the opening of the first seal, which in turn ushers the start of the tribulation period. Chapters 6 through 18 have been taught to relate to this period. There have been many questions that have arisen over the past thirty years of teaching this book that have plagued this author. Some pieces of the puzzle just did not seem to fit properly into the overall picture. These pieces were put into place and did not fit so they were turned around in all directions to see if they would fit in another direction. Sometimes they did fit as looked at differently. Other times they were just pondered and put back into the heart waiting for a future time when historical events may reveal something new that would enhance the meaning to these questions. Some of these questions will be enumerated in the following paragraphs.

The man riding the white horse under the first seal is personified and represents the antichrist as he rises into power. Why are not the men riding the next three horses personified and if so whom do they represent? Must we not be consistent in our interpretations?

Can all of the events occurring in chapters 6 through 18 happen in a seven-year period? The conclusion of many is that all things are possible with God and when the end time events start they will proceed with the action of a trip hammer. During this time many events must occur. The world must be divided into ten nations. The last world ruler must overthrow three of these nations and he in turn must rule for a period of time. This world ruler must sign a treaty with Israel before the tribulation can start. The 144,000 must evangelize the entire world. Is it not more likely that these events will take a much longer time to unfold?

If the tribulation period starts immediately following the rapture of the church then where does the ten-kings-kingdom fit into the picture? How can the rapture of the church be imminent if the signing of a peace treaty between the antichrist and Israel initiates the beginning of the tribulation period and he is not even on the scene? The antichrist must be in power in order to sign a treaty and he cannot be in power until after the ten king's kingdom, when he is to subdue three of these kings. He will thereby be elevated into his position of authority as world dictator. It appears that a period of time and a kingdom are missing from the traditional interpretation. If this period of time and this kingdom do not fall between the rapture and the start of the tribulation then the rapture cannot be imminent.

Why are the trumpet plagues and final vial plagues poured out on the same kingdom when they are so very similar? It seem more logical that the trumpet plagues will be extended to the kingdom of the ten kings and then God will in like manner pour out similar plagues via the vials upon the final antichrist kingdom.

Chapter 13 reveals two beasts, one out of the sea and one out of the earth. These beasts are commonly referred to as the antichrist and the false prophet respectively. In the book of Daniel we interpret beasts to represent kingdoms and horns to represent rulers of that kingdom. When we come to the Revelation of Jesus Christ we personify beasts and make them into the antichrist and false prophet while the two horns of the beast out of the earth are mostly ignored. Why are we not again consistent in our interpretations and allow the beasts to represent kingdoms and the horns represent rulers of that kingdom?

One other question that arises is how does the antichrist and Satan elevate themselves into a place of authority where they will be worshiped by the whole world? It is commonly taught that they just miraculously appear on the scene. Every other diplomat is elevated to a place of authority through his own efforts and political machinery that he has developed around him. Satan is no different as he has been using the already established political systems that have existed since the time of the Tower of Babel. We will be looking at the existing human governments of the world that Satan has and will continue to use as we look at chapters 13 and 17.

It is the purpose of this book to answer these questions and at the same time reveal to the Christian community that the bridegroom is even at the door. In order to put many of the pieces of the puzzle into place we must first endeavor to allow the scriptures to interpret themselves. One of the most important portions of scripture that will enable us to understand God's plan for the future is found in Rev. 17: 9-13. We will endeavor to look at this in detail in the context of this book. We will also show the relationship of the prophecies in the book of Daniel and Matthew chapter 24 to the prophecies in The Revelation of Jesus Christ.

The world is on the verge of being placed under the control of the UN or some other global organization. If the Book of Revelation is chronological in nature this can only happen after the rapture of the church. The church must be in heaven and when the Lamb appears he will open the first seal allowing the entire world to be conquered. Wake up Christians and get excited for the bridegroom is coming. Where is the cry *The Bridegroom Cometh, The Bridegroom Cometh?* He is even at the door. *Behold I Come Quickly.* Even so, come, Lord Jesus.

All references to and quotations of the scriptures used in this book will be from the *Authorized King James Version.*

This writing is in no way intended to be a history lesson. All references to the history of the seven churches in chapters 2 and 3 are taken from *Through The Bible* with J. Vernon McGee. He has personally visited the sites of the seven churches in Asia Minor and has given much information concerning their history and existing condition. Any information included in the messages to the seven churches is only to show how their history should give them insight and understanding into the message that God has sent to the angel of each church.

Much of the eschatology of this writing has been derived from *The Revelation of Jesus Christ,* A Commentary by John F. Walvoord. He is a very well known and respected author concerning Bible prophecy and is a former president of Dallas Theological Seminary.

CHAPTER 1

The Things Which Thou Hast Seen
The Revelation of Jesus Christ

An omniscient God has given us an outline for the book of Revelation 1:19. As we endeavor to understand the meaning of this book we will be viewing it with this outline in mind. Chapter 1 reveals to us **"the things which thou hast seen."** This is one of the most comprehensive descriptions of the Lord Jesus Christ given anywhere in the scriptures. The descriptions given here reveal to us the answers to the problems that are encountered by the churches in chapters 2 and 3. These two chapters correspond to the next great division of the book **"the things which are."** Chapters 4 through 22 are apocalyptic in nature and represent the final division of the book **"the things which shall be hereafter."** These chapters reveal to us all of the events that will follow the age in which we are presently living, commonly known as the "church age." These events will include the period between the rapture and the tribulation period, the tribulation period, the appearing of the Lord Jesus Christ in power and glory, Satan bound in the bottomless pit, the millennial kingdom, the great white throne judgment, and the new heaven and earth.

The Revelation of Jesus Christ, which God gave unto him, to show unto his servants things which must shortly come to pass; and he sent and signified it by his angel unto his servant, John, Who bore record of the Word of God, and of the testimony of Jesus Christ, and of all things that he saw.

Rev. 1:1-2

Chapter 1 opens with the statement that this is the "Revelation, or unveiling, of Jesus Christ." This signifies to us that the writer of the book is about to reveal something that has been hidden from mankind for centuries but is about to be manifest. The thing that is about to be manifest is none other than a very comprehensive revelation of Jesus Christ as He manipulates the events that will culminate in the end of this age. The origin of the revelation is from God himself as He is about to show those things to his servants. The things that He is about to unveil "must shortly come to pass." This does not mean that these things will appear immediately but that when they do begin to happen they will be completed in a short period of time.

The one to convey the message is an angel. He reveals the Revelation to John, the servant of Jesus Christ. The John spoken of here is commonly believed to be the apostle John. The description does fit since he did bear witness of the Word of God. He was one of the few that bore witness of The Son of God as He became flesh and dwelt among us. He was the one that declared that "*In the beginning was the Word, and the Word was with God, and the Word was God.*" And again "*And the Word was made flesh, and dwelt among us.*" (John 1:1, 14a) Throughout the book of John he declares that he is the one that bore witness of the One that he is writing about. He is one of a few that bore record of the testimony of Jesus Christ. He not only bore record of His testimony but also lived with Him on a daily basis, and bore record of the things that he saw. It is no wonder that God chose such a faithful servant to be the recipient of this final revelation and declare to him the things that must surely come to pass.

Blessed is he that readeth, and they that hear the words of this prophecy, and keep those things which are written in it; for the time is at hand.

Rev. 1:3

This book opens like no other book in the scriptures. It not only opens with a beatitude but also closes with a beatitude. There are seven beatitudes in all contained within the book. They are found in: 1:3; 14:13; 16:15; 19:19; 20:6; 22:7, and 22:14. The blessing found here is three-fold in nature.

First there is a blessing to one that reads this book. Isn't it ironic that this is one of the least read books in the scripture? God has given assurance to any one that reads this book that they will receive a special blessing.

Second there is a blessing to those that hear the words of this book. It was intended that the writings of this book should be read to the congregations of the churches to whom it was addressed and to all future congregations.

Thirdly there is to be a blessing to those that keep the things that are written in the book.

In these last days how important is it for us to read the Word of God and particularly of that portion that pertains to the end of this age and the events leading up to the return of our blessed Savior. We are living in an age in which the reading of the Word of God is very much neglected. The hearing of the word is omitted in many of our churches today. Certainly it is not politically correct to keep the things written in the book. No wonder today's church is lukewarm, without faith and just like what the Lord declared that he would find when he returns at the end of this age. This will be discussed further as we look at the letters to the churches in chapters 2 and 3.

The word here is declared to be prophesy. This is true to the majority of the book. Even chapters 2 and 3 were prophetic when they were written. The phrase "for the time is at hand" signifies that the prophetic revelation is near. It does not indicate that the events will immediately appear, however the events of chapters 2 and 3 did follow shortly after this revelation. Nearly two thousand years have passed since the revelation. Today we are waiting for the next big event, the rapture of the church and the fulfillment of the remainder of the book. As we explore these prophecies we will discover that this time is near, even at the door.

> *John, to the seven churches which are in Asia: Grace be unto you, and peace, from him who is, and who was, and who is to come, and from the seven spirits who are before his throne…*
>
> Rev. 1:4

The book is addressed to the seven churches in Asia. These seven churches were located in the western half of what is now known as Turkey. John uses the two familiar terms used by Paul in his writing of the epistles. The first term, "grace" is an expression of God's great love whereby He can declare us not guilty only due to the fact that His Son has paid the penalty for our sins. This is an experience that we may receive, by faith, even though we do not deserve it. It is commonly referred to as "unmerited favor." This represents our standing before a Holy God. The second term, "peace" is what we experience after we have been shown God's grace and know that our sins have been forgiven. This represents our experience with a righteous God.

This grace and peace originated from the very throne of a triune God; God the Father, God the Son, and God the Holy Spirit for they are all three described here. God the Father is sitting upon the throne, Jesus is portrayed as the eternal one, "the one that was, the one that is, and the one that is to come," and the Holy Spirit is described as the seven spirits before the throne. There can be no peace until we first attain grace. These two experiences must always appear in this order. The eternal triune God is the source of both grace and peace.

There has been much speculation as to what is meant by "the seven spirits who are before his throne." Some believe this to be a reference to the Holy Spirit. Others feel this refers to special angels in places of high authority before the throne of God. Isaiah 11:2-3 gives us the idea that they represent the Holy Spirit that indwells the Lord Jesus Christ. Revelation 3:1 indicates that Jesus Christ is the one that has the seven spirits of God. Again Revelation 5:6 tells us that there is a Lamb standing before the throne *"having seven horns and seven eyes, which are the seven spirits of God sent forth into all the earth."* This is not the place to be dogmatic; however, it would appear that these seven spirits should represent the Holy Spirit. If that is indeed true then the triune Godhead is in view here as the source of this revelation since the eternal God the Father, the Son, and the Holy Spirit are all three mentioned here.

> *And from Jesus Christ, who is the faithful witness, and the first begotten of the dead, and the prince of the kings of the earth. Unto him that loved us, and washed us from our sins in his own blood...*
>
> Rev. 1:5

The grace and peace mentioned in verse 4 is again from Jesus Christ for without him there could be no grace extended to mankind. This is only available to those that accept Him by faith for what He has done on the cross for an undeserving world. Grace is extended to the world because Jesus Christ is the faithful witness. He was faithful to represent and do the will of his Father, to be made lower than the angels and become a man. He was faithful to withstand all of the temptations that this world has to offer. He was faithful and obedient to go to the cross and give his life in order to meet all the demands that the Father required for the consequences of sin.

The proof of the fact that he is the first begotten of the dead is the truth that he arose from the dead; *death had no dominion over Him.* Because he arose from the grave we know that we too shall rise from the grave at His appearing. This is the blessed hope of the believers. There would be no hope for this world if He had not risen from the grave. There would be no righteous kingdom for this world to look forward to without His resurrection. There would be no eternity for believers to look forward to without His resurrection.

In order to be the prince of the kings of the earth he must literally be the ruler of the kings of the earth. He will be the ruler over all the kings of the earth in a righteous kingdom that will last for 1,000 years. The condition of this kingdom will depend solely upon the condition of the ruler of the kingdom. If the king is unrighteous then the kingdom will be unrighteous, or if the king is righteous then the kingdom will be righteous.

There is no human being on this earth that can meet this requirement, only Jesus Christ the Son of the living God can meet the criteria of a righteous King. He will rule with a rod of iron and at the same time be righteous, fair and just. What a change from anything this world has ever been accustomed to.

He is the one that loved us enough that while we were yet sinners he died for us. No greater love can a man express than giving one's life for his friends. This great love is expressed in the fact that he has washed us from our sins in his own blood. He not only died for us; He also made it possible for our sins to be forgiven because they are washed and covered by His blood. Since the wages of sin is death (separation), then this is what every man has earned, because all have sinned and come short of the glory of God. However because of God's grace, he can declare us not guilty only because of the fact that the blood of His beloved Son covers our sins.

And hath made us a kingdom of priests unto God and his Father, to him be glory and dominion forever and ever. Amen.
Rev. 1:6

A prophet is a person that declares the words of God to mankind and a priest is a person that represents or stands between man and God. An omniscient God decided in the beginning that a man should be the one to represent and teach other men about himself. God chose Abraham to be the father of a nation that had one major purpose in mind, and that was to show the rest of the world who he is and reveal his majesty and glory as they lived by faith on this earth. He also ordained the church to perform the same duty. Unfortunately both parties have failed miserably in performing their duties.

All that we do should bring glory and dominion to our God and Savior. If the Hebrew nation and the church would have been the priests that they were ordained to be then this is exactly what would have been accomplished. We will see this in more detail as we look at the messages to the seven churches in chapters 2 and 3.

> *Behold, he cometh with clouds, and every eye shall see him, and they also who pierced him; and all kindreds of the earth shall wail because of him. Even so, Amen.*
>
> Rev. 1:7

Behold means to look in amazement. When Jesus Christ returns with power and glory at the end of the tribulation period he will appear in the clouds of the sky and every eye shall see Him. At his appearing in the clouds for his church the only ones to see him will be those that are looking for him. With the technical knowledge that man has come up with today it is not a surprise that every man on earth will be able to see him when he appears in the heavens with the hosts of heaven and the saints. All of the major TV station on earth will be broadcasting every detail of the event.

The ones that have pierced him refers to the Jewish nation. At that time they will have realized that he was the one that was pierced on the cross for them, and they will accept him as their Messiah.

As for the rest of the world, they will be judged directly in accordance to what they have done to those believers in Christ that are being persecuted at that time. Those that have done nothing for the suffering will be ordered to depart from him. Those that have helped the faithful will be invited into the kingdom and live with the Lord for 1,000 years. Because of this judgment all nation of the world will wail. Even so, Amen means that these things surely will be because the Omnipotent one has spoken.

I am Alpha and Omega, the beginning and the ending, saith the Lord, who is, and who was, and who is to come, the Almighty.

Rev. 1:8

Jesus is saying that he is the first and last letter of the Greek alphabet and everything in between. He is all-inclusive and nothing can be added about him that is not already declared. He is without beginning and without end, he is eternal. He is eternal because of His resurrection. History has proven that he was, and his word declares that he will come again and rule this world. If he were not Almighty (omnipotent) he would not have risen from the dead, be seated at the right hand of the Father interceding for us, and come again with power and authority.

I, John, who also am your brother, and companion in tribulation, and in the kingdom and patience of Jesus Christ, was in the isle that is called Patmos, for the word of God, and for the testimony of Jesus Christ.

Rev. 1:9

John identifies himself as a brother in the Lord, and also suffering in tribulation as many other brothers were doing at the time. He is patiently waiting the time when Jesus Christ will set up his kingdom and he can be a participant in that kingdom. He has been put in exile on the isle of Patmos because of his faith in Jesus Christ and because of the testimony he has had for the Lord.

*I was in the Spirit on the Lord's day, and heard behind me
a great voice, as of a trumpet...*

Rev. 1:10

Even though John was in exile and was being persecuted due
to his faith, he had not forgotten his Lord. He was worshiping
the Lord through the aid of the Holy Spirit as had been his cus-
tom since his first falling in love with him.

As he was worshiping the Lord he heard a loud noise like a
trumpet behind him. The trumpet is a very loud instrument and
would surely get your attention if it were blown directly behind
you. Someday soon the noise of a trumpet will sound and all
those that are looking for his appearing will be caught up in the
air to be with Him.

There are times in our lives, like John's, that we think that we
are all alone and in despair due to our circumstances; however
like with John, the Lord has promised that he will never leave us
nor forsake us.

*Saying, I am Alpha and Omega, the first and the last; and,
What thou seest, write in a book, and send it unto the seven
churches which are in Asia: unto Ephesus, and Smyrna, and
unto Pergamum, and unto Thyatira, and unto Sardis, and
unto Philadelphia, and unto Laodicea.*

Rev, 1:11

The voice that sounded like a trumpet behind him spoke to
him and revealed that he was the Eternal Son of God. He was
told that he was about to see some remarkable things and that
he should write them down in a book and to send them to the
seven churches in Asia. As we know these seven churches are the
ones that Paul had visited on his missionary journeys throughout Asia Minor, or in what is known as Turkey today. We will be
looking at each one of these churches individually as we study
chapters 2 and 3.

And I turned to see the voice that spoke with me. And being turned, I saw seven golden candlesticks, And in the midst of the seven candlesticks one like the Son of man, clothed with a garment down to the foot, and girdled about the paps with a golden girdle.

Rev. 1:12-13

John naturally turned around to see the one that was talking to him. What a surprise it must have been to see seven golden candlesticks. We don't have to wonder what the candlesticks represent because, as usual, the scriptures interpret themselves. In verse 20 of this chapter we are told that *'the seven candlesticks which thou sawest are the seven churches"*

Not only did John see seven golden candlesticks but he also saw *one like the Son of man.* This can be none other than the Lord Jesus Christ. He is described as the Son of man since he was born of a virgin and in so doing God became a man and dwelt among his people. While he was on earth the first time he was performing his ministry as a prophet. When he was crucified and gave his life for the sins of the world the Vail between the Holy place and the Holy of Holies in the temple was rent in twain. After his Resurrection he was seated at the right hand of his Father to intercede for us. At this time we have access into the very presence of God only on the basis of what he has done for us. What is about to be revealed to us is that Jesus Christ is performing his ministry as priest during the church age. This is very significant because as we will see in chapters 2 and 3, Jesus Christ is dealing with his church while he is away preparing a place for her. When he comes back in power and glory at the end of the tribulation period we will see him as King of Kings.

Our High Priest is revealed as having a garment down to the foot. This is similar to the priestly robe that was to be worn by the priests in the Old Testament. He is also girded about the breast with a golden girdle. This indicates that he is not only just any ordinary High Priest but that he is Deity since gold usually signifies deity.

It is very significant that he is in the midst of the candlesticks. He is to be the very center of attention in the midst of his bride, the church, while he is performing his priestly duties. He is to be the head of the church and everything in the church should revolve around Him. Unfortunately as will be seen in chapter 3 he is found outside the church knocking to be invited in.

His head and his hair were white as wool, as white as snow; and his eyes were like a flame of fire…

Rev. 1:14

When we think of a person's head and hair being white as wool and as white as snow we immediately think of a person that is old, ancient of age and has much wisdom. Jesus Christ certainly fits into this category since he was with the Father in the beginning, is without beginning or end and is omniscient or all knowing. As we think of white as wool and white as snow we also are reminded of the purity signified in its whiteness.

"Come now, and let us reason together, saith the Lord: though your sins be as scarlet, they shall be as white as snow; though they be red like crimson, they shall be as wool."

Isaiah1:18

We see indicated in this verse that our sins can be made clean and pure like snow or wool if they are under the blood of Jesus. If our High Priest is to be representing sinful man before a holy and just God then he must have these attributes. He must be all knowing, wise, and just in his dealings with his bride the church.

With eyes like a flame of fire we see him as one that sees everything. Nothing is hidden from his sight. He not only sees everything but he also judges all things. When something is thrown into a fire it is burned up and consumed. The one that is standing in the midst of the churches sees their entire goings on and will judge them according to his justice and righteousness.

All of man's works will be tried in the fire and only the gold, silver, and precious stones will remain. The fire will consume the wood, hay, and stubble. What kind of works will you have when you stand before Him?

> *And his feet like fine brass, as if they were burned in a furnace; and his voice like the sound of many waters.*
> Rev. 1:15

Since brass speaks of judgment, as seen in the brazen alter of the tabernacle, we see here that the Lord Jesus Christ will bring swift judgment upon the church for their sins and upon the world for their unbelief. This does not mean that the judgment will come soon, but that when it does come it will be accomplished in a short period of time.

His voice will be spoken with much authority and with power. He must, because of his holiness, keep his word and do exactly as he has said that he would do. If he could speak this world into existence then surely he can judge it according to his will and in accordance with His word.

> *And he had in his right hand seven stars; and out of his mouth went a sharp two-edged sword; and his countenance was as the sun shineth in its strength.*
> Rev. 1:16

Verse 20 tells us that "*the seven stars are the angels of the seven churches.*" Angels are messengers and no doubt represent the ministers or pastors of the seven churches. Isn't it interesting that he holds them in His right hand? The right hand is representative of the strength of a person. These pastors are in a very sure and secure place since no one is able to pluck them out of His hand.

The two-edged sword proceeding out of his mouth is the word of God. It is two-edged since it can bring forth judgment and at the same time forgiveness, hope and eternal life. When he opens his mouth to speak, the whole world will tremble before him, and what he says must surely come to pass because he cannot lie.

When the Lord comes back to earth in power and glory his countenance will shine brighter than the sun. The one that created the sun must be much brighter than what he has created. Who will be able to stand before the one with the two-edged sword and with a countenance brighter than the sun?

> *And when I saw him I fell at his feet as dead. And he laid his right hand upon me, saying unto me, Fear not; I am the first and the last...*
>
> Rev. 1:17

John could not stand before him. When Ezekiel saw the glory of the Lord he fell upon his face. Moses hid in a cleft of a rock and could only see the backside of the Lord. When he came down from the mountain his face shone from the glory that he had seen. If it were not for the grace of God no man would be able to stand before Him. When he appears for his church and we stand before him at the judgment seat of Christ we will all fall upon our faces and cast our crown at his feet because he alone is worthy.

In reassurance the Lord laid his mighty right hand upon John. What a comfort this must have been as his Lord told him to "*fear not.*" John had experienced such comfort many times before when he was with his Lord during his ministry here on earth.

When he said, "*I am the first and the last*" he was indicating that he is the eternal one. He has no beginning or end. He is the one that created all things and he is the one that will bring all things to an end either in final judgment or final glory.

> *I am he that liveth, and was dead; and, behold, I am alive for evermore. Amen, and have the keys of hell and of death.*
>
> Rev. 1:18

Jesus Christ was obedient to his Father and became lower than the angels to be born as a man in Bethlehem. He was tempted in all points as we are, yet without sin. Our Lord was tempted in all three categories in which all sins fall; the lust of the eyes, the lust of the flesh and the pride of life. He was persecuted, ridiculed, spit upon, falsely accused, without a place to lay his head, and hated by the religious leaders of the day. This is the one standing in the midst of the churches as their High Priest and he is the one that will be judging the church and the world according to how they have lived their lives. What a righteous judge he will be since he has experienced all of life's trials and understands our infirmities!

He was also obedient to go to the cross and give his life for the sins of the world. He became death for us, in that he suffered for the penalty for our sins and received upon himself what we deserve to receive upon ourselves. His life was not taken from him but he gave his life because he loved those in the world so much. Three days he spent in the grave and experienced the sting of death that all individuals must go through if He tarries. How can we have a Savior that loves us any more than this and understand all of our sufferings and even death?

Since he is the Son of God the grave could not contain him and he arose on the third day. What a display of Gods power! He walked around Jerusalem, appeared to his disciples, and ascended into heaven. Today he is seated at the right hand of his Father interceding for us. In the future he will come back for those that are looking for his appearing. He will execute judgment upon this world during the tribulation, and he will appear on a white horse with all the hosts of heaven behind him to bring judgment upon the nations of the world and usher in his kingdom that shall last for one thousand years. At the end of the thousand years he will judge all of the people of this earth according to their works, create a new heaven and earth and so shall we forever be with our Lord. Amen.

The keys have reference to authority and power. Hades speaks of the unseen world, a place of torment and a place that is waiting for all those that have experienced physical death without receiving Jesus Christ as their savior. Our Lord has authority and power to determine where all that have walked through the valley of death shall spend eternity. He alone is all knowing, searches and knows what is in the heart of every man. Have you made a decision to trust in the one that has such power and authority?

> *Write the things which thou hast seen, and the things which are, and the things which shall be hereafter…*
>
> Rev. 1:19

John is instructed to write down the things that he is about to have revealed to him. An omniscient God does not want the world to be surprised at what is in store for them in the future. *The things that thou hast seen* refers to this first chapter of the Revelation. John the apostle had lived with and experienced all of the things talked about here. *The things that are* refers to the church age as described in chapters 2 and 3. *The things that shall be hereafter* refers to the remainder of the book.

> *The mystery of the seven stars which thou sawest in my right hand, and the seven golden candlesticks. The seven stars are the angels of the seven churches; and the seven candlesticks which thou sawest are the seven churches.*
>
> Rev. 1:20

God wants us to know when he is talking about symbolic things and when he is talking about literal things so he uses the word mystery here to help us understand that this is something that has not been previously revealed. The words written in the remainder of this book had not been revealed to any other person prior to this revelation. There is some reference to this period in history written in the books of prophecy in the Old Testament; however the church age is not mentioned and many of the details given here were never mentioned there. We have already discussed the significance of the seven stars and the seven churches so we won't go into further detail here.

What is important here is to realize the fact that in this chapter Jesus Christ is unveiled to reveal himself as the High Priest during the church age and that he should be the central figure in all that pertains to the churches of chapter 2 and 3. Every church has a need or a problem, or both, and we will endeavor to show that Jesus Christ is the answer to every need and to every problem. The descriptions of him in chapter 1 will solve every problem and more than meet every need of the churches.

CHAPTER 2

The Things Which Are

Ephesus, Smyrna, Pergamos And Thyatira

Chapters 2 and 3 of Revelation have to do with seven specific churches, each one with a unique problem. As we explore their problems we will be looking at each one from four different viewpoints. At first we will look at the specific church that is addressed. Second, we will look at all churches in general. Third, we will be looking at how these churches represent church history. And fourth, we will be looking at how the message speaks to individual church members.

Always keep in mind that Jesus Christ is dealing with these churches as their High Priest. He knows everything about them and he can meet their every need. We will see that all of the churches have a specific characteristic about them that is unique from all of the rest of the churches.

In the message to each individual church the Lord first of all identifies himself from one of his descriptions expressed in chapter 1. In all seven churches he states that he knows their works. With all of the churches with exception to Smyrna and Philadelphia he has found something against them. In all cases he gives the solution for overcoming their specific problem and tells them what the reward for overcoming will be to those that have an ear to hear.

The church is the central theme in chapters 2 and 3 and is significantly not mentioned again until 22:16. We will discuss this further as we explore chapters 4 through 22 and discuss "the things which shall be hereafter."

Ephesus: The Church That Lost Its First Love

Ephesus was a beautiful city on the shores of the Aegean Sea in western Turkey. It was one of the greatest cities in Asia in its day. She was called "the Vanity Fair of Asia" and "the Light of Asia." Ephesus was both the religious and commercial center of the entire area of both Asia and Europe. The city was formed around the temple of Diana, the goddess of fertility. The statue of Diana was many-breasted, had a club in one hand and a trident or three-pronged spear in the other hand. Diana was the most sacred idol of heathen worship. The original temple was a wooden structure built by the edge of the sea; however, due to the enormous soil erosion in the area the temple had to be moved to higher ground.

Alexander the Great constructed a new temple, which became the largest Greek temple that was ever constructed. It was four times larger than the Parthenon in Athens, with over one hundred green columns about fifty six feet in height of which thirty-six were hand carved. The Goths finally destroyed the temple in AD 256. Around the temple of Diana were performed some of the most vile forms of sexual perversion and the wildest of orgies. The ruins of the city may be visited today and some of the original columns may be seen in Istanbul at the Hagia Sophia, which was built by Justinian.

Paul visited Ephesus on his third missionary journey and remained there for two years. His description of his experience there is expressed in his first letter to the Corinthians where he stated *"for a great door of effectual is opened unto me, and there are many adversaries"* (1Cor. 16:9).

The apostle John came later to become the pastor of the church. He was in exile on the isle of Patmos for approximately ten years and then returned to Ephesus where he is believed to have died and was buried at the present site of the Basilica of Saint John.

> *Unto the angel of the church of Ephesus write: These things saith he that holdeth the seven stars in his right hand, who walketh in the midst of the seven golden candlesticks.*
>
> Rev. 2:1

Each message is directed unto the angel of that particular church. Revelation 1:20 informs us that the seven stars are the angels of the seven churches. Since angels are messengers then the ones mentioned here are most likely the pastors of each church. The message was not intended only for the pastor to read, but also it was to be read before the whole congregation. In each case John is instructed to write.

The one informing John to write is *"he that holdeth the seven stars in his right hand."* The angel is informed that he is in a secure place in the Lord's right hand. He is to be completely controlled by him and under his absolute authority. How unfortunate that the church at Ephesus, many of the churches of our day, and many Christians throughout history, have lost sight of this most important fact.

The message is also from the one *"who walketh in the midst of the seven golden candlesticks."* Jesus Christ is alive today, because he rose from the grave, and he has not forgotten his bride, the church, but is walking up and down observing every movement and decision that she makes with anticipation of his return for his bride. There is no limit to the love that he has bestowed upon his bride and there is no limit to the love that he is waiting to extend to her throughout eternity. How blessed we are to have a Savior who is so attentive and concerned about each and every one of his loved ones.

I know thy works, and thy labor, and thy patience, and how thou canst not bear them who are evil; and thou hast tried them who say they are apostles, and are not, and hast found them liars; And hast borne, and hast patience, and for my name's sake hast labored, and hast not fainted.

Rev. 2:2-3

Seven words of commendation for the church at Ephesus are expressed here:

1. Works

In every message to every church the Lord reminds them that *"I know thy works."* He is the Omniscient One walking up and down observing their every movement. When God speaks of works he is always speaking of the works of righteousness that follow the salvation of believers. The works of self righteousness performed by unbelievers prior to salvation appear as *filthy rags* before the Lord.

2. Labor

The difference between works and labor is that labor carries a meaning of weariness in it. A person can work without getting weary, but he can't get weary without working. The Christians at Ephesus not only worked, but they worked until they were weary.

3. Patience

This is a fruit of the Spirit and it should be applied to our attitude towards others, all of life's circumstances, and in looking for our Lord's return. What a wonderful attribute to possess.

4. Can't Bear Them That Are Evil

The church at Ephesus had evil all around them; however, they did not participate in that evil nor did they tolerate those that made it their life practice. We are to be in the world but not of the world.

5. They Tried Them That Say They Are Apostles And Are Not

Every one that came to Ephesus and claimed to be an apostle was tested to see if he was telling the truth. They were not gullible nor did they accept everyone for what he claimed to be or accept every wind of doctrine that came along. The church was well-grounded in doctrine and was not easily led astray. Oh what a shame that this is not true of many of our churches today.

6. Hast Borne…..For My Name's Sake Hast Labored

For His name's sake they were preaching the gospel of Jesus Christ, the One who died for the sins of the world. They believed in and were preaching that he was virgin born, he was Deity, he died a sacrificial death and he was resurrected. For this they were paying a price.

7. And Hast Not Fainted

This means that they did not grow weary in proclaiming the gospel of their Lord and Savior. Earlier it was said that they grew weary in their works. The difference here is that they never grew weary *of* their work, but they grew weary *in* their work. A person can get very tired when he works hard. This does not mean that he is not enjoying his work and that he would like to change his occupation.

> *Nevertheless, I have something against thee, because thou hast left thy first love.*
>
> Rev. 2:4

Even though the early church had works, labor, patience, hated evil, questioned false teaching, had borne for His name's sake, and had not fainted; they also had one main condemnation. That condemnation was to become the signature characteristic problem in their lives. They were beginning to lose their enthusiastic devotion for their Lord.

Sometimes it is hard for us, in our day of skepticism, to understand how a church could have such devotion for the one who gave himself for them and was willing to give his life for them. We, however, have not had the opportunity like the apostles, to walk and talk with him on a daily basis while he was upon this earth. This church had a personal relationship with Jesus Christ like no other church. They had an opportunity to reach out to all of the many dignitaries and world leaders that passed through this beautiful and commercial city. Their light could shine brighter in this environment than anywhere else in the known world. This church took advantage of their situation, however. The worldly conditions that existed in Ephesus began to creep into the church and they gradually lost the love that they had had in the beginning. How easy for the pull of the world to creep into our lives and rob us of our devotion for Him. This is the first step toward backsliding and eventually leading to total apostasy. As we progress through the messages to the seven churches we will see the steps that will lead us on a downward spiral that will eventually cause us to end up lukewarm and indifferent.

> *Remember, therefore, from where thou art fallen, and repent,*
> *and do the first works, or else I will come unto thee quickly,*
> *and will remove thy candlestick out of its place, except thou*
> *repent.*
>
> Rev. 2:5

The first thing that we need to do when we begin to become complacent is to remember. Remember where we were in our walk with the Lord and do whatever is required to climb back up to the place that we have fallen from. The next thing that is required is that we repent. To repent means that we turn about face and proceed in the opposite direction, in a direction that will lead us back to the place from which we have fallen. The next step is to again do the works that we were doing when we first fell in love with our Lord.

If we do not remember and repent then the Lord will come quickly and remove our light that is supposed to be shining in this sinful world. This is apparently exactly what happened to the church at Ephesus since if you go there today the only things that you will find are the ruins of this once beautiful and prosperous city. What a travesty that this would be the end of such a testimony in the world. This is a very real possibility for every believer that gradually loses his love for the Lord and turns his affection on the things of the world.

But this thou hast, that thou hatest the deeds of the Nicolaitans, which I also hate.

Rev. 2:6

Some scholars believe that the word *Nicolaitans* is a compound word comprised of *Nikao*, which means, "to conquer" and *laos* which means "the people." These scholars also believe that a priestly order was beginning to form that exalted themselves above the laity which thing God would hate. If indeed this is true then they should be commended for such action.

The other explanation for what this means is that there was a person by the name of Nicolaus of Antioch who believed that the only way a person can know what sin is, is to indulge in it. They gave themselves over to sensuality, thinking that their sin did not touch their spirit; therefore, it was doing them no harm. This is probably the best explanation for the meaning of this phrase. The church at Ephesus should be commended for hating this doctrine. We will later learn that the church at Pergamos embraced this false teaching. It should be noted that the church at Ephesus did not have a problem doctrinally, but had a heart problem that would eventually cause them to lose their light in the world.

He that hath an ear, let him hear what the Spirit saith unto the churches: To him that overcometh will I give to eat of the tree of life, which is in the midst of the paradise of God.

Rev. 2:7

Only the one who knows the Lord as his personal savior can have an ear to hear. *But the natural man receiveth not the things of the Spirit of God; for they are foolishness unto him, neither can he know them, because they are spiritually discerned. (1 Cor. 2:14)* The natural man is one who has never come to the saving knowledge of the Lord Jesus Christ and has not received the Holy Spirit into his life. This person can, therefore, not hear what the Spirit is saying to him because he does not possess the Spirit in his life.

The only way to be able to hear what the Spirit has to say is to realize that you have sinned and have earned death (separation from God), and can never come into His presence. You must confess (agree with God) that you are lost and in need of a savior. Then you must believe (have faith) that Jesus Christ is who he said he is (The only begotten Son of God), and decide to trust him as your savior. If you do this then the Holy Spirit will make you a new creation and give you understanding of spiritual things.

If you know Jesus Christ as your savior then you should let the Spirit talk to you about your spiritual condition. In this case he wants to talk to you about your love for Jesus Christ. If you are losing this love then you are in danger of backsliding and losing your light. Again, this is the first step in a downward spiral.

If you listen to the Spirit and remember from where you have fallen and then repent, only then will the Lord allow you to eat of the tree of life. Since this tree is in the paradise of God the only place to partake of it is in the eternal paradise and new heaven that God has prepared for us. The tree of life will enable us to enjoy life to the fullest and will provide healing for the nations. In this life we cannot begin to enjoy life to the fullest extent that God has intended for us due to our old sinful nature and the frailty of our bodies.

Applications

1. Specific Church

When we look at the message to the church at Ephesus we see that this specific church is in danger of losing its first love. Only history can bear out that this is probably what happened to them, because God has removed their witness in their place of influence.

2. Churches in General

When we look at Christendom in general we have seen many churches go down this path, and they no longer have an impact in this world. We see this in many of our universities that were founded on Christian principles, but have been taken over by liberal ideals and no longer have a witness for Jesus Christ. God has removed the light that was supposed to shine through the churches upon a lost world, to reveal to the world that he is who he is. Many of our churches have succumbed to the influence of the world and have lost their first love and their light has been extinguished. Consequently the world is living in darkness with no hope for the future.

3. Church History

The church at Ephesus represents that period in church history from about 33 AD until about 100 AD. During this period of history the original twelve apostles were alive and had a great influence upon the church. By the time this period in history had come to a close the church was beginning to lose its fervor for the Lord and drift into complacency. As we look at how this represents church history, we need to keep in mind the fact that throughout history the church experienced some or all of the characteristics mentioned in these messages. However, as we look at the main characteristic of each church then it seems to indicate that a certain age is in mind for each church and this coincides with the main characteristic of that age.

4. Personal

Individually we need to listen to what the Spirit is saying to each one of us. Have you experienced a lack of love for your Lord and Savior and started on, or continued on, that downward spiral toward apostasy? If you have then it's time to remember and repent or else you are in danger of having your light removed.

Solution

The solution to the problem in this church is found in the fact that Jesus Christ loved them enough to die for them and he is the one holding them in his right hand and walking in their midst. If we remember that he is our strength and security and that he wants to walk in our midst then how can we do anything but repent and remember from where we have fallen and re-fall in love with him? In each case the description of the Lord at the beginning of the message to each church becomes the solution to the problems found in that church.

Smyrna: The Suffering Church

Smyrna was located approximately 65 miles north of Ephesus in one of the most beautiful harbors of western Turkey. The original city was founded by the Hittites around 2000 BC. During the reign of Alexander the Great the city was transformed into one of the most beautiful cities of its day.

It had wide double boulevards with many beautiful temples. The temples of Zeus, Cybele (Diana), Aphrodite, Apollo, and Asclepius were all constructed in this city. The acropolis, being encircled with flowers, a hedge, and myrtle trees, gave the city the names of *flower*, *ornament* or *the crown of all Asia*.

There was also a theater and music center that made it known as the home of music. The city boasted one of the largest stadiums of its time. It was at this stadium that Polycarp, bishop of Smyrna and a student of John the apostle, was martyred and burned alive in 155 AD. This city is still in existence today, however it has been renamed Izmir. Today Izmir is a very large, prosperous and commercial center in the area. There are a few Christians in the city today, but they have been driven underground due to the persecution of Christians in modern Turkey.

Smyrna comes from the word "myrrh," and has the meaning of suffering. When Jesus addressed this church he mentioned their suffering and poverty. There is no condemnation given to this persecuted church or to the church at Philadelphia, and they are the only two that have had a continuous existence.

As we look in detail to the message to the church at Smyrna we will notice that it is the shortest message to any of the churches and that it contains only praise or commendation.

> *And unto the angel of the church in Smyrna write: These things sayeth the first and the last, who was dead, and is alive.*
> Rev. 2:8

This church in Smyrna was to experience poverty and persecution like no other church. The Lord knowing this because of His foreknowledge, presented himself as the one who can and will meet their every need. This description is taken from 1:17, 18. There he is described as *the first and the last,…he that liveth, and was dead,…and alive forevermore."* As always, he gives a description of himself that is fitting for that particular church and its specific need.

"The first and the last" means that there was nothing before him and there will be nothing after him. He will have the final say in what will happen to his creation. He will demonstrate this fact in what he has to say in the remainder of this book. The persecuted church needs to realize that he is the one who is in charge of all things, and that even their persecution was in his planning and purpose. The troubles that they were to experience would only be for a season. Then there will be no more pain and suffering when they meet their Lord in eternity.

"Which was dead, and is alive" indicates to a suffering church that he too understands what they are going through since he lived on this earth and was persecuted like no other. He was put upon a cross, the cruelest form of punishment ever contrived by man, and suffered to the point of giving his life. No one knows our infirmities better than he does. He not only gave his life for us but he also was resurrected and is alive today interceding for us. What an assurance that we too shall be resurrected and there will be no more suffering and pain, for all eternity, for them that are faithful to him in this life.

> *I know thy works, and tribulation, and poverty (but thou art rich); and I know the blasphemy of them who say they are Jews, and are not, but are the synagogue of Satan. Fear none of those things which thou shalt suffer. Behold, the devil shall cast some of you into prison, that they may be tried, and ye shall have tribulation ten days; be thou faithful unto death, and I will give thee a crown of life.*
>
> Rev. 2:9-10

In these two verses we see seven things that the Lord commends.

1. Tribulation

The tribulation mentioned here is not the Great Tribulation that is to come upon the world in the end time, but simply means that they shall experience "trouble" in their lives. The tribulation that the church suffered at the hands of the Roman emperors is not referred to as the Great Tribulation, so surely the trials that we go through in our lives is also not that Great Tribulation. The church at Smyrna did endure much tribulation and many suffered even unto death for the Lord Jesus Christ.

2. Poverty

This poverty has reference to the lack of any earthly possessions. When the early church believed in Christ as their savior then their earthly possessions were taken from them. Even though their earthly possessions were taken, they were declared to be rich in spiritual blessings. What a contrast, as we will see, to that of the church of Laodicea. They thought that they were rich, but the Lord declared that they were poor and didn't know it. We need to understand that our spiritual welfare is not any indication of, neither is dependent upon, any earthly possessions or wealth.

3. The Blasphemy of Them Which Say They Are Jews… But Are The Synagogue of Satan

In Romans 9:6, Paul states that "they are not all Israel, who are of Israel." What he is trying to say is that just because you are born into the Jewish family it doesn't make you a Jew. The thing that made a Jew a Jew is his religion and faith in his God. He must be a Jew inwardly as well as outwardly. In Smyrna there were those who had given up their belief in the Old Testament. In so doing they gave up their faith in God's promises to the Jews, and in particular the promise of their Messiah coming through the Jewish family.

One cannot give up his foundational beliefs without losing the very basis upon what his faith is established. To do so is to worship something other than the truths that God established with Abraham. This consequently will end up causing them to worship some false religion. This is demonstrated by the fact that they were worshiping at the synagogue of Satan.

4. Fear none of those things

What an encouragement to those that are going through trials and tribulation in this life. We don't need to fear those that can only kill the body but we are told to fear Him that can kill the soul.

5. The Devil Shall Cast Some Of You Into Prison

From this statement we are to understand that Satan is the one responsible for their suffering. He is the root problem for all of

BEHOLD, I COME QUICKLY

our trials so we need not blame those who are being used by him and are his tool in bringing these immediate trials upon us.

6. Ye Shall Have Tribulation Ten Days

Some believe that this means that their trials would only last for a short period of time. Some scholars believe that this has reference to the ten Roman emperors that ruled during this period of time in history. There has never been a time when the church was persecuted more than under their rule. These emperors were Nero, Domition, Trajan, Marcus Aurelius, Severus, Maximinius, Decius, Valerian, Aurelian and Diocletian.

Paul was beheaded under Nero's reign. John was exiled under the reign of Domition. Ignatius was burned at the stake under the reign of Trajan. And Polycarp was martyred under the rule of Marcus Aurelius.

7. Be Thou Faithful Unto Death

These believers were faithful unto death. Many of them were martyred because of their faith in their Savior. To those who were faithful, he promised a "crown of life." He is not promising a crown of flowers like the one surrounding the acropolis, but a crown that is eternal and that is only given to those who are faithful. This is a crown that will let the person who possesses it experience life to its fullest throughout eternity. What a reward waiting for those that have suffered trials and even martyrdom in this life! It will be worth it all when we see Jesus and receive the rewards that He has waiting for us.

> *"He that hath an ear, let him hear what the Spirit sayeth unto the churches: He that overcometh shall not be hurt of the second death".*
>
> Rev. 2:11

Have you heard Him today? Do you have an ear to hear? The overcomer shall not be hurt by the second death. Dwight L. Moody said it like this: "He who is born once will die twice; he who is born twice will die once." In other words, if you do not know Jesus Christ as your Savior then you have only been born once, and when the final judgment comes you must experience the second death.

At the first death, your body will die and you will be separated from that body and from your loved ones on this earth. The second death is a spiritual death when you will be resurrected, judged according to your works, and separated from God for all eternity. If you have trusted Christ as your savior then you will only die once. This will happen when your body dies and you leave this world. You will not experience that second death and separation from God. The first death concerns the body while the second death concerns the soul.

Applications

1. Specific Church

As we look back on the church at Smyrna we know that it suffered more persecution than the other churches. It was here in the midst of paganism that many Christians were martyred by being burned at the stake, beheaded, cast to the lions or many other heinous means of death. Even though this is the history of this church, some have overcome and there is a remnant of believers in existence in Izmir today.

2. Churches in General

There are many faithful churches today that are suffering persecution due to their love of the Savior. These churches should remain faithful because of the promise that there is a crown of life waiting for them. There is nothing in this world that can equal the rewards in store for them.

3. Church History

This period in church history represents that time between about 100 AD and 314 AD. According to *Fox's Book of Martyrs,* five million believers died for Christ during this period in history. There has never been a time in history when such persecution of the church has taken place. Many believers during this time in history were faithful even unto death and a special reward is awaiting them. The main problem facing the church during this age was suffering and martyrdom as depicted in the church of Smyrna.

4. Personal.

If you are suffering trials or even persecution in your life then you need to know that Jesus Christ is the answer to your problems. He has suffered in like manner as you have suffered and was willing to give His life for you. He is the first and the last and was dead but is alive. Our trials are only for a short period of time. When we become overcomers we shall receive a crown of life. There is hope for those believers that are infirmed, crippled and maimed in this life because they too shall be resurrected with a new body that shall never experience pain or sorrow for all eternity.

Solution

When we realize that Jesus Christ is the beginning of all things and that He will bring all things to a rightful conclusion, then we have nothing to fear in this life. Since He lived, died, and rose again, we are assured that we too shall live, die, and be resurrected with a new body. There is nothing in this world that He has not already experienced because He was faithful even unto death. What more can we give to Him than our very lives. Suffering and persecution can be the next step in that downward spiral to apostasy. When suffering and trials come into our lives the most common way to find relief is to begin to compromise. As we look at the church at Pergamum we understand that compromise is the central theme of that church.

Pergamos: The Church in Compromise

In the King James text this church is called Pergamos; however, in Turkey it is called Pergamum. We will assume that this is the proper pronunciation of the name and we will endeavor to use it in the context of this writing.

Pergamum lies approximately seventy miles north of Smyrna. These first three cities were the royal cities of the area and they competed with each other for their position in the area. Ephesus was the political center, Smyrna was the commercial center, and Pergamum was the religious center. Unlike Ephesus and Smyrna, Pergamum was not a seaport. Neither was it built on the trade routes from the east. It was built, however, in a very secure and fortified location. The acropolis (highest and most fortified portion of the city) remains today with the ruins of the temples and the city on top of it. In this city was built a magnificent temple in honor of Caesar Augustus which according to Sir William Ramsay made it "a royal city." When the climate got cold in Rome, Augustus would go there to enjoy the beauty and warmth. Because the city was built upon a mountain it was a fortified and safe location to visit. Augustus had a problem with alcohol and he would go there to "dry out."

Pergamum was noted for its great library. It was the greatest library in the pagan world and boasted having over two hundred thousand volumes. This library is the one that Mark Anthony gave to Cleopatra; she took it to Egypt where it was considered the greatest library in the world. The city got its name from the parchment (pergamena) that was used in making these many books.

There are two other facilities that were very prominent in Pergamum. The first is the temple of Dionysius. This temple was built along the side of the mountain and was the place to worship Dionysius, also known as Bacchus (the god of wine, the goat-god). He was depicted with horns, with his upper part as a man and his lower part as a goat, with cloven feet and a tail. This is where the modern picture of Satan originated.

When you come down from the promontory you would see the second great facility which was the temple of the god Asklepios. The Greek god Asklepios was depicted as a man; however, the Oriental Asklepios was depicted as a serpent. In Pergamum he was depicted as a serpent. This temple was known as the greatest hospital in the ancient world. The temple was constructed in a round configuration. In the temple was practiced every means of healing imaginable. They used medicine and psychology and anything else that could be imagined to perform healing.

There were holes in the ceiling of the temple and as the patients walked through the corridors, sultry voices would be coming from these holes saying, "You are going to get well," "You are going to feel better," "You are going to be healed."

If this did not work, they were given a shock treatment by turning loose nonpoisonous snakes in their rooms during the night. If this didn't heal them, it would probably drive them crazy. The serpent on a pole is where the symbol for modern medicine originated. For seven hundred years this temple was the place that people came from all parts of the world to be healed.

"And unto the angel of the church in Pergamos write: These things saith he who hath the sharp sword with two edges."
Rev. 2:12

As is the case in every message to every church it is addressed to the angel of the church. Again this is no doubt the messenger or pastor of that church. Here Jesus reminds them of one of the descriptions of himself found in 1:16 where He stated that "out of his mouth went a sharp two-edged sword." This is exactly what the church at Pergamum needed to hear since they were in the midst of every form of false religion. The sharp two-edged sword represents the Word of God. It is portrayed as two-edged because it can bring both judgment and salvation. Only the Word of God can reveal the truth and give mankind answers concerning their false religious beliefs and have an answer to their needs and man's sin.

> *"I know thy works, and where thou dwellest, even where Satan's seat is; and thou holdest fast my name, and hast not denied my faith, even in those days in which Antipas was my faithful martyr, who was slain among you, where Satan dwelleth.*
>
> Rev. 2:13

Again, the Lord knew the situation in which the church of Pergamum found itself. He knew that it was a very difficult and worldly place to dwell. It was not only difficult but was also the place in which Satan had his seat (dwelling place). The many temples, palaces, theaters, library and hospital were all designed to proclaim that there was a religious and satanic influence in Pergamum. With this influence all around them it would be very difficult to not be led into a place of compromise.

It should be pointed out at this juncture that Satan's throne is not yet in Hell but upon this earth where he dwells. He is "the prince of the power of the air" and "he walks around seeking whom he may devour." In this way he can influence mankind to follow his pernicious ways. As we will see later on in our studies he will eventually be locked into the bottomless pit for one thousand years and then cast into the lake of fire for eternity. In the meanwhile he is going to do everything in his power to deceive mankind with false religions, false literature and witchcraft.

They are commended for some of them holding fast to the name of Jesus, and not denying their faith, and believing in his deity. The true believers were faithful to uphold the doctrines in which they were taught.

They were faithful even though Antipas (a person we know nothing about) was martyred by the followers of false religion and paganism. Antipas no doubt was the first of many to be martyred in the city of Pergamum. They were reminded that the

Lord understands that they were living in the place that Satan dwells, and if they remained faithful, it could very well cost them their lives.

This concludes the portion describing their commendation and now we will proceed to see that they are about to be condemned on two counts.

> *"But I have a few things against thee, because thou hast there them that hold the doctrine of Balaam, who taught Balak to cast a stumbling block before the children of Israel, to eat things sacrificed unto idols, and to commit fornication. So hast thou also them that hold the doctrine of the Nicolaitans, which thing I hate.*
>
> Rev. 2:14-15

The first condemnation comes from the failure to be faithful in correct doctrine. There were some in Pergamum who embraced the doctrine of Balaam. We need to understand that there is a difference between the *doctrine* of Balaam, the *way* of Balaam, and *error* of Balaam.

In 2 Pet. 2:15 we see that the way of Balaam has to do with his covetousness since he thought that he should be paid for his prophecy against Israel.

Jude 11 talks about the error of Balaam where he thought incorrectly that God would curse Israel. Here the way of Balaam has to do with the corrupt advice that he gave to Balak in telling him that the way to defeat Israel is to have their men marry heathen women. In so doing they would be led into idolatry, which would result in their eating things offered to idols, and to commit fornication. This is promoting the doctrine of compromise, and this is exactly what was happening in the church of Pergamum.

With all of the false religious beliefs going on around the believers, it was very easy to fall into the trap of compromising, especially when they were seeing fellow believers being martyred right before their eyes. The temples made it easy to eat things offered to idols. The temples, with their sexual orgies, made it very easy to commit fornication, as was the norm with the non-believers. Most of the literature in their library was teaching about false gods and heathen philosophy. Even though their hospital was satanic in nature, where else could they go for healing? Are we any different when it comes to compromising with the things of this world?

The second condemnation has to do with them holding the doctrine of the Nicolaitans. In both condemnations we are dealing with false doctrinal teachings. It is very important that the church understands true doctrine and that they live in accordance with these doctrinal teachings. We discussed in 2:6 the meaning of the doctrine of the Nicolaitans and that it was hated by the Ephesian church. Here we see that the thing that was hated in Ephesus is embraced in Pergamum. In both cases we are told that the Lord hates this doctrine. In Pergamum it would have been very easy to believe that one could engage in sin in order to understand what it is all about and in so doing it would only hurt the body, which is mortal, but it would have no effect upon the soul. What a damnable doctrine this is! No wonder it is hated by God.

> *"Repent, or else I will come unto thee quickly, and will fight against them with the sword of my mouth.*
>
> Rev. 2:16

The only thing for them to do is to repent, change their mind, turn around, and go the right way. If they did not repent he would quickly appear and fight against them. The thing that he will fight with is none other than the Word of God that comes out of his mouth. It is important that this church learn that God's Word, and the doctrines expressed in it, is his final word, and no one is able to stand if he deliberately disobeys his Word. What a mistake it is to think that the church has the authority to determine what is right and wrong. The church must realize that Jesus Christ and his Word is the only authority in its midst.

> *"He that hath an ear, let him hear what the Spirit saith unto the churches: To him that overcometh will I give to eat of the hidden manna, and will give him a white stone, and in the stone a new name written, which no man knoweth saving he that receiveth it.*
>
> Rev. 2:17

May we all have an ear to hear what the Spirit is talking about! The promises waiting the faithful believer are hidden manna and a white stone. The hidden manna is none other than the Lord Jesus Christ. He is hidden from the world and from many believers today. He said "I am the bread of life." The believers of Pergamum had a choice to either eat things offered to idols or partake of the Bread that will give them life and nourishment for their souls.

Likewise, they could either receive a black ball and be condemned for their failure to live in accordance with His doctrines, or they could receive the white stone of acquittal when they were faithful. The crowns will be given to those who are faithful in certain areas of their life or who have gone through martyrdom, or some other thing that others have not experienced. Everyone will be given a name that can in no way apply to anyone else. That name will have special meaning to that person and only he can appreciate his new name.

Applications

1. Specific Church

The church of Pergamum was living in the midst of paganism and where Satan dwelt. They had the opportunity to either let their light shine brighter than any other, or they could compromise and fail to have a witness in their midst. Unfortunately, they chose the latter because they could not resist the influence that was being placed upon them from the worldly, pagan, heathen community. It was easier for them to compromise than to face martyrdom or persecution. The results of their failure are manifest in the fact that the only thing left in Pergamum is an acropolis with the ruins of a once beautiful city.

2. Churches in General

Many of our churches today have chosen to compromise with the world and follow after false doctrine. Unfortunately, this has led the way for false doctrines to be taught in their midst and many churchgoers to be led astray. The Word of God is not the authority in their midst and they are blown about with every wind of doctrine. Because of their compromise many members will never experience what it is like to eat of the hidden manna or have a white stone with a name written in that no one but themselves can know.

3. Church History

The church of Pergamum is representative of that period in history from approximately 314 AD to 590 AD. It was during this time in history that the church began to move away from the person of Christ and the influence of the world entered into its midst. The Edict of Toleration by Constantine in 314 AD brought about the end of persecution and ushered in an era of compromise. It was during this time that the church was accepted by the state of Rome. This led to a belief that Christianity would be universally accepted and that it would be popular to be called a Christian. The true doctrines of the Word of God were not adhered to and many false doctrines were accepted as the truth.

4. Personal

As we Christians proceed down that spiral that leads to apostasy, the next step after suffering will be compromise with the world.

There are many Christians today who have abandoned the Word of God and the doctrines that are taught therein. Today it is popular for the church to be caught up in worldly practices and disregard the Word of God.

For many of our professing Christians it has become the norm to move in with some one of the opposite sex prior to marriage. Many engage in pornographic material, or watch sexually explicit programs or movies. Rock music has become the accepted music both in our churches and among our Christian youth. Most of the literature found in our Christian bookstores are centered around Psychology or trying to make one feel good about oneself.

All of these things show that we live in a day of compromise. We are no different than the church of Pergamum where they engaged in eating things offered to idols, and committed fornication, and filled their minds with pagan literature. The church engages in holding to the doctrine of the Nicolaitans where it is all right to indulge in sin as long as it only hurts the body and does not have an effect upon the Spirit. Don't be fooled into thinking that anything that hurts the body does not hurt the Spirit. "Know you not that your body is the temple of the Holy Spirit" and anything that defiles the body also quenches the Spirit? If you have a problem with compromise then repent and return again to the fellowship of your Lord Jesus Christ through the study of his Word. He wants to have total authority in your life.

Solution

Jesus is presented as the one with the two-edged sword in His mouth. His Word is the final authority concerning doctrinal truths. If you are having a problem with the influence of the world upon your life, and you are compromising with the affections of this world, then remember that Jesus and His Word are a cure for those desires. Repent and come to him and he will take away all desires for worldly things. If we love him then we have no time to love the world and the things that are in it. He expects your undivided attention and he alone is the one that can reward you for your faithfulness.

Thyatira: The Church That Tolerates Apostasy

Thyatira was located inland about forty miles southeast of Pergamum. It was situated on a high plateau in the ridge that separates the Hermus and Caicos rivers. Because the valleys stretched east and west it provided an easy traverse for the early trade route to the east. Much commerce had traveled through these valleys over the early centuries. Today a railroad travels through these valleys east and west through Turkey.

Thyatira was located in a very strategic location and the elite guard was situated there to provide defense. The main purpose of the city was to provide defense for the caravans traveling the main trade route to Asia. Other cities were built upon an acropolis or promontory with walls around them to provide for their defense. Thyatira did not have an acropolis to build upon so their only defense was the elite guard.

The city was built by Lysimachus and rebuilt by Seleucus I, the founder of the Seleucid dynasty. If you were to go to this city today you would only find the ruins of a once great city. No city in the area has been so completely destroyed.

Thyatira became very prosperous under Vespasian, the Roman emperor. It became the headquarters for many of the ancient guilds. It was the center of the dying guild, the tanners' guild, the weavers' guild, the potters' guild, and the robe makers' guild. Lydia the seller of purple and Paul's first convert in Europe was from Thyatira. The purple for the dye was taken from a plant that grows in the area. Apollo, the sun god, was worshiped as Tyrimmos in Thyatira.

And unto the angel of the church in Thyatira write: These things saith the Son of God, who hath his eyes like a flame of fire, and his feet are like fine brass.

Rev. 2:18

Here the description of our Lord is taken from 1:14, 15. He is described as "The Son of God" in chapter 2, while He is described as "one like the Son of man" in 1:13. Jesus Christ, the Son of God, is the one that has authority to bring judgment upon this church and eventually upon a sinful world.

Fire speaks of judgment since it consumes the objects that are burning. Brass is a symbol of being able to withstand judgment since it is not consumed in a fire. The Son of God has eyes like a flame of fire. This indicates that he sees everything going on in the church and the church will be judged for their wrongdoings. His feet are the object whereby he brings judgment as he stomps them with his feet yet the feet are not hurt in the fire of judgment.

This church in Thyatira is going to be judged for their toleration of apostasy. Since the Lord Jesus Christ went through every temptation known to man, yet without sin, he is righteous in his judgment of a church that is tempted and then yields to that temptation. Even though the church will be judged there are a few words of commendation for the church.

> *I know thy works, and charity, and service, and faith, and thy patience, and thy works; and the last to be more than the first.*
>
> Rev. 2:19

We will see that there are six words of commendation for this church. Even though the church as a whole was basically led astray by false doctrine, there were a few believers in this church who remained faithful and they were distinguished by their works. As in every church the Lord sees and recognizes that they have works of commendation. These six words of commendation are:

1. Works

Works are the credentials of true believers. "Yea, a man may say, Thou hast faith, and I have works: shew me thy faith without thy works, and I will shew thee my faith by my works" (James 2:18).

A remnant of believers lived righteously and demonstrated their faith by their works of righteousness.

2. Charity

Charity (love) was manifest in the church by the true believers even though the church in general had tolerated apostasy.

3. Service

Service (ministry) indicates that there were some who were faithful in their service to the Lord in this church.

4. Faith

Faith is placed behind works, love, and service; however, it is the very thing that motivates these works.

5. Patience

Patience means that there were those who were enduring during this time of apostasy in their midst. They were patiently waiting for the appearing of their Lord.

6. The Last Works Were More Than The First

The last works were more than the first, indicates that their works increased rather than decrease during this time.

All six virtues are a product of an indwelling Holy Spirit. As we shall see in the letter to the church in Laodicea, it is the responsibility of each and every believer to live according to the Word of God no matter what the circumstances that surround him.

> *Notwithstanding, I have a few things against thee, because thou sufferest that woman, Jezebel, who calleth herself a prophetess, to teach and to seduce my servants to commit fornication, and to eat things sacrificed unto idols.*
>
> Rev. 2:20

This church had six words of commendation; however, it received one scathing word of condemnation. Apparently there was a woman by the name of Jezebel in the church that was self-proclaimed to be a prophetess. She was a counterpart for the Jezebel of the Old Testament; the wife of Ahab, king of Israel. Ahab's wife caused him and his kingdom to worship the god of Baal.

And Ahab, the son of Omri, did evil in the sight of the Lord above all who were before him. And it came to pass, as if it had been a light thing for him to walk in the sins of Jeroboam, the son of Nebat, that he took as his wife Jezebel, the daughter of Ethbaal, king of the Sidonians, and went and served Baal, and worshiped him. And he reared up an altar for Baal in the house of Baal, which he had built in Samaria. And Ahab made an idol; and Ahab did more to provoke the Lord God of Israel to anger than all the kings of Israel who were before him.

I Kings 16: 30-33

The Jezebel of Thyatira was guilty of the same sin that Ahab's wife was guilty of. The thing God hates most is for one to seduce his people to the point that they commit spiritual fornication. To seduce means a fundamental departure from the truth. To mix the true doctrines of the church with pagan practices is an abominable thing in the sight of the Lord. This is exactly what was going on in the church of Thyatira. What a contrast between this woman and the faithful Lydia!

And I gave her space to repent of her fornication, and she repented not.

Rev. 2:21

The Lord has been very patient with this church down through history and he has given her space (time) to repent, but she has refused to repent. This will be the case with the final apostate church in the end time, as we shall see later in our study of this book.

> *Behold, I will cast her into a bed, and them that commit adultery with her into great tribulation, except they repent of their deeds.*
>
> Rev. 2:22

The church is to be the Bride of Christ; however, this church is committing adultery in that she is unfaithful to her betrothed. She will be cast into the bed of adultery with those with whom she is committing adultery, and they will be cast into Great Tribulation. The Great Tribulation probably has reference to the Great Tribulation that is to follow the removal of the true church from this world. The apostate church that has been in existence for centuries will be left after the true church is gone, and it will be judged during the Great Tribulation. The only salvation for this church is to repent; however, we have already learned that she will not repent of her evil ways.

> *And I will kill her children with death; and all the churches shall know that I am he which searcheth the reins and hearts; and I will give unto every one of you according to your works.*
>
> Rev. 2:23

The children mentioned here are those in the church who have been born out of an adulterous relationship, and have been raised under its corrupt system. The only thing to look forward to is to be killed with death. To be put to death with death has reference to the second death. These illegitimate children will not only experience physical death here on earth, but will also experience eternal death (separation from God).

All the churches refers to the true churches down through the ages. The true church will know that Jesus Christ is the one that knows them even better than they know themselves, and he is the one that searches the "reins" (literally the kidneys), and the heart.

The kidneys refer to the total psychological makeup of a person—the thoughts, the feelings, the total purposes of their lives. When we combine the kidneys with the heart it includes our total makeup. When it comes time for the final judgment that is to come upon every human being that has walked upon this earth, they can be assured that they will be judged by one that is just, has been tempted in all points as we, and that he will judge in accordance with what he knows to be in the reins and heart of every individual. While there is still life and breath there is time to repent of your fornication.

But unto you I say, and unto the rest in Thyatira, as many as have not this doctrine, and who have not known the depths of Satan, as they speak, I will put upon you none other burden.
Rev. 2:24

The Lord here is speaking to the rest in Thyatira, to those who have not been seduced to commit fornication and eat meat offered unto idols. These are the believers who have adhered to the faith and true doctrines that were established by the apostles. The false doctrines taught in the church were originated from Satan himself and designed to bring the members of the church under his control and dominance. In so doing they shall experience the depths of his illusions and deceptions. To the true and faithful, they need no other burden placed upon them and the Lord assures them that this will indeed be the case.

But that which ye have already, hold fast till I come.
Rev. 2:25

Here our Lord is reminding his church that he is coming to take her out of this world and that she should patiently wait for that day. In the meanwhile hold fast to the true doctrines taught in his Word and be found faithful when he comes.

*And he that overcometh, and keepeth my works unto the
end, to him will I give power over the nations…*

Rev. 2:26

The promise given here to those that overcome and keep His
works is that they shall rule with Him during the Kingdom age.
His works shall be in contrast to the works of Jezebel. His works
are those works wrought by the Holy Spirit in the believer's life.
Jezebel's works are the works of the flesh, and those works done
in one's own power. Believers overcome by faith and not by effort
or works of the flesh.

*And he shall rule them with a rod of iron; as the vessels of
a potter shall they be broken to shivers, even as I received of
my Father.*

Rev. 2:27

During the millennial kingdom the Lord will rule with a rod
of iron. He will rule with ultimate control and authority. What
a reminder to those who have been unfaithful to him in this life.
If we know this, then how much more we should love him and
live for him today.

Remember that there was a potters' guild in Thyatira, so the
people of that city understood what he was talking about when
he told them that the vessels of the potter shall be broken to
shivers. When a potter made a vessel that was below standard
or below his expectation he would break it to pieces and throw
it away. The Lord will do the same thing to those who listen to
Jezebel and follow after her adulterous ways.

And I will give him the morning star.

Rev. 2:28

Jesus Christ is that Bright and Morning Star that shall appear
in the near future to receive his own unto Himself. The hope of
the church is his returning for his own at the rapture. "Looking

for that blessed hope, and glorious appearing of the great God and our Savior Jesus Christ" (Titus 2:13).

He that hath an ear, let him hear what the Spirit saith unto the churches.

Rev. 2:29

Only those who are the children of the Lord Jesus will hear, because it is the Holy Spirit speaking. In contrast, the children of Jezebel will not hear what is being spoken to this church, and will not repent, or hear his shout when he comes for his own.

Applications

1. Specific Church.

The church at Thyatira allowed that woman Jezebel to come in and teach false doctrine in their midst and allowed it to abound. They were given a time to repent but they repented not. Because of this the Lord of judgment has seen their apostasy and they have been judged according to what He has seen. Today there is no church in Thyatira.

2. Churches In General.

There are many churches in the world today that have followed after the doctrines of Jezebel. What a tragedy when churches embrace false doctrine and lead their followers astray! The only thing for these churches to look forward to is for their children to be killed with the second death.

There is hope for those who will listen to the Word of God and repent. How important it is for our churches to teach the Word of God and people of the churches to know his Word. This is the only thing that will protect us from falling prey to Satan and his false doctrines.

3. Church History.

The church at Thyatira represents that period in church history from about 590 AD through 1100 AD. During this period in church history many damnable heresies were allowed to be brought into the church and be embraced by the church. Pagan practices and idolatry were brought into the church. Under Gregory I (590 AD) and under Gregory VII (1073-1085 AD) the papacy was elevated to its place of power. Rituals, traditions, and church doctrine replaced personal faith in Jesus Christ. Worship of the Virgin Mary and her Child, and mass was made a definite part of church services. Purgatory and mass said for the dead became a doctrine of the church. Many documents were established and circulated to give power to the pope. The church put many of God's people to death during this period in history. This is very similar to what Jezebel (the wife of Ahab) did when she killed Naboth and persecuted many of Gods prophets during her time.

4. Personal

The next step in falling into total apostasy is embracing false teachings. If you are caught up in a church that teaches false doctrines, and you do not know what the Word of God says about the danger of committing spiritual adultery, then you should make every effort to know what is in the Word of God and repent while there is still time. Remember that the Lord Jesus is watching what is going on in your life, and you will be judged according to your works in accordance to what is written in his Word.

Solution

The problem in this church was allowing false doctrine to be accepted into the church. The solution to this problem is found in the person of Jesus Christ. As was the case with every other problem encountered by the church, Jesus Christ is the answer to that problem.

Man and his philosophical endeavors can in no way solve this problem. When we understand that Jesus is the final Judge in the affairs of man, and that he sees everything that is going on in our lives, then we must have a desire to please him and keep his commandments.

If he knows the reins and the heart of every man, how important it is to know him and have a desire to love him and please him. For those who do know his Word and abide by his true doctrines, there is hope in his coming for those that love his appearing. There is hope that we shall rule and reign with him during the kingdom. For those who are faithful to him there is no fear of the second death (eternal separation from God).

CHAPTER 3

Sardis, Philadelphia, and Laodicea
Sardis the Church That is Dead

Sardis is located approximately 25 miles south-southeast of Thyatira. This city was one of the oldest and most important cities in Asia Minor and she became the capitol of Lydia. The city was inland and built upon a small, elevated plateau. The rock walls of the acropolis were smooth, steep, and unscalable on all sides except the south side.

As civilization and commerce grew in the area, the small plateau did not have room for expansion so a second city was built on the westerly side. The old city was then used only as an acropolis. She actually became two cities, thus the plural name Sardis.

The city became very wealthy due to the carpet industry situated there. Coins were first minted in Sardis. Cyrus captured their last prince (Croesus) and at the time of his capture he was considered to be the wealthiest man in the world. Sardis has been ruled by the Persians, Alexander the Great, Antiochus the Great, and finally by the Romans. An earthquake destroyed the city during the reign of Tiberius.

There were two major temples in the city. One was the temple of Cybele and the other was the temple of Apollo. The remains of these two temples can be seen today and they are one of the few double temples that exist in the world. Cybele was known as

Diana (the god of fertility) in Ephesus; however, in Sardis she was known as the nature god or the god of the moon. Apollo was the god of the sun and they were believed to be brother and sister. The worship of these two gods was very sensual and corrupt, much like the worship of Diana in Ephesus. Today there is very little left of the city of Sardis, however there is some excavation of the city going on.

And unto the angel of the church in Sardis write: These things saith he that hath the seven spirits of God, and the seven stars. I know thy works, that thou hast a name that thou livest, and art dead.

Rev. 3:1

John is again instructed to write to the messenger of the church. This time He is speaking to the church in Sardis. The one speaking to John is the Lord. He is the one who possesses the seven Spirits of God and holds the seven stars in His hand. Jesus Christ sent the Holy Spirit into this world and he is the one and only person who can provide life to the fullest in the believer. Without the Holy Spirit in our lives we would be dead and lifeless. Isn't it wonderful that the Lord is also the one that holds and protects each and every believer?

There is only one work that is to be commended in this church. That work was indicated by the fact that they had a name that they were alive. Many churches and individuals have tried to impress the world that they are alive simply by using the name of Jesus. Just because we use the name Jesus, or Christian, in association with our names, organizations, or titles, does in no way mean that we have the Holy Spirit in our lives and posses life.

Even though the church at Sardis indicated by their name that they were alive they could not fool the omniscient One who knows their works and everything there is to know about them. He also in the same sentence condemns them for being dead. It is very easy to fool most of the people of this world and convince them that you are something that you are not. But the Lord has the Spirit of God and cannot be deceived.

> *Be watchful, and strengthen the things which remain, that are ready to die; for I have not found thy works perfect before God.*
>
> Rev. 3:2

To be watchful is a warning to the people of Sardis. On two occasions they thought that their city was impregnable, but found to their dismay that someone had gone to sleep and let the enemy enter the city from its weak south side. Sardis was warned to be watchful because they knew not when their enemy would come upon them. They were also warned to be watchful because they were about to lose what little spiritual life that they had remaining. We are told to watch and pray since we know not when our Lord will come. We also need to be on guard that we do not lose our knowledge of the truth. There is always danger in losing the influence of the Holy Spirit in our lives.

"Strengthen the things that remain," tells us that this church was not completely dead, because there were a few things remaining. Hang on to those things with all that you have, or they, too, will slip away. The things that do remain need to be strengthened. They were to build upon what they had and be encouraged over the fact that there was still some life left in them. As long as there is life there is hope!

When a person is seriously ill the only thing that can be done to restore one back to good health is to nourish the body and build upon what little strength remains. This same thing is true in our spiritual lives. The little strength that remained in this church was about to die, and if they did not give it some nourishment it would die.

None of the works that were being performed in Sardis were completely satisfying to God. There was something missing in all that they were endeavoring to accomplish. This something was the life that only comes through the power of the indwelling Spirit.

Remember, therefore, how thou hast received and heard, and hold fast, and repent. If, therefore, thou shalt not watch, I will come on thee as a thief, and thou shalt not know what hour I will come upon thee.

Rev. 3:3

The church at Sardis was in trouble spiritually. They were on the verge of losing the vitality that was supposed to be in their lives. In the situation that they found themselves, they were told to do the best thing that they could do, and that was to remember. They needed to remember how they had heard about the Lord and how they had received Him. They no doubt had heard about salvation through faith in Jesus Christ from Paul the apostle on one of his missionary journeys through their country. The message would have been given with power and authority of the Holy Spirit. When they heard, they were convicted and believed. Their belief gave them a new life; however, they did not grow spiritually and they were Christian in name only and did not express any power in their lives.

Remember and hold fast to what you have. Hang on to the memories of knowing that your sins have been forgiven. Hang on to the fact that you will be with the Lord in eternity. Hang on to the fact that he died, but the grave could not hold him and he arose from the grave to live forever to intercede for you. After you remember, the next thing to do is to repent. Turn about-face and go back to the place from where you have fallen and build upon the things that you remember changed your life.

If you do not watch, I will come to you as a thief. The city of Sardis very well knew what he was talking about. As indicated earlier, they had gone to sleep and the enemy had come in on two occasions and conquered them. The Lord Jesus Christ is coming back to receive his bride. If you are not watching he will come as a thief, when you least expect. If you are watching and anxious for his coming you will keep yourself dressed in white (remain pure). You won't be surprised or ashamed when he comes. The next great event to take place on this earth will be the rapture of the church. Don't be lulled to sleep and miss out on the excitement of His coming.

> *Thou hast a few names even in Sardis that have not defiled their garments, and they shall walk with me in white; for they are worthy.*
>
> Rev. 3:4

In every church, and even in Israel, there has always been a remnant that has remained faithful to their Lord. These faithful ones do not deliberately defile their garments. They do not habitually indulge themselves in sin-defiling activities or fleshly activities.

Those who have been faithful in this life shall walk with Him in white garments. White garments represent the righteousness of the saints. In a country where the main dress was black wool, a person dressed in all white would really be a standout. When a person lives a righteous life in the midst of a sinful world, he too will be a spectacle. Those who are faithful are given white clothing because they are worthy. The white clothes are not given for self-righteousness, but for the righteousness that is accomplished through the power of the Holy Spirit.

> *He that overcometh, the same shall be clothed in white raiment; and I will not blot his name out of the book of life, but I will confess his name before my Father, and before his angels.*
>
> Rev. 3:5

All those who remember where they had heard and believed, and have repented, shall be given the same clothing for they, too, are worthy. How difficult it is to repent and change your way of life in the midst of an evil environment and with peer pressure all around. What a reward for those who have the strength to take that step of faith. Those who overcome, never has reference to those who overcome in their own strength, but refers to those who overcome by the Power of the Spirit.

And I will not blot his name out of the book of life. There has been much speculation concerning the meaning of this statement. The subject will come up several more times in this book and we will discuss the meaning more fully in the future.

It should be noted here that there are two types of books that will be opened at the final great white throne judgment. The first books will reveal the works that have been accomplished by every individual, and the second book will be the book of life. Every man will be judged according to his works; however, if his name is not written in the book of life, he will be cast into the lake of fire. When a person accepts Jesus Christ as his savior, his name is written in the book of life. This is a book that indicates that the name of the person written in the book will be given eternal life. Even in Sardis, where the majority of the church is dead, there were those who had their names written in the book of life. They are assured that their name will never be blotted out. Instead, at that great judgment our Savior will look at the book and declare to his Father and to his Father's angels that their names are written in the book.

He that hath an ear, let him hear what the Spirit saith unto the churches.

Rev. 3:6

Again, this only applies to those who have the indwelling Spirit for without Him you cannot hear or understand what He is trying to say.

Applications

1. Specific Church

The church in Sardis declared to be Christian; however, they lived like the world and appeared to be dead. They had very little influence in teaching the community that they should live righteously. They were reminded that they should remember and repent. There were a few who were faithful in spite of the circumstances surrounding them, and there will be some that will be clothed in white and declared righteous at the final judgment. There is no Christian influence in the area today, for the city has been completely destroyed.

2. Churches In General.

There are many churches today that are just like this church in Sardis. Many of our churches claim to be Christian, are named after Jesus Christ, and do works in the name of Jesus. These same churches are as dead as a mackerel and smell about as bad. They have no idea where spiritual life comes from, or how they can find it. Everything is done in man's strength and it has no eternal value. If they ever had some sort of spiritual life, then they should remember where that life came from and repent. There is a great reward waiting for those who repent and find life in the Spirit.

3. Church History.

This church represents that time in church history during the period between about 1100 AD and 1500 AD. This period is commonly known as the dark ages. During this time in history the church declared itself to be the true Christian church at the same time denying justification and sanctification by faith. Salvation was attained by works and being obedient to the church. They had a name but were dead. Even though the main church was dead there were those within the church who remained faithful. This was the time that great men like Peter Waldo, John Wycliff, and John Huss were faithful and wrote many great truths. These men remembered from where they had heard and first believed. They will have their names in the book of life because they were faithful in a very trying time.

4. Personal.

We have finally reached the end of that downward spiral toward total apostasy. The first step is losing your love for Jesus. The second step is when persecution comes into your life and you take the third step to compromise the situation. The fourth step is tolerating apostasy or false doctrine to influence your life. These steps will lead you to a point in your life where the Holy Spirit cannot work and you will appear spiritually dead. If you have once made a commitment to Jesus Christ, and accepted Him as your savior, and have since then drifted back into a life like the one you had prior to salvation, then the Spirit is speaking to you. He said that you should remember where and how you heard about him and repent. It is never too late to start over and let the Spirit control your way of life and renew your spiritual life. The reward will make it all worthwhile when we see Jesus, even though it may be very difficult in this world of sin and despair.

Solution

Jesus Christ is presented to this church as the one who has the seven Spirits of God and holds the stars in his hand. The Spirit of God is the only person that can give meaning in this life and assure that you will experience eternal life. If you are a person who has professed to be a Christian, but find yourself spiritually dead then it is time to repent and invite the Holy Spirit to take control of your life and he will revitalize your life. The Lord is also the one who holds the stars, or messengers of the churches, in his hand and he will also hold you in his hand of security and strength.

Philadelphia
The Church with the Open Door

Philadelphia is located about 20 miles East-Southeast of Sardis. Today it is a fairly prosperous little Turkish town located in a wide and very beautiful valley. The valley runs North and South with the Cogamis River flowing through it. Much of the country is uninhabited today because it is subject to severe earthquakes. In A.D. 17 a great earthquake struck this town and totally destroyed it along with Sardis and many other surrounding cities. Tiberius, the emperor at the time allocated a huge sum of money to have these cities restored.

The city got its name because Attalus had a great love and respect for his brother Eumenes, king of Pergamum. Because of his love for his brother, he named the city, "Philadelphia, the city of brotherly love."

The city was a fortress city to protect the larger cities on the coast (Ephesus, Smyrna and Pergamum) from invaders from the east. It was on the main trade route from the east and always had an open door to the caravans. The gospel of Jesus Christ and the Word of God was upheld and preached to the surrounding communities and to strangers as they passed through their city.

> *And to the angel of the church in Philadelphia write: These things saith he that is holy, he that is true, he that hath the key of David, he that openeth, and no man shutteth; and shutteth, and no man openeth.*
>
> Rev. 3:7

John is instructed to write to the messenger at the church in Philadelphia. As always, it is the risen Lord Jesus Christ who is giving the instructions. He is reminding John and the church that he is holy (set apart, consecrated). He was born holy, lived holy, died holy, and is holy as he performs his priestly duties before the throne of God. He is declaring that he is truth. All truth is based upon the person of the Lord Jesus Christ and his word.

Having the key of David gives him the rightful authority to be the King over all of his creation. He will sit upon the throne of David during the millennium. Today he is sovereign as he is sitting at the right hand of his Father waiting for his enemies to become his footstool.

He has given this church an open door to preach the gospel to all who pass by. He alone can open doors that no man can shut and close doors that no man can open. Even today, doors can be opened when we are willing to be faithful to him and declare that he is holy, true, and sovereign over all of his creation.

I know thy works; behold, I have set before thee an open door, and no man can shut it; for thou hast a little strength, and hast kept my word, and hast not denied my name.
Rev. 3:8

For this church there is no word of condemnation. They are the faithful church and he knows their works. He has set before them an open door that no man can shut. This door has been opened to them because they have a little strength. They had a little power because they were walking in the Spirit and in obedience to his word. The door was open because they kept his word. They were faithful to the truth of the word and were faithful to reveal the truth to others. They had a door opened to them because they did not deny his name. The church knew who the Lord was. He was the Creator of his universe, he is almighty, he is all knowledge, he is everywhere present, and he is sovereign, just, righteous, true and holy. He is God come in the flesh to provide salvation for all those who believe in his mane.

Behold, I will make them of the synagogue of Satan, who say that they are Jews, and are not, but do lie; behold, I will make them to come and worship before thy feet, and to know that I have loved thee.
Rev. 3:9

Because this church is faithful to the Lord he will show the Jews that he loves this church and they will have to come and worship before their feet. The Jews can no longer rely upon the Law for salvation, justification, and sanctification. They must now come to the cross just like everyone else to be saved. God will show them the truth because this church is faithful to declare the truth of the Word of God.

Because thou hast kept the word of my patience, I also will keep thee from the hour of temptation, which shall come upon all the world, to try them that dwell upon the earth.

Rev. 3:10

Jesus is telling this church that they have been faithful to keep his word. They have been patiently waiting for his return, for the rapture of his church according to his word. Because they have been patient, he will deliver them prior to the tribulation period that is coming upon the world to try them to see if they will follow the works of Satan or follow the Lord of the entire universe. Most of these people will choose to follow Satan because he is the ruler of this world. They will be deceived because their dwelling place is this world. We know that we are only sojourners here and that our home and dwelling place is in the heavenlies, in the presence of our Lord and Savior.

Behold, I come quickly; hold that fast which thou hast, that no man take thy crown.

Rev. 3:11

When Jesus says that he is coming quickly, it does not mean that he is coming right away in the near future. It does mean that when he comes it will be suddenly, in the twinkling of an eye, at the last trump. Hold fast to the Word of God with its promises that he is coming back for his church. If we hold fast and cling to the truth of the word, there is a crown of victory for all those that are faithful to the end.

Him that overcometh will I make a pillar in the temple of my God, and he shall go no more out; and I will write upon him the name of my God, and the name of the city of my God, the new Jerusalem, which cometh down out of heaven from my God; and I will write upon him my new name.

Rev. 3:12

Jesus said that the one who overcomes the false teachings of the world, and holds to the truth of the word and teaches his holiness, that he will make them a pillar in the temple of God. A pillar is part of a structure that has strength and gives support to other members of the structure. To be a pillar in the temple of God is to be strong in the word and give support to other members of the church.

To go no more out means that we will never again be separated from the presence or fellowship with God. He will write upon us the name of his God. Jesus always uses the phrase, "my God" when speaking about his Father. He has a special relationship with his Father that none of us shall ever know.

We will have special access to the New Jerusalem because we have the name of the city written upon us. The New Jerusalem is that city that comes down from heaven and is the dwelling place of God and all believers in Jesus Christ after the creation of the new heaven and new earth.

He will write upon us his new name that only he knows. This is a new name that he has given each one of us that assures a special, personal relationship with him.

He that hath an ear, let him hear what the Spirit saith unto the churches.

Rev. 3:13

The Spirit is speaking to those who know Jesus Christ as their personal savior for only they can hear the Spirit speaking to them. Listen carefully to what the Spirit is saying to you.

Applications

1. Specific Church.

Jesus is telling this specific church that they have been true to his word and declared his holiness. They have not denied his name; therefore, he has given them an open door that no man can shut. The Jews will sit at their feet for they shall know that he loves this church. The members of this church have been patiently awaiting the rapture of the church and are assured that they will not go through the tribulation that is to follow. They are warned to hold fast to what they have so no man can take it from them. He will make them a strong support for other believers. They will have a special name given to them and they shall ever be dwelling in his presence. What wonderful promises to those who are faithful to his word and to his person.

2. Churches In General.

There have been many churches that have been faithful to Jesus Christ and declared his holiness to the rest of the world. The members of these churches will receive the same blessings that the local church of Philadelphia shall receive. Woe to the many churches that have watered down the gospel and have taught a social gospel of good works for they will be deprived of all of these blessings.

3. Church History.

The period in church history that represents this church is the church age from about 1500 AD to 1850 AD. This was the period that God opened the door for the great missionary movement in all parts of the world. The doors were opened in China, Africa, and many other places that the gospel had never before been preached. It was during this period that many great men of God wrote about spiritual things. There has never been a time when so much had been written about the truth of the word and about the holiness of God. If we want to read great commentaries about the word we must go back to the books that were written by the great men of God during this age. The men of God who lived during this age will have a special blessing from God because of their faithfulness to him.

4. Personal

We have seen a downward trend in the lives of the individuals in the five previous churches. This church gives us hope in knowing that we too can be like the church in Philadelphia and be faithful to the Lord and declare his holiness. There are many blessings in store for those who make the effort to spend time in his word and learn of his greatness. May we have ears to hear what the Spirit is saying to us from the study of this great church.

Solution

Jesus is portrayed here as the one who is holy, true and the one who holds the key of David. If we want to be faithful to him in these trying times we must spend time in his word which is the truth and teaches us about his holiness. He alone is the one that shall rule the world with peace and justice as he sits upon the throne of David for 1000 years. There are no shortcuts to a spiritual life in Christ. It takes a lot of effort on our part but it will be well worth the time and effort. May God bless you as you listen to the Spirit teach you what he wants you to know.

Laodicea
The Church That is Lukewarm

In the beautiful Lycus River valley lies the ruins of the once great and prosperous city of Laodicea. It was noted for its commerce and Greek culture. Some of the things it was noted for are science and literature, medical school, eye salve, banking and manufacturing of clothing. The medical school was very primitive and the eye salve has been found to have no known medicinal purpose.

Surrounding the valley were high snow-capped mountains, and downstream from the city were hot springs that were so hot that much of the water came out as steam. The city was named after Laodice, the wife of Antiochus. The city was abandoned because of the many earthquakes in the area.

> *And unto the angel of the church of the Laodiceans write: These things saith the Amen, the faithful and true witness, the beginning of the creation of God.*
>
> *Rev. 3:14*

Again the Lord Jesus Christ tells John to write to the messenger of the church, this time to the church at Laodicea. He portrays himself as the Amen. This is the only time in the scriptures that Amen is used as a proper name. He is telling this lukewarm church that he is going to have the final word in all things. He is the alpha and omega. He is the only one that can fulfill all of the promises of God. He is the one that will reward all believers at the judgment seat of Christ.

Jesus declares himself to be the faithful and true witness. He was faithful to become lower than the angels and become a man so he could shed his blood on the cross for the remission of the sins of the whole world. He declares himself to be the truth. He is absolute truth for there is no deceit or deception in him. When it comes time for him to testify before the Father at the judgment seat he will be a faithful and true witness for he alone knows the thoughts and intents of our hearts. He knows all that motivates us to do the things we do. Are the things that we do motivated by pride, money, and self glory, or are they done out of a fervent love for our savior?

This world was created by Jesus Christ. He knows all about his creation, even every little detail about the heart of man. Since he is the Creator, then he has a sovereign right to do with his creation as he chooses. This is his world and he is about to reclaim it from the clutches of Satan. He gave dominion of the world to Adam, but he relinquished his dominion when he yielded to the temptation of Satan and followed him instead of being obedient to God.

I know thy works, that thou art neither cold nor hot; I would thou wert cold or hot.

Rev. 3:15

Since Jesus is the Creator of man and knows their hearts then he certainly can know about their works. What a scathing condemnation that is proclaimed to the church of Laodicea. They knew very well what he was talking about when speaking about being lukewarm. One of the most detestable things for man is to have lukewarm water to drink. In the mountains above their city there were snow-capped mountains with very cold water flowing from their springs. The people of Laodicea had built an aqueduct from the mountains to the city to provide them with water. By the time the water reached the city it had become lukewarm. They also transported water from the hot springs downstream back to their homes for their household use. By the time they reached home this water was also lukewarm. This was a detestable situation for the people of Laodicea.

Some people prefer hot water to drink and others prefer cold water. Not very many prefer the taste of lukewarm water. The Lord is no different when it comes to the spiritual condition of his bride-to-be. He prefers her to be hot or cold, not indifferent to his love and affection toward her in his absence while he is preparing a place for her.

So, then, because thou art lukewarm, and neither cold nor hot, I will spew thee out of my mouth.

Rev. 3:16

To be cold is to deny the basic doctrines of the church. To be hot is to love the Lord with all your heart and obey his commandments. The condition of this church was that they were trying to ride the fence. They had lost their love for the Lord and had gotten away from the doctrines that kept them obeying the truth. This makes the Lord want to vomit them out of his mouth.

Because thou sayest, I am rich, and increased with goods, and have need of nothing, and knowest not that thou art wretched, and miserable, and poor, and blind, and naked…
Rev. 3:17

Here is a church that receives no commendations but only accusations. This is the most severe accusation of all. You say that you are rich, but I say that you are wretched. You say that you have increased in goods, but I say that you are miserable and poor. You think that you have need of nothing, but I know that you are blind and naked. To be wretched is to be miserable to the point of being pitiable or to the point of being a beggar. This church that thinks that it has everything that it could possibly need is found wanting in everything that God counts as glorifying to himself. They are lacking in spiritual riches; they are miserable because of their lifestyle; they are poor in rewards and blessings; they cannot see or understand spiritual things; and they are undressed because they do not have on the righteousness of Christ. It is possible for a church to be so caught up in materialism that they cannot understand that spiritual blessings far outweigh the pleasures of this world.

I council thee to buy of me gold tried in the fire, that thou mayest be rich; and white raiment, that thou mayest be clothed, and that the shame of thy nakedness do not appear; and anoint thy eyes with eye salve that thou mayest see.
Rev. 3:18

The Lord Jesus strongly urges this church to buy from him gold tried in the fire. He is telling them that they need to come to him and understand that he is Deity. He is pure gold since he has been through the trials of life and has come out 100% pure with no dross in him. He came righteous even as a baby, he lived righteous, he died righteous, he arose righteous and he sits at the right hand of God as our righteous intercessor. If we understand who he is and accept him as our Lord and Savior, then we are rich. If we reject his deity then we are wretched, miserable, and poor.

This church needs to be clothed in white raiment. White raiment speaks of righteousness. In this case it is speaking of the righteousness of Christ. If we are clothed in his righteousness then we will not appear naked before the world, or before God, when they look at us as we go through our daily duties. When we appear in our own righteousness, the shame of our nakedness is seen by all.

You are noted throughout the world for your eye salve, but you do not apply any eye salve to your own spiritual eyes so you can see spiritual things. This spiritual eye salve comes only from the reading and understanding the word of God and through the aid of the Holy Spirit. He is the one who illuminates us and gives us understanding of the things of God.

As many as I love, I rebuke and chasten; be zealous, therefore, and repent.

Rev. 3:19

God loves his own children. If he loves them, he is bound by his duty as our Father to discipline us when we are disobedient to him. God always disciplines his children with love through rebuke and chastening so we will be and do what is best for us. It is never too late, even for this self righteous church, to be zealous and repent and turn from their evil ways.

Behold, I stand at the door, and knock; if any man hear my voice, and open the door, I will come in to him, and will sup with him, and he with me.

Rev. 3:20

Behold, stand in amazement, this same Jesus seen in chapter one standing in the midst of the churches and here he is standing outside the church knocking on the door. There is no knob on the outside of the door so he will not let himself in. He must be invited into the church by those who are on the inside, by those that want to have fellowship with him. He never forces himself upon anyone. The invitation is to individuals that hear his voice. "If any man" hears his voice and opens the door he will come in. He will not only come in but he will sup with them and them with him. This means that he will be invited to the main supper of the day. To sup with him is to spend time in his word and let him speak to your heart about himself.

When we read of the condition of this church in the previous verses, it is no wonder that he is on the outside of this church. They are lukewarm and he would spew them out of his mouth. He wants nothing to do with a church that is in such a condition. He does, however, in his grace and love for his children reach out to those individuals who are interested in his Deity and the truth of his word.

To him that overcometh will I grant to sit with me in my throne, even as I also overcame, and am set down with my Father in his throne.

Rev. 3:21

Jesus promises those that have overcome being lukewarm to the things of God, that he will give them permission to sit with him in his throne. He alone has the authority to grant someone to sit with him. His throne is a place of authority during his reign during his kingdom age.

He overcame all the temptation of this world and was obedient unto his Father, even to his death on the cross. Because of his obedience he is now seated upon his Father's throne in the heavenlies interceding for us as our High Priest.

He that hath an ear, let him hear what the Spirit saith unto the churches.

Rev. 3:22

The Spirit of God is especially interested for this church to listen to what is being said to them for there is nothing good to say about a church that is indifferent to the things of God. Every future reward and blessing is dependent upon their faithfulness and obedience to Christ as they go through their lives here on earth.

Applications

1. Specific Church.

The church in Laodicea was found lacking in their zeal and desire to know the truth about the things of God. They thought that they had everything they needed because they had become rich through the commerce of the traders from the east. They had all kinds of nice clothes to wear and eye salve for their sore eyes. They had an abundance of hot and cold water available to them; however, by the time they could get the water into their homes it would become lukewarm.

This church needed to get their eyes off of the material things of life and start looking at the Deity of Christ and his word. Then, and only then, would they see that they were spiritually destitute in their wealth of the knowledge of God, and were naked, and were blind to what God wanted them to be. Because of their spiritual condition, Jesus will spew them out of his mouth.

The only hope for this church is for individuals to repent and fall in love with Jesus and invite him to come into their lives to sup with him and him with them.

2. Churches In General

There are many churches that have turned their backs on the fundamental doctrines of the word of God and have become very liberal in their teachings. They think that they have the world by the tail but they will be found wanting.

There are some churches that have remained faithful to the Lord and they will be invited to sit with him in his kingdom.

3. Church History.

The church of Laodicea represents the church in history from about 1850 AD until the coming of the Lord in the air for his church at the rapture. The churches of Philadelphia and Laodicea overlap in that the changes between the two have been very gradual. The decline began when a few men decided that the church was having too much influence in the world and it must be diluted and striped from such influence. During the 1850's many cults were established to accomplish this purpose. Many churches have been influenced by the doctrines of these cults and they have become very liberal in their theology.

If we want to find good books on the Deity of God and the major doctrines of the scriptures we have to go to the authors that wrote around the middle of the 1800's until the turn of the twentieth century. Today we have many damnable heresies taught in our churches such as the prosperity doctrine, dominionism, and replacement theology. Many of our churches think they are rich, and they are rich in the things of this world but poor in the understanding of the truth about the Deity of Christ and the need to be clothed in his righteousness. Many have become rich through the writing of many books on things that will make people feel good about themselves. We don't need to feel good about ourselves, but we need to know what we are in Christ and what he wants us to be.

The church today has become lukewarm and he would spew it out of his mouth. There has never been a time in church history when the church has been so rich in the things of this world, but so poor when it comes to the knowledge of God and the truth of his word. The invitation is still available today for those who want to have fellowship with the Lord for them to open the door and invite him into their lives. If they open the door he has promised that he will come in and dine with them.

4. Personal

We as individuals become complacent to the things of God and are swept away by the riches and pomp of the churches today. We get to thinking that we are rich in knowledge and worldly goods and have need of nothing. We too are seen as blind, poor, and naked when it comes to our understanding of God's Word and the understanding of who he is. We as individuals need to make the decision on what we want to be and open the door and let the Lord do a work in our lives. When we open the door he will come in and teach us the truth and eventually grant us to sit with him in his place of authority.

Solution

The solution for the church in Laodicea, and for all churches throughout history that have become lukewarm and have watered down the truth of God's Word, is to repent. We need to buy of him gold tried in the fire. We need to understand that he is Deity and that he has been tried and proven to be the Son of God. We need to understand that he is the Amen, the final word in all things. He is the faithful and true witness that was faithful to his Father when he came to earth, and showed us who his Father is, and then gave his life that we might live. We need to fall on our faces before him and worship him for all that he has done for us and for all that he is going to do for us in the future.

Won't you open the door and invite the Lord into your personal life today? If you do, you will be blessed in this life and have many blessings in the life to come.

CHAPTER 4

The Things Which Shall Be Hereafter

A Door Is Opened In Heaven

At the end of chapter three the church is not mentioned again until Rev. 22:16. The viewpoint of the remaining portion of this book is from heaven. Since the church is not mentioned again it is the opinion of many that the rapture of the church takes place between chapters 3 and 4. Enoch is a picture of the rapture of the church and God removed him prior to the destruction of the world by means of the flood of Noah. Lot was removed prior to the destruction of the two evil cities. God promised the church of Philadelphia that they would be delivered from the hour of temptation that would come upon the world.

Because of the examples set forth in the word of God we will be taking the approach that the church will be taken out of this world prior to the time of the Great Tribulation. For a description of the removal of the church called the rapture; read I Cor. 15; 51-52 and I Thes. 4:13-18. This is the hope of all believers that the Lord will appear in the air and shout like the sound of a trumpet. The dead in Christ shall rise first and those that remain shall be caught up with them in the air and ever be with our Lord.

After this, I looked and, behold, a door was opened in heaven; and the first voice that I heard was, as it were, of a trumpet talking with me; which said, Come up here, and I will show thee things which must be hereafter.

Rev. 4:1

After this, or after the church age described in chapters 2 and 3, John looks and, behold, a door is opened in heaven. The vantage point for John from this point on will be from heaven. The first thing that he experiences is hearing a voice like a trumpet talking to him. This is the same experience that he had on the isle of Patmos in chapter 1 when a voice like a trumpet talked to him and when he turned he saw seven golden lamp stands. Here the one sounding like a trumpet says that he will show him things that must be hereafter. This ushers in the third division of this book as outlined in chapter 1:19. Everything remaining in this book will be future in nature and follow (or be hereafter) the church age.

And immediately I was in the Spirit and, behold, a throne was set in heaven, and one sat on the throne.

Rev 4:2

Immediately John is in the Spirit and he sees a throne in heaven and someone is sitting on the throne. The throne in heaven represents the place from which Almighty God is sovereign over the affairs of his creation.

And he that sat was to look upon like a jasper and a sardine stone; and there was a rainbow round about the throne, in sight like an emerald.

Rev. 4:3

John is impressed with the beauty and glory of the one sitting upon the throne. He is described as appearing like precious stones, the first being like jasper. The jasper is believed to be in appearance like a diamond. The second is described as being like sardine or like the stone found in Sardis which is brilliant red in color. Round about the throne is a brilliant emerald green rainbow. The glory of his appearance and the beauty of the New Jerusalem, his creation, are beyond description and hard to imagine.

An invisible God is sitting on the throne. The only thing that John could see was his beauty and glory as seen in the precious stones and rainbow. The one sitting is the triune God consisting of God the Father, God the Son, and God the Holy Spirit. We see in chapters 4 and 5 that all three persons of the Godhead are described here.

> *And round about the throne were four and twenty seats, and upon the seats I saw four and twenty elders sitting, clothed in white raiment; and they had on their heads crowns of gold.*
>
> Rev. 4:4

John sees twenty four seats with twenty four elders sitting upon these seats that are round about the throne. It is commonly believed that these twenty four elders are representatives of the church age, from its beginning on the day of Pentecost until the rapture. This is another indication that the church is established in heaven seated before the judgment throne of God prior to the tribulation that is to follow. These elders are clothed in white raiment which indicates that they are in their eternal state and clothed in the righteousness of Christ. They have been given their rewards since they have a crown of gold upon their heads. The rewards will be given out at the Judgment seat of Christ immediately following the rapture. These are temporary rewards since we will see in verse 10 that the elders cast them before the feet of him that is seated upon the throne.

> *And out of the throne proceeded lightnings and thunderings, and voices; and there were seven lamps of fire burning before the throne, which are the seven spirits of God.*
>
> Rev. 4:5

The lightning and thunder coming from the throne indicates the omnipotence of God. Thunder and lightning usually precedes a storm and the severity of the storm is shown by the magnitude of the lightning and thunder. The indication presented here is that the storm of judgment is about to begin on planet earth.

The voices indicate that the judgment that is to begin is not just an ordinary one but is one that is directed by the one sitting upon the throne. There is a lot of organizing and coordination to be done in preparation for this judgment. Since it is going to be performed by God, it must be just, righteous, and done in mercy.

The seven lamps of fire burning before the throne are declared to be the seven Spirits of God. This is a clear indication that the Holy Spirit is going to have his part in the final judgment.

> *And before the throne there was a sea of glass like crystal; and in the midst of the throne, and round about the throne, were four beasts full of eyes before and behind...*
>
> Rev. 4:6

The sea usually indicates that there is turmoil, tossing of the waves, and confusion of life. Here we see that the sea is of glass like crystal. This indicates that it is smooth like glass and will reflect all of the beauty and glory of God as he is sitting upon his throne. This is assurance of the tranquility and peacefulness that is experienced by the elders as they are in the presence of God.

In the midst of the throne and all around the throne there are four living creatures (beasts). These living creatures are discussed in the next two verses so we will look at them before we comment about them. The living creatures are full of eyes in front and behind. The implication is that they see all things and nothing gets past them.

> *And the first beast was like a lion, and the second beast like a calf, and the third beast had a face like a man, and the fourth beast was like a flying eagle.*
>
> Rev. 4:7

As we look at these four living creatures we are going to relate them to Jesus Christ as he is presented in the four gospels. The attributes of Jesus as presented in the gospels will forever be in the midst of the throne and round about the throne reminding us of who he was and who he is going to be throughout eternity. We should never tire of hearing of the things that he has done for us.

The first beast is like a lion. The lion is declared to be the king of beasts. In the gospel of Matthew we see Jesus portrayed as the King of Israel. He was born a king, he lived a king, he died a king, and he will be king when he returns to earth.

The second beast is like a calf. The calf will grow up to be an ox or domesticated beast of burden and a servant of mankind. In the gospel of Mark, we see Jesus portrayed as the servant. There is no genealogy of him written in the book of Mark. When we hire a servant it is not necessary for us to know his heritage. All we need to know is if he is qualified to do the job that he is being hired to do. In the book of Mark, Jesus is declared to be faithful to accomplish the task that God the Father sent him to perform.

The third living creature has a face like a man. In the gospel of Luke, the physician, Jesus is portrayed to be the Son of Man. He was truly God but at the same time he was truly man. Because he became a man he can understand our infirmities and be a faithful judge.

The fourth living creature is declared to be like a flying eagle. An eagle soaring in the heavens reminds us that Jesus is the one who came down from the Father and again ascended back to God in Heaven. In the gospel of John we see Jesus portrayed as the Son of God. He is the one who came down from his Father and arose again to sit at his Father's right hand to intercede for us. He declared that if you have seen him then you have seen his Father.

And the four beasts had each of them six wings about him, and they were full of eyes within; and they rest not day and night, saying, Holy, holy, holy, Lord God Almighty, who was, and is, and is to come.

Rev. 4:8

The four living creatures have six wings and they are full of eyes. The wings indicate mobility and the fact that they are omnipresent. The eyes indicate vision in all directions which declares that they are omniscient. They never quit declaring that Jesus is holy, holy, holy, and that he is Lord God Almighty. We know this is speaking of Jesus because this is how he was portrayed in chapter 1, (who was, and is, and is to come). Throughout eternity, Jesus will be worshiped for the wonderful salvation that he has wrought for you and me. We should never tire of hearing and declaring his praises.

In this verse Jesus is declared to be Holy (set apart or consecrated), almighty (omnipotent), mobile (omnipresent), all seeing (omniscient), and never changing (immutable).

And when those beasts give glory and honor and thanks to him that is seated on the throne, who liveth forever and ever, The four and twenty elders fall down before him that is seated on the throne, and worship him that liveth forever and ever, and cast their crowns before the throne, saying, Thou art worthy, O Lord, to receive glory and honor and power; for thou hast created all things, and for thy pleasure they are and were created.
Rev. 4:9-11

In this scene we get a little picture of the worship that will be going on in heaven for all eternity. The four living creatures will never tire of declaring the glory, honor, and thanks for the things that our savior has done for us. When the living creatures give thanks then all of the members of the redeemed will fall on their faces before the one who is eternal and cast their crowns before him. Any crowns that we may have are ours only because of what Christ has been able to do in and through us.

We are so undeserving so we will cast our rewards at the feet of him who lives forever. In doing so we are declaring that he is the one to receive glory and honor and power. He is worthy because he is the one who created all things. All things were created according to his will to bring honor to him. They are and were created for his own pleasure. All of his creation was created to worship him because they want to worship him. He never forces himself upon any of his creation. He gave us a free will to make a conscious decision to worship him.

What a wonderful God and Savior we have to bestow upon his creation the grace to be in his presence for all eternity even though we are so undeserving. How can we ever stop loving and worshiping him?

CHAPTER 5

Worthy Is the Lamb

In chapter 5 we will continue the heavenly scene that began in chapter 4. We will see God the Father sitting on the throne and holding a book, or scroll, with seven seals. It cannot be opened except by the one who has authority to remove the seals and open the scroll. This scroll is going to declare what is going to happen upon this earth following the rapture of the church until the creation of a new heaven and new earth. Since Jesus Christ is the Creator of this earth and the earth belongs to him, then he alone has the right to open the seals and reveal to us the things that must be hereafter. Worthy is the Lamb of God to reclaim the earth for himself, and set up his kingdom that shall last for one thousand years upon this earth, and then he will continue to care for those who love him for all eternity. The narrative is about to continue because there is one that is worthy to open the seals.

> *And I saw in the right hand of him that sat on the throne a book written within and on the backside, sealed with seven seals.*
>
> Rev. 5:1

John looks at the one sitting on the throne, who has the appearance of a sapphire and sardine stone with an emerald rainbow around about, holding a scroll. This scroll is written on both sides of the parchment, within and without. It also is sealed with seven seals. When a king had a document that was not to be opened, he would seal it with a putty-like substance and then press his signet ring into the putty. By doing so this would signify that he had the authority to seal the document and he alone had the authority to remove the seals and open the document.

It should be noted here that none of the events that are recorded on this scroll can progress until someone worthy is found to open the seals and allow things to proceed.

And I saw a strong angel proclaiming with a loud voice, Who is worthy to open the book, and loose its seals?

Rev. 5:2

Everyone in the presence of the one sitting upon the throne is anxious to have the seals opened so the events that are to follow on this earth may be revealed and begin to proceed. A strong angel proclaims with a loud voice, Who is worthy to open the seals. Who is worthy, has the authority, or earned the right to open the seals? If there is no one worthy to open the seals then the world will never be warned of the doom that is about to fall upon it. We shall see that the God of mercy has prepared someone worthy, even before the foundation of the earth, to open the seals.

And no man in heaven, nor in earth, neither under the earth, was able to open the book, neither to look on it.

Rev. 5:3

As they searched for someone to open the seals they discover that there is no **man** who is able to do so. They looked in heaven where all the great saints of God were in the presence of the one sitting upon the throne and no one was found worthy. They looked upon the earth to see if there was someone left after the rapture who was worthy, and again, they found no one. Maybe there has been some great person who has lived upon the earth and has passed on and is buried beneath the earth that will fit the requirement to open the seals, but to their dismay there was none. There was not nor has there ever been a man who is worthy to open the seals. They didn't even qualify to look upon it.

And I wept much, because no man was found worthy to open and to read the scroll, neither to look on it.

Rev. 5:4

John was full of sorrow and he wept much because no man was found worthy to open the seals and read and look upon the events that are to follow. If the seals are not opened, then the world will not know how a just and righteous God is going to deal with the ungodly nations of the earth.

And one of the elders saith unto me, Weep not; behold, the Lion of the tribe of Judah, the Root of David, hath prevailed to open the book, and to loose its seven seals.

Rev. 5:5

One of the elders came along side of John to comfort him and said weep not. Behold (look in amazement), for the Lion of the tribe of Judah has prevailed and is found worthy to open the seals. There are three requirements revealed here about the one that is to open the seals that must be met. The first requirement is that he must be a lion. A lion is the king of beasts and this is signifying that the one found worthy must be a king. The entire gospel of Matthew declares that Jesus is King of the Jews. The second requirement is that he must be from the tribe of Judah. Both the gospels of Matthew chapter 1 and Luke chapter 3 declare that Jesus is from the tribe of Judah. The third requirement is that he must be of the Root of David. Again both Matthew and Luke declare that Jesus is a descendant, or of the Root of David. The one that is to come and be the messiah during the millennial reign must be a descendent of David. Jesus alone has met the qualifications required to prevail and has been found worthy to open the seals.

> *And I beheld and, lo, in the midst of the throne and of the four beasts, and in the midst of the elders, stood a Lamb as though it had been slain, having seven horns and seven eyes, which are the seven spirits of God sent forth into all the earth.*
>
> Rev. 5:6

As John stops weeping and begins to look around, he sees the glory of the throne with the four living creatures and the twenty four elders around about. And, lo and behold, in the midst of the elders there is The Lamb of God standing with his blood-stained robe and nail-pierced hands and feet and looks as though he had been slain. He was seen in the midst of the candlesticks in chapter 1, and here he is in the midst of the saints of God. It is the desire of our savior to be the central figure and center of attention for those who have been covered by his shed blood.

Before Jesus ascended to heaven he promised to send the comforter, the Holy Spirit, into the world. Here we see the Holy Spirit having seven horns. Seven is the number of completeness and horns represent strength. John must have been reminded of the promise that when the Holy Spirit comes he would give him power to perform the works that Jesus had commanded him to do. The eyes were a reminder that the Holy Spirit is the one who taught him all things and illuminated his life. The Lamb of God is the one who died for my sins, and for your sins, and through his Spirit he gives us power to live our lives pleasing to God and illuminates our understanding of the word of God. We owe to him everything that we are, and he alone is worthy to open the seals and reveal what he is going to do to his world.

> *And he came and took the book out of the right hand of him that sat upon the throne.*
>
> Rev. 5:7

From this verse we learn that it is the Father who is sitting upon the throne and the Son, the Lamb of God, comes and takes the scroll out of his mighty right hand.

> *And when he had taken the book, the four beasts and four and twenty elders fell down before the Lamb, having every one of them harps, and golden vials full of odours, which are the prayers of saints.*
>
> Rev. 5:8

Through the symbolic gesture of the Lamb taking the scroll from the Father, we are taught that the Son will be in charge of the events that will happen through the remainder of this book. When he receives the scroll, the four living creatures and the twenty four elders fall down in worship before the Lamb. He is deserving of the praise and adoration that is bestowed upon him. Each one of the living creatures and elders is given a harp. The harp is a symbol of worship. Each one of them has a bowl of incense in his hand which is declared to be the prayers of the saints. It should be the prayer of each and every saint that we may see him as he truly is. Here we see that their prayers have been answered as they see him in his glorified body and with great power and authority and he is found worthy.

> *And they sang a new song, saying, Thou art worthy to take the book, and to open its seals; for thou wast slain, and hast redeemed us to God by thy blood out of every kindred, and tongue, and people, and nation…*
>
> Rev. 5:9

The group before the throne begins to sing a new song. For the first time they can sing praises to Jesus because he has received power and authority to take the scroll and open the seals so that he can begin to take control of his creation that has been under the control of Satan for such a long time. He is declared to be worthy because he is the one who gave his life that we might live.

He is the one who shed his blood on the cross of Calvary for our sins. He is the one who bought us (redeemed us to God) from every corner of the earth. He is so deserving of our praise because he is found worthy.

And hast made us unto our God a kingdom of priests, and we shall reign on the earth.

Rev. 5:10

He is the one who has made it possible for us to be priests, the one who represents man before a Holy God. This will happen when we rule with him during his millennial reign on this earth.

And I beheld, and I heard the voice of many angels round about the throne and the beasts and the elders, and the number of them was ten thousand times ten thousand, and thousands of thousands...

Rev. 5:11

John hears the voices of many angels that are surrounding the throne of God and around the living creatures and twenty four elders. The number of these angels is one hundred million and millions. The number is innumerable and beyond comprehension.

Saying with a loud voice, Worthy is the Lamb that was slain to receive power, and riches, and wisdom, and strength, and honor, and glory, and blessing.

Rev. 5:12

All of the heavenly hosts are shouting with a loud voice that the Lamb who was slain is worthy. He is worthy to receive power to open the seals and power to perform the task that is set before him. That task is to reclaim the earth for himself. He is worthy to receive praises for the riches that he has created and are his to have and enjoy. He is worthy to be praised for his wisdom and strength for he is both omniscient and omnipotent. Because of who he is and what he is about to do, he will receive honor, glory and blessing for all eternity. We will join our voices with the heavenly hosts and praise the Lord Jesus because he is worthy to receive our praise forever and ever.

> *And every creature that is in heaven, and on the earth, and under the earth, and such as are in the sea, and all that are in them, heard I saying, Blessing, and honor, and glory, and power be unto him that sitteth upon the throne, and unto the Lamb forever and ever.*
>
> Rev. 5:13

All of God's creation that is in heaven, on earth, under the earth, or in the sea begin to praise the Lord Jesus Christ because he alone, along with his Father, is worthy to receive blessing, honor, glory, and power. They will be praised forever and ever for their great salvation and grace that they have bestowed upon the earth to all those that trust in their name.

> *And the four beasts said, Amen. And the four and twenty elders fell down and worshiped him that liveth forever and ever.*
>
> Rev. 5:14

The four living creatures say amen to the praises that are echoed by all of God's creation upon the Creator of heaven and earth. To say amen, is to agree with what has been said and to confirm that it is the truth. The twenty-four elders fall down and worship the eternal God and Savior who loves them so much. May we never tire of praising the one who has given us such salvation and eternal life! If you are not in the habit of praising him every day then you should start today because that will be your theme in glory. The one who is deserving of our praise and is found worthy is about to open the scroll with the seven seals. Aren't you glad that "worthy is the Lamb"?

CHAPTER 6

The Lamb Opens the Seals

B etween chapters 3 and 4, the rapture of the church has just taken place, and in chapters 4 and 5, the church is seen in heaven with the Lamb of God, the twenty-four elders and the four living creatures. We have just learned the narrative cannot proceed until the Lamb, the only one worthy, is able to open the seals. The events that are to follow are the "things that shall be hereafter."

At this point we will proceed in a different direction than what is traditionally taught. Traditional teaching states that the seven years of tribulation will follow immediately after the rapture. Since there are many prophecies yet to be fulfilled before the tribulation can start, then either the rapture is not imminent and could not have happened, as stated above, or by necessity there must be a period of time between the two. We, in general, believe that there is nothing that must happen prior to the rapture, and that it is imminent. Therefore we must conclude that there must be some period of time between it and the beginning of the tribulation. If there is no time between the two events then we must conclude that the rapture must be postponed until all of the prophecies referring to the tribulation are fulfilled.

In this discussion we will agree that there are no prophecies to be fulfilled prior to the rapture and that it is imminent. We will also look at the events that must be accomplished prior to the start of the tribulation.

The events that must be accomplished prior to the tribulation are as follows:

1. Daniel 7:7-8 *After this I saw in the night visions, and, behold, a fourth beast, dreadful and terrible, and strong exceedingly, and it had great iron teeth; it devoured and broke in pieces, and stamped the residue with its feet; and it was diverse from all the beasts that were before it, and it had ten horns. I considered the horns, and, behold, there came up among them another little horn, before which there were three of the first horns plucked up by the roots; and, behold, in this horn were eyes like the eyes of man, and a mouth speaking great things.*

2. Daniel 7:23-24 *Thus he said, The fourth beast shall be the fourth kingdom upon the earth, which shall be diverse from all kingdoms, and shall devour the whole earth, and shall tread it down, and break it in pieces. And the ten horns out of this kingdom are ten kings that shall arise; and another shall rise after them, and he shall be diverse from the first, and he shall subdue three kings.*

3. Daniel 9: 27 *And he shall confirm the covenant with many for one week; and in the midst of the week he shall cause the sacrifice and oblation to cease,*

4. *Rev. 17:3 So he carried me away in the spirit into the wilderness and I saw a woman sit upon a scarlet colored beast, full of names of blasphemy, having seven heads and ten horns.*

5. Rev. 17:7 *and the angel said unto me. Why didst thou wonder? I will tell the mystery of the woman, and of the beast that carrieth her, which had seven heads and ten horns.*

6. Rev. 17:12 *and the ten horns which thou sawest are ten kings, who have received no kingdom as yet, but receive power as kings one hour with the beast.*

The scriptures indicate that there will be a world confederacy consisting of ten kings that shall devour the *whole* earth and stomp the residue with his feet. There will arise a world dictator who will confirm the covenant with Israel for seven years, which shall start the tribulation period. This dictator comes out of a ten-king confederacy that has never existed prior to this time. The dictator must subdue three of these ten kings in order to establish his kingdom. This kingdom is described as the fourth kingdom in Daniel and, therefore, must be the revived Roman Empire.

Throughout history there have never remotely existed situations like those described above. There have been several attempts to create a world government that would control the entire world. One such attempt was following World War I (the war to end all wars). In 1920 the League of Nations was established to join the nations of the world in order to cure all world problems. Hitler made another attempt in the 1930s just prior to World War II. This attempt resulted in one of the worst wars ever experienced by mankind. Yet another attempt was made when the United Nations was created in 1940 following that same war. None of these attempts could be accomplished because the Lamb of God had not opened the seal to let the narrative progress.

Before we begin the dialogue on chapter 6 we must also look at the events that must be fulfilled as spoken of in Matthew chapter 24. These events consist of people coming in His name, wars and rumors of wars *but the end is not yet,* famine, pestilence, earthquakes in divers places, and the gospel of the kingdom preached throughout the world *and then shall the end come.*

All of these disasters are only the beginning of sorrows. They are commonly referred to as the "birth pangs." We are also informed that "this generation shall not pass away until all of these things are fulfilled." A generation is considered to be the time from when a person is born until he starts to produce children of his own. This time period is usually between 25 and 40 years. The children of Israel spent 40 years in the wilderness waiting for their "generation" to pass away before they could enter into the Promised Land. From this we can assume that a generation could be as much as 40 years.

And the beast that was, and is not, even he is the eighth, and is of the seven, and goeth into perdition.

Rev. 17:11

It is commonly understood that the "beast that was, and is not, yet is," refers to the revived Roman Empire, since it was, but does not exist today, and will reappear in the future. This verse tells us that there will be eight kingdoms on the earth, however there will only be seven heads. These seven heads (kingdoms) consist of Egypt, Assyria, Babylon, Media-Persia, Greece, Rome and the final world dictator kingdom.

So what about the eighth kingdom? Since it is "the one that was and, is not" then it must be the revived Roman Empire. Then where does it fit into the scheme of things and how long will it last? If it is the revived Roman Empire, it must fall in between the Roman kingdom and the final kingdom. It is of the seven so it does not produce another head; however, it is a separate kingdom and requires a time for it to be in existence.

The tribulation period consists of a time of seven years, two periods of three and one half years each. If the "birth pangs" mentioned above could cover a period of up to 40 years then they cannot fit into the tribulation period. Could it be that there would be a period of 40 years, more or less, between the rapture and the tribulation for the events of chapters six through ten to take place?

The United Nations has never been agreeable to step into world situations that consist of famines, genocide or other world problems that would save millions of human lives. Instead, it has been the policy and goal of the United Nations to reduce the population of the world by 50% through the means of wars, famine and pestilences. It has long been their goal to accomplish this goal by the year 2000. The year 2000 has come and gone; however, their goal has not diminished one bit.

We hear on the news that the world is overpopulated and something must be done about it before it is too late. This goal is being carried out today through abortion, homosexual lifestyle and now the necessity to have no more than one child per family. Does this all sound familiar when we read Matthew 24 and Revelation 6?

In this study we will be looking at the events in chapters 6 through 10 as the time of the revived Roman Empire (The New World Order). If this is not true then we may be waiting 40 years for the rapture of the church if the tribulation is to immediately follow the rapture and continuing for the next seven years.

The First Seal (Control)

And I saw when the Lamb opened one of the seals, and I heard, as it were, the noise of thunder, one of the four living creatures saying, Come.

Rev. 6:1

As we learned in chapter 5, the Lamb is the only one worthy to open the seals and advance the narrative. There will be no events following the rapture of the church that the Lamb does not have under his complete control, and they cannot happen until he says it is time for them to happen. There is no man who is able to begin any of these events until the Lamb says it is time. The Lord Jesus Christ is about to start the process of reclaiming his earthly creation as his own. One of the four living creatures announces the event that is about to take place.

In this chapter we will look at the comparison between Revelation 6 and Matthew 24.

And I saw and, behold, a white horse; and he that sat on him had a bow; and a crown was given unto him, and he went forth conquering, and to conquer.

Rev. 6:2

And Jesus answered and said unto them, Take heed that no man deceive you. For many shall come in my name, saying I am Christ; and shall deceive many.

Mat. 24:4-5

There is fast approaching a time when the world will be brought under control. This is definitely the emphasis portrayed in the first seal. The United States of America is the last frontier for freedom and liberty and these are fast disappearing right before our eyes. The whole world must be brought under control prior to the appearance of the final world dictator. Many laws enacted by our congress that override the restrictions laid out by our founders are usurping our constitution. Most of these laws have to do with controlling and financially destroying our nation.

There have been those, for many years, who have wanted a health care plan that would provide the means whereby the government can control every aspect of the lives of the masses. The contrived economic crisis has led to the failure of the stock market.

Trillions of dollars have been robbed from the investors. The bailouts of our auto industry, the banks, and insurance companies have led to an enormous national debt that in no way can be sustained.

The global warming hoax will generate laws and taxation that will devastate our people. The health care plan will not only control every aspect of our lives but will create an enormous taxation upon every citizen in our nation. These things are all for control, and there is no better way to control the masses than to have them broke and hungry. This control is happening all over the world and the masses *will* be brought under control. That is what is portrayed with the opening of the first seal.

When we look at the opening of the four seals we will see that the whole world will be brought under control. This will lead to political and economical unrest and the people will rebel and there will be many wars and skirmishes that will follow due to the loss of individual sovereignty. Famines most generally follow wars and pestilence follow death and destruction. The New World Order will have many problems on its hands; however, it will accomplish its purpose in reducing the population of the earth to a point where it is manageable.

The traditional teaching is that the man on the white horse is the antichrist and he is going forth setting up his kingdom. This will usher in the beginning of the tribulation period. There are a couple of problems with this interpretation. First being that if we personify the man on the white horse then we must personify the men on the red, black, and pale horses. We *must* be consistent in our interpretations. No one has come up with an explanation as to who these men are.

The second problem is the short time allowed for all of the remaining prophecies in the book of revelation to be fulfilled. First the antichrist must subdue three kings and come into power. He must confirm the covenant with Israel for three and one half years. (Some believe that this will usher in a period of peace on earth.) There will be a period of wars and rumors of wars. Then there will be a period of famine.

Next there will be pestilence and death over the entire earth. These three periods will result in a population reduction of about one fourth the population of the earth (about one and one half billion people). Not one of these periods is likely to happen during a short time frame. After this, there will be many martyred on the earth.

The next thing to happen is earthquakes in diverse places and other physical changes on the face of the earth. After this, there will be one hundred and forty-four thousand Israelites sealed and preaching the "gospel of the kingdom" throughout the entire world. (There will be many saved through the preaching of this gospel.) A third part of the trees and all the grass will be burned up. A third part of the sea will be turned to blood. A third part of the fresh water will be turned bitter.

Next a third part of the sun, moon and stars will be smitten so that a third part of them is darkened. There will be a period of time that locust will come out of the bottomless pit and torment mankind. There will be an invasion of an army from the river Euphrates consisting of two hundred million soldiers.

The two prophets will live, die, and be raised back to life. All the people who have taken the mark of the beast or worshiped his image shall befall foul and painful sores. The sea will turn into congealed blood. All of the fresh water will be turned to blood. Men will be scorched with fire because the sun has been smitten. The throne of the beast will be smitten with darkness.

The river Euphrates will be dried up making way for the kings of the east. Three unclean spirits, like frogs, appear to pave the way for the great battle of Armageddon. There will be voices, thunder, lightning, great earthquake (like never before on the earth), every island fled away, the mountains were not found, and hail the size of a talent (about 100 pounds). Mystery Babylon will be destroyed.

It is highly unlikely that the entire situation mentioned above would occur in what some scholars believe to be a three and one-half year period of time, or even in the seven-year duration of the tribulation period.

The trumpet plagues of chapters 8 and 9 are very similar to the bowl plagues of chapter 16. It has always been very troubling as to why God would send such similar plagues upon the earth in such a short period of time. Since there are to be eight kingdoms, wouldn't it be more logical that the trumpet plagues would be sent upon the first kingdom and the bowl plagues poured out upon the final kingdom?

This author will be taking the position that chapters 6 through 10 apply to the "New World Order" kingdom and that the tribulation does not start until chapter 11 when God measures (surveys) the temple and claims it for his people.

It should be noted that the man is riding upon a white horse with a bow in his hand going forth conquering and to conquer. The symbol of the Council on Foreign Relations (CFR) is a man riding upon a white horse with a bow in his hand and the sign of the ram in his other hand. The goal of the CFR through the organization of the United Nations is to conquer the world and bring forth a leader, or leaders, who will control the entire world and reduce its population by one half. The revived Roman Empire must appear upon the scene and be led by ten kings.

One of the most significant things about the Roman Empire is that all of their leaders were declared to be gods and were worshiped as such. This kingdom shall have great iron teeth and stomp the residue with his feet. Matthew states that many shall come in His name and deceive many. The Club of Rome is a global organization that was established in 1986 and has drawn a map dividing the world into 10 regions. Isn't this interesting since the Word declares that there will be 10 kings who have not had a kingdom as yet? This kingdom with ten kings must first appear on the scene and then three of those kings will be subdued and one will rise greater than them all and become the final world dictator.

The movement in today's world is toward a global society. This is being accomplished by controlling the masses through legislation and treaties with other world governments. The establishment of a World Bank is one way to control all of the economy of the world. The fair trade agreements between many nations are dividing the world into several economical regions. This will continue until the world is divided into ten regions and a king is set over each one. The environmental treaty, due to so-called global warming, is preparing a method in which the effluent countries can support a global society through taxation.

In our country we have established the clean water act, the clean air act, and the endangered species act in order to control every aspect of our lives. We are about to pass legislation that will control every person's health from the cradle to the grave. Also the cap-and-trade bill will control how much energy any and all people can use. Both of these last bills will tax the people to the point that we will not be able to pay for them. Then the immanent domain laws will set in where the government can confiscate our property in order to satisfy our tax requirement.

The natural question that should be asked at this time is "how can a sovereign nation like the United States, or any other sovereign nation, lose its sovereignty to a world organization like the United Nations that has the authority to create the New World Order that can develop into the Revived Roman Empire?"

The United States is the last nation to enjoy liberty and freedom. This liberty and freedom must be abolished before the other nations of the world can emerge into a world government. The sovereignty of all nations must be done away with. The cry of other world leaders is that "there will be a world government and the United States must follow along with them or be left behind."

The European leaders know that there are loopholes in our constitution that can allow them to enforce their laws and regulations upon us. The first loophole is for the President of the United States to sign a *treaty* with any other nation or entity and if the treaty is ratified by the Senate then it will supersede our constitution and become the law of the land.

The United Nation leaders have been working overtime in writing treaties in order to overthrow the government of the United States and bring them under UN control. Several treaties have been signed by our presidents, but they have never been sent to the Senate for ratification. In 1998 the "Rome Statute" was written by the UN and signed by President Clinton but due to some flaws in the treaty it was never sent to the Senate. In 2002, the treaty was rewritten and was titled "International Criminal Court" (ICC). President Bush refused to sign the treaty and informed the UN that they would not ratify the Rome Statute.

Our current President Obama is leaning toward signing the ICC and there are those in the Senate who have expressed their desire to ratify the treaty. If this is signed and ratified then all criminal law will be under the authority of the UN and in accordance with Old Roman Empire laws. There will no longer be any protection under our constitution and bill of rights. There will no longer be any presumption of innocence until proven guilty, the right to a speedy trial, the right to be heard by a jury, or the right to face your accuser. All criminal cases would be heard by one man that becomes your judge and jury just like it was in the days of the Roman Empire.

It will also be illegal for any president or leader of any country to declare war upon another nation without UN approval. If he does he will be subject to be tried for "War Crimes." This stipulation can be retroactive back to 2002 when the law was written which could allow President Bush to be tried and convicted of war crimes for going to war with Iraq without UN approval.

There are many other treaties being written such as the "Law of the Sea Treaty" (LOST) that are just as devastating to our sovereignty. All it will take is the stroke of a pen of the President of the United States to sign these treaties and have a liberal Senate to ratify them for us to lose our sovereignty and become under the complete authority of the UN. There are over one hundred nations of the world that have already signed onto some of these treaties. With Roman law being established as the law of the world, and with the rise of ten kings that declare themselves to be gods, just as the Roman Emperors did, it is easy to see how the Revived Roman Empire can reemerge into being. It is already raising its ugly head.

The second way that our constitution can be suspended is through the ability to declare *martial law*. This can be executed through an executive order written by the president if he determines that an emergency exists. This does not have to be a national emergency such as an atomic attack upon the United States, but could be anything that the president determines to be a national emergency such as a social disorder of any kind. An example facing us today is the created crisis that may, and most likely will, arise from the loss of hundreds of thousands of health care plans under "the affordable care act." This may lead to rioting in the streets of America and civil unrest throughout the nation.

If the president determines that this is creating an emergency then he can suspend the constitution and he alone can direct all of the affairs of the nation through his secretaries to their departments to issue regulations that will bring the masses back under control. He can write executive orders at will and each one will become the law of the land 15 days following his signature. At this point our country will be under the control of a dictator that can do as he pleases. Thousands of executive orders have already been written by previous presidents that have mostly all extended more authority to the executive branch and taken away authority from the legislative branch.

As you can see, most all of the laws are in place to control every aspect of our lives and to bring us under control. And he went forth conquering and to conquer. He has great iron teeth and will stomp the residue with his feet.

This kingdom will not be limited to the region of the Old Roman Empire, it will however, encompass the entire world and will be ruthless, evil and satanic in nature. It will destroy the wealth of the world and bring it all under subjection to a world government. This government has been referred to as "The New World Order" by George H. W. Bush (41st president) and others. A global society is talked about freely by many and our children are taught that we are to be a global community. Aren't you thrilled that an omniscient God has determined that the rapture of His Church will happen prior to these events and that they cannot happen until the Lamb who is Worthy has opened the seal?

There is someone riding on this horse with a bow in his hand. The bow is an instrument of warfare and indicates that this one has ultimate military might. He also is given a crown indicating that he has been given ultimate political power to rule over the people of the world.

It should be noted at this point that there is a significant difference between how the disasters, caused by the four horsemen and the plagues of the trumpets and bowls, are accomplished. In every trumpet and bowl plague we see that an angel is the one to administer them. In the four horsemen we see that it is a man that is in control and riding on a horse. This is very similar to the woman riding on the beast in chapter 17. This woman is believed to be in control of the beast. Then should we not be consistent and believe that the man on the horse is in control and directing its every move?

The Second Seal (War and Bloodshed)

And when he had opened the second seal, I heard the second living creature say, Come. And there went out another horse that was red; and power was given to him that sat on it to take peace from the earth, and that they should kill one another; and there was given unto him a great sword.

Rev. 6:3-4

And ye shall hear of wars and rumors of wars; see that ye be not troubled; for all these things must come to pass, but the end is not yet. For nation shall rise against nation, and kingdom against kingdom…

Mat. 24:6-7

Wars are a terrible thing and cause destruction in the areas where they are fought. We have experienced the devastation caused during World War I, World-War II, Korean War, Vietnam, and the wars in the Middle East. It takes years for the nations involved to recover from such disasters. The loss of human lives is phenomenal.

Many of the nations of the world will be very unhappy about the establishment of a world government and they will rebel. One of the strongest desires of the people of the world is to maintain their individual sovereignty. When this is threatened there will be many nations protesting such a movement and this will result in "wars and rumors of wars."

There is no indication how long this period of bloodshed shall last. If past wars are any indication, it takes months to prepare for war and mobilize manpower and equipment. Once the war is started it usually takes several years before its conclusion.

Here we have plural wars meaning that there will be at least two major wars and other rumors of wars. How does this fit into the last three and one-half years of the Great Tribulation?

The second living creature introduces us to the fact that the second seal is being opened. The opening of this seal reveals a red horse with a rider that was given power to take peace from the earth. Again it is the rider who has the power to take peace from the earth. There will be many people killed through wars and the use of a great sword. Just because the Lamb is worthy to open the seals does not in any way indicate that He is the one who is executing the events under the seals. Again we must be consistent and personify this rider if we try to personify the rider on the white horse. There does not appear to be anything in scripture that could be represented by such a person.

All is not well in the newly established New World Order. There will be rebellion from all corners of the world because nations have lost their sovereignty and they show their rebellion through many wars and conflicts throughout the world. Kingdoms shall rise against kingdom and nations (nationalities or languages) will war against each other. It will be a terrible time on planet earth until the nations can be brought under control and a semblance of peace once again established.

These wars on the earth and the destruction of millions of people will play into the hand of a government that is bent on reducing the population of the earth. The inhabitants of the earth are considered "human cattle" by the elitists that are in control. They are only allowed to live as long as they are producing something to contribute to the elitist's comfort and well being. Once their usefulness no longer exists they will be slaughtered just like an animal. This kingdom will have great iron teeth and stomp the residue with his feet.

The Third Seal (Famine)

And when he had opened the third seal, I heard the third living creature say, Come. And I beheld and, lo, a black horse; and he that sat on him had a pair of balances in his hand. And I heard a voice in the midst of the four living creatures say, A measure of wheat for a denarius, and three measures of barley for a denarius, and see thou hurt not the oil and the wine.

Rev. 6:5-6

...and there shall be famines...

Mat. 24:7

There have been several nations that have experienced devastating famines in recent years. The people had become emaciated and died, as well as the animals in the area affected by these famines. There is not anything much more heart-wrenching than to look upon the people and animals that are starving to death because of famine. It will be most difficult for the whole world to stand by and watch the suffering and death of tens of thousands, or even millions, suffering from malnutrition and die of starvation.

It is beyond comprehension how a government, consisting of ten kings who profess to be gods, can engineer such a diabolical method of total control and population control to the extent that the population is reduced to a "manageable" size. The suffering will be beyond the thinking of any sane individual. Again there is no mention of the duration of this plague. If it doesn't last for at least two years then it will have little effect upon the people of the earth. The great famine in Egypt, during the time of Joseph, lasted for seven years. How would this fit into the time frame that is commonly taught?

There was no person on earth, under the earth, or in heaven worthy to open the seals, only the Lamb. He opens the third seal and the third living creature invites us to come and see what is under the seal. We are introduced to the third horse, which is black in color. The one sitting on the horse has a balance in his hand. This indicates that he has the authority to weigh out whatever he is in control of. We find that he is in control of wheat and barley. This is produce that is used to sustain life. He will produce one measure of wheat for a denarius. Wheat is a product that can be used to produce bread. This is the mainstay of most people's diets. He will also produce three measures of barley for a denarius. Barley is a less valuable commodity than wheat; however, if one has a family to support there will be three measures instead of one. The denarius is the wage that is earned for one day of work. Anyone that provides a day's work will be provided with either one meal of wheat or three meals of barley. But don't hurt the oil or the wine. There will not be any of the finer things in life available such as oil or wine.

Since there is someone riding on the black horse, there is the indication that the rider is in control of all food produce. The rulers, who declare themselves to be gods, will continue to live high on the hog while they watch the population expire. The rulers will measure out a small ration of food, at a high price, for the common people, but the finer items that would normally be consumed by the population will only be available to be enjoyed by the elite. The self-elected gods and elite class will continue to eat, drink, and be merry while they watch the population dwindle away, because of starvation.

Famine is one of the common things to occur following a war since the earth is usually parched and scorched following such an instance. There are almost no heirloom seeds available to the general public in which to grow their own produce. The elite own all of the heirloom seeds and they produce hybrid seeds from them to be used by the common man. These hybrid seeds will not reproduce for any length of time, so these seeds will gradually run out and people will go hungry unless they can obtain the original seeds.

The Fourth Seal (Pestilence and Death)

And when he had opened the fourth seal, I heard the voice of the fourth living creature say, Come. And I looked and, behold, a pale horse, and his name that sat on him was Death, and Hades followed with him. And power was given unto them over the fourth art of the earth, to kill with sword, and with hunger, and with death, and with the beasts of the earth.

Rev. 6: 7-8

…and pestilences…

Mat. 24:7

There have been several great disasters caused by pestilence throughout history. Many of these have been very devastating, killing millions of people. There is much talk about a pandemic occurring almost every year during the flu season. Some people believe that the HIV-Aides epidemic that occurred in Africa was started in a test tube and used for population control. Even if it was not developed in a test tube, there are many known diseases that are stored in laboratories under control of individuals so they can be used for experimentation. These diseases will be used in the end time for biological warfare and population control. There are those individuals that are not beyond using such deadly forces for their own gratification and control. Most pandemics take months or even years to spread throughout the world. If that is the case here then how can the disasters that occur by the opening of the second, third, and fourth seal be completed in three and one half years?

The Lamb of God opens the fourth seal and the fourth living creature says, "Come and see what is about to unfold." Upon looking, a pale horse is revealed with a rider with the name "death." This may indicate that the other riders also have a name. The black horse may be called "famine," the red horse may have the name of "war and bloodshed," and the white horse may be called "control." This pale horse has Hades following with him. Hades is the place that all unbelievers go upon death awaiting the final "Great White Throne Judgment."

There will be one-fourth of the population of the earth killed under the control of these human-caused disasters. First there will be many killed with the sword, indicating war and bloodshed. Next there will be many killed by hunger, which speaks of famine. Following the famine we see many killed by death, indicating pestilence. And finally there will be those killed by beasts of the earth.

There are many depraved individuals on the earth that are in control of all kinds of biological warfare. It should not be any surprise that these evil men would use these weapons on the inhabitants of the earth.

All of these disasters naturally follow starvation caused by first wars and rumors of wars and then famine. The famine will not only affect human kind but also the animal kingdom. We have seen this recently when we observe the effect of famine on TV showing the emaciated humans and their cattle in countries across Africa. The dead bodies left unburied will cause all kinds of pestilence. The hungry animals that have no vegetation or natural prey will attack mankind and devour whatever they can find to eat.

We have seen in the "four horsemen" the New World Order coming into power and that ruthless diabolical kingdom setting up ten kings to rule over the entire earth. Their desire is to reduce the population of the earth by as much as 50% (some say as much as 90%). They plan on accomplishing this population control through wars, famine, and pestilence. That is exactly what is described in God's Word in chapter 6 of Revelation and chapter 24 of Matthew. Out of this kingdom that "has great iron teeth and stomps the residue with his feet," will arise another horn diverse from the ten and he will become the ruler of the seventh and final head as spoken of by Daniel in chapter 7. Three of the original kings must be subdued before the final dictator can come into power. None of these events can happen until the Lamb of God who is worthy to open the seals, begins to open them and let the four horsemen ride forth upon the earth.

The Fifth Seal (Souls Under The Altar)

And when he had opened the fifth seal, I saw under the altar the souls of them that were slain for the word of God, and for the testimony which they held. And they cried with a loud voice, saying, How long, O Lord, holy and true, dost thou not judge and avenge our blood on them that dwell on the earth? And white robes were given unto every one of them; and it was said unto them that they should rest yet for a little season, until their fellow servants also and their brethren, that should be killed as they were, should be fulfilled.

Rev 6:9-11

Then shall they deliver you up to be afflicted, and shall kill you; and ye shall be hated of all nations for my name's sake. And then shall many be offended, and shall betray one another, and shall hate one another.

Mat. 24:9-10

There has never been a time in history when God has not provided a witness to those upon the earth. At most times the natural man has hated the witnesses, and in many cases these witnesses have been killed by ungodly men because of their faithfulness. Here we see many saints killed due to their testimony, and for their faithfulness to the word of God. They will be hated by all *nations* for their testimony, because they have just witnessed one of the greatest catastrophes that ever struck the world, the rapture of the church.

They have been deceived and made to believe a lie and they are not interested in hearing that the Lord Jesus Christ is coming back to set up his kingdom. The world does not want to hear about an omniscient, omnipotent God who is about to bring judgment upon such a diabolical evil kingdom. In order to quell their outcry they will kill those who are proclaiming what the word of God has to say about the end time events and the coming kingdom.

These souls are of those who have been killed due to the disasters caused by the four horsemen. They are under the altar in heaven and are asking God how long before he avenges their blood upon these evil men. The answer is that there are more martyrs that must be killed in the near future. There are apparently more souls to appear before the altar from another period of Great Tribulation in the future. The ones to follow are souls that come from the events caused by the opening of the sixth seal and the trumpet plagues. This is another indication that this is speaking of the time of sorrows prior to the Great Tribulation. There will be many more souls to follow, consisting of those that will die during the Great Tribulation and will come directly back with the Lord into the millennial kingdom. We will see that God does avenge their blood by turning the sea and water into blood. Is he not just in his vengeance?

White robes were given unto them indicating that they were clothed in the righteousness of Christ. They are to rest for a little while until it is time for their brethren to be killed.

The Sixth Seal (Earthquakes)

And I beheld, when he had opened the sixth seal and, lo, there was a great earthquake, and the sun became black as sackcloth of hair, and the moon became like blood; And the stars of heaven fell unto the earth, even as a fig tree casteth her untimely figs, when she is shaken of a mighty wind. And the heaven departed as a scroll when it is rolled together; and every mountain and island were moved out of their places. And the kings of the earth, and the great men, and the rich

men, and the chief captains, and the mighty men, and every
slave, and every free man, hid themselves in the dens and in
the rocks of the mountains, And said to the mountains and
rocks, Fall on us, and hide us from the face of him that sitteth
on the throne, and from the wrath of the Lamb; For the great
day of his wrath is come, and who shall be able to stand?

Rev. 6:12-17

…and earthquakes, in divers places.

Mat. 24:7

We are reminded of many earthquakes that have occurred throughout history. To mention a few we are told of a mighty earthquake during the reign of the kings of Israel, a mighty earthquake that occurred at the crucifixion of our Lord resulting in three hours of darkness on the earth. There have been earthquakes in Alaska, California, Mexico, Japan, Indonesia, Italy, Haiti, and other regions of the world. As devastating as these were it is nothing compared to what is described when the sixth seal is opened. There is not anything more destructive and devastating than the effects of an earthquake. Thousands of people are trapped, injured, and killed in the collapse of structures during an earthquake. Rescue methods are hampered because of total devastation of the infrastructure. Hospitals and emergency facilities are destroyed thus bringing to naught any means of rescue or care for the injured.

Many times an earthquake is accompanied with volcanic activity. When this occurs, the devastation is much more severe. There is not only the earth shaking to contend with but also the fear of ash and magma covering the victims. Darkness is created when the ash enters the atmosphere. The sun is darkened and the moon is turned to the color of blood.

The time is right for the Lamb to open the sixth seal and there will be a great earthquake. Matthew states that there will be earthquakes in diverse places. This earthquake will be different than all others before it. Many earthquakes will occur in different places at the same time. One earthquake can create much devastation. How much more devastation will many earthquakes at once create? It will result in a worldwide disaster. Millions of people will be killed and many millions injured.

Either the earthquake will set off volcanic activity or volcanic activity will set off earthquakes. In either case the sun will be darkened and the moon will turn to blood.

At the same time there will be solar activity resulting in many stars falling from heaven. A similar phenomenon happen in the early 1900's resulting in the death by suicide of many people.

The heaven (our atmospheric heaven) will disappear like a scroll being rolled up because of the ash cloud surrounding the earth. Every mountain and island (coastlands) will be moved out of their places. Many of our island and mountains have been created by volcanic activity and they can be destroyed by volcanic activity. Many of our coastlands are on or near tectonic plates that can disappear into the ocean due to severe earthquakes.

The devastation and destruction will be so great that all men, rich and poor, free or slave, will rather have the mountains fall on them than face the one that is on the throne. The devastation will be so horrific that many will lose their minds from the grief caused by the loss of loved ones. There will be those who have lost appendages, and crushed to death under the rubble. The stench from dead bodies and the smell of death will be everywhere. They would rather have the mountains fall on them than face tomorrow. There is no sign of repentance on the part of any man. They will hide themselves in the rocks and caves of the mountains. They want to hide themselves from the wrath of the Lamb. They understand where the source of destruction is coming from.

The great day of destruction has come and there is none that can stand against the power of an omnipotent God. The end time destruction has been prophesied for thousands of years by the prophets of old, the Lord when He was here on earth and by the New Testament writers so it should be no surprise to those who have read His Word.

In this chapter we have seen the rise of the revived Roman Empire (The New World Order). The control established by this kingdom through the establishment of ten kings that claim to be gods and controlling the entire world. These kings will create a situation where nation shall rise against nation and wars and rumors of war will abound. They will create famines throughout the world in order to reduce the population of the earth dramatically. Next there will be pestilence, animal attacks, and bloodshed. There will appear many souls under the altar in heaven from the people who have been killed during this reign of terror. Then we have seen that Almighty God begins to avenge the blood of those slain by sending a great earthquake and stars falling from the heavens.

There must be a space between the rapture of the church and the start of the tribulation. Let's not help perpetrate the lie (of the antichrist) concerning the rapture of the church by saying that the tribulation will immediately follow the rapture. How easy it will be for the newly established antichrist kingdom to say, "The church did not know what was going to happen." "The tribulation did not happen the way they had predicted so the rapture is also a hoax perpetrated by the church."

The world will be so happy to see the troublemakers gone that there will be a great celebration. Now they can continue with their utopia without any opposition.

During all of this suffering and devastation there appears to be no help or hope from the human point of view. A loving God has made a way of escape for all those who will put their trust in him and his Son. They may lose their life but they need not also lose their souls. All have sinned and come short of the glory of God. The wages (what we have earned) of sin is death (separation), but the gift of God is eternal life through Jesus Christ our Lord.

For God so loved the world that he gave His only begotten Son that whosoever believeth in Him should not perish but have everlasting life.

John 3:16

Have you asked forgiveness for your sins and asked Jesus to be your Lord and savior? If you have then there is no fear of facing tomorrow because men may kill the body, but they cannot destroy the soul. If you have not made that decision, then you need to do so today so you may know that whatever happens in this life that you will be with the Lord for all eternity.

Behold, I come quickly. Even so, come, Lord Jesus.

In the next chapter we will see the evangelization of the entire world through the message of the gospel of the kingdom by the one hundred and forty four thousand Jews. *And then the end shall come.*

CHAPTER 7

The 144,000 and Tribulation Saints

All these are the beginning of sorrows.

Mat. 24:8

All of the disasters that occurred in Revelation chapter 6 are, according to Matthew, only the beginning of sorrows. Matthew 24:6 tells us that the end is not yet; there must be more sorrow before the end can come. The next few verses in Matthew tell us of the tribulation that shall come upon the nation of Israel during this time.

> *Then shall they deliver you up to be afflicted, and shall kill you; and ye shall be hated of all nations for my name's sake. And then shall many be offended, and shall betray one another, and shall hate one another. And many false prophets shall rise, and shall deceive many. And because iniquity shall abound, the love of many shall wax cold. But he that shall endure unto the end, the same shall be saved. And this gospel of the kingdom shall be preached in all the world for the witness unto all nations; and then shall the end come.*
>
> Mat. 24:9-14

During this time the Jews will be delivered up to be afflicted and many shall die because of the great persecution. The Jews will be hated by all other nations because they are preaching the gospel of the kingdom—that Jesus is coming soon to set up his kingdom. Because of the persecution many will turn on each other and betray and hate one another.

There will arise on the world scene many false prophets who will deceive multitudes into not believing that Jesus and his kingdom is about to replace the newly founded "New World Order." Because the Holy Spirit has been set aside as a restrainer, the world will be gripped in iniquity of the worst kind. The love of many shall grow cold and people shall be indifferent to each other.

Those who remain faithful to the end shall be invited by Jesus to enter into his kingdom that shall remain for one thousand years. The gospel of the kingdom shall be preached in every corner of the world as a witness against the evil nations that have taken control.

And then shall the end come. The end cannot come until all of these things are fulfilled.

The seventh chapter tells about the 144,000 Jews that are sealed with God's seal in their forehead so they cannot be killed during this horrible time of persecution. There will be, however, a great multitude of believers who will be killed and they will be seen in heaven before the throne of God.

> *And after these things I saw four angels standing on the four corners of the earth, holding the four winds of the earth, that wind should not blow on the earth, nor on the sea, nor on any tree.*
>
> Rev. 7:1

> *And they cried with a loud voice, saying, How long O Lord, holy and true, dost thou not judge and avenge our blood on them that dwell on the earth? And white robes were given unto every one of them; and it was said unto them that they should rest yet a little season, until their fellow servants also and their brethren, that should be killed as they were, should be fulfilled.*
>
> Rev. 6:10-11

God has heard the prayers of those who were killed in chapter 6 and he is about to fulfill his words and let there be a time when the gospel of the kingdom is preached throughout the whole world. Many will repent and believe that the Messiah is coming soon. In accordance to his word he sends four angels to stand on the four corners of the earth. The four corners are north, south, east, and west. These angels are holding the four winds of the earth. Strong winds are very destructive forces that cause terrible disasters wherever they blow. Winds here represent destruction and disasters that are about to come upon this earth.

The angels are instructed to not let the winds blow on the earth, or on the sea, or on any tree. The trumpet plagues that are coming must wait until God's words are fulfilled. They cannot bring disaster to the earth, sea or trees until many people of every nation hear the gospel of the kingdom and come to have a personal relationship with the Savior.

> *And I saw another angel ascending from the east, having the seal of the living God; and he cried with a loud voice to the four angels, to whom it was given to hurt the earth and the sea, Saying, Hurt not the earth, neither the sea, nor the trees, till we have sealed the servants of our God in their foreheads.*
> Rev. 7:2-3

We see another angel coming from the east holding the seal of God and crying with a loud voice to the four angels that are holding the four winds. He cries for them to hold their winds and do not hurt, or bring destruction upon the earth, sea, or trees until the servants of God have received God's mark in their foreheads.

We have no idea what this mark might be, but we know that it will be some mark that will identify these servants to be the servants of the living God and that they are under his control and protection. This mark will assure each one of them that they will survive the attacks and destructions that are to come upon the earth. They will each one be here at the end of the Great

Tribulation period for God has put his seal of protection upon them. We will see later on in this book that Satan imitates this symbol and he makes all of his followers to take a mark in their right hand or in their forehead. This mark will symbolize that those that have taken his mark are worshipers of him and are under his control.

> *And I heard the number of them which were sealed; and there were sealed an hundred and forty and four thousand of all the tribes of the children of Israel.*
>
> Rev. 7:4

The ones who are sealed are from all the tribes of Israel. God knows each and every member of the children of Israel and he knows what tribe they belong to. He is going to seal twelve thousand from each of the twelve tribes for a total of one hundred and forty four thousand. They will be listed in the following verses.

> *Of the tribe of Judah were sealed twelve thousand. Of the tribe of Reuben were sealed twelve thousand. Of the tribe of Gad were sealed twelve thousand. Of the tribe of Asher were sealed twelve thousand. Of the tribe of Naphtali were sealed twelve thousand. Of the tribe of Manasseh were sealed twelve thousand. Of the tribe of Simeon were sealed twelve thousand. Of the tribe of Levi were sealed twelve thousand. Of the tribe of Issachar were sealed twelve thousand. Of the tribe of Zabulon were sealed twelve thousand. Of the tribe of Joseph were sealed twelve thousand. Of the tribe of Benjamin were sealed twelve thousand.*
>
> Rev. 7:5-8

There are a few things of interest about this list of the twelve tribes that should be explained. Reuben was the firstborn and should have been listed first, but because of his gross sin of sleeping with his father's concubine, he has lost his right to be the first in line to rule Israel. God has chosen Judah to take his place and the kings of Israel all came from the tribe of Judah. The Messiah also came through the tribe of Judah.

There is the absence of the tribe of Dan from this list. That is because the tribe of Dan was the tribe that first introduced idolatry into the nation of Israel. They are not mentioned here, but are mentioned in the list of those who will inherit the land during the millennial reign of Christ. This shows that our God is a forgiving God to those that repent and seek his forgiveness.

Manasseh is the second son of Joseph, and he is listed in the place of Dan. Ephraim, his brother, should have been listed ahead of Manasseh, but he led a rebellion against the two southern tribes of Israel and caused the split between the northern ten tribes and the two southern tribes. Because of this sin God rejected him from being sealed during this time. There are consequences to our sins so we must be on guard to avoid sin in our lives that will cause us to miss out on God's blessings.

Before we proceed into the next portion of scripture we must look at and remember what is going on upon planet earth at this time. The rapture of the church has taken place and those *troublemakers* have been removed from the earth. The restraining effect of the Holy Spirit has been set aside to pave the way for anarchy, deception, and iniquity to abound. The world has been conquered by ten ungodly kings that have set themselves up to be dictators and to be worshiped as gods. They have ushered in wars, famines and pestilences to reduce the population of the earth to a manageable amount of people. According to the book of Daniel, their kingdom will be part iron and part clay. The iron represents the rule of iron by a socialistic, dictatorial government, and the clay represents democratic controlled government of the people. A dictator form of government is the strongest form of government that can exist since it is controlled by one person, while a government controlled by multitudes of people is the weakest form of government. That doesn't mean that a dictator is better than a democracy it only says that it is stronger.

We are seeing a socialistic government ruled by the vote of the people appearing throughout the world right before our eyes. The people will believe that they have power to choose the leaders that they want in power; however, their votes won't count because of corruption and voter fraud perpetrated by their own government.

There will be no love and compassion for the inhabitants of this earth because the government will be an ungodly government. God is love and without him there can be no love for the people of this world. The Government has seen the elimination of the Christian influence in the lives of individuals since the time of the rapture and they do not want any Judeo-Christian theology to ever raise its ugly head again.

With these things in mind let us look at the next portion of scriptures that reveals to us the effect of the preaching of the gospel of the kingdom.

> *After this I beheld and, lo, a great multitude, which no man could number, of all nations, and kindreds, and peoples, and tongues, stood before the throne, and before the Lamb, clothed with white robes, and palms in their hands, And cried with a loud voice, saying, Salvation to our God who sitteth upon the throne, and unto the Lamb.*
>
> Rev. 7:9-10

After the sealing of the one hundred and forty-four thousand of the tribes of Israel, and after the events of chapter 6, John sees a multitude of people standing before the throne and before the Lamb. There are so many that they could not be numbered. They have come from every corner of the earth. They have come from every nation, kindred, people, and tongue. The gospel of the kingdom had not only reached the more inhabited and civilized portions of the earth, but also to the remotest tribes of the jungles. The gospel has had its effect upon multitudes of people and they have believed and been redeemed by the blood of the

Lamb. Because of their faith in Christ they have been killed by their ungodly government and are clothed in white robes, which signify that they are in their spiritual, eternal bodies. They appear with palms in their hands which indicate that they are victorious.

They cry with a loud voice, saying, "Salvation to our God who sits upon the throne and Salvation to the Lamb." They have been saved and redeemed from the terrible persecution and carnage that has taken place on this earth. They know where their salvation has come from and they are forever grateful.

And all the angels stood round about the throne, and about the elders and the four beasts, and fell before the throne on their faces, and worshiped God, Saying, Amen! Blessing, and glory, and wisdom, and thanksgiving, and honor, and power, and might be unto our God forever and ever. Amen.
Rev. 7:11-12

All one hundred million, plus millions, of the angels that are gathered around the throne, where the elders and the four living creatures are standing, fall down on their faces before the throne and worship God. They worship him because he has redeemed multitudes of martyrs who have suffered persecution and tribulation at the hands of sinful men. They worship him because all blessings are initiated at the throne of God. They worship him because there is no glory like the glory of God. God is worshiped because there is no wisdom that can match his knowledge, and him knowing how to use that knowledge. All of creation will be forever thankful for his mercy and grace. He will be praised because he has kept his honor in keeping his word and redeemed his people from tribulation. God is all powerful and almighty, for that he will be worshiped and praised forever and ever. So be it.

And one of the elders answered, saying unto me, Who are these who are arrayed in white robes? And from where did they come?

One of the elders wants to make sure that John knows where these people, arrayed in white robes, have come from. So he asks John if he knows who they are and where they have come from.

And I said unto him, Sir thou knowest. And he said to me, These are they who came out of great tribulation, and have washed their robes, and made them white in the blood of the Lamb.

Rev. 7:14

John said to the elder that he had no idea from where these came let alone who they are, but he knows that the elder knows where they came from and who they are. The elder then tells him that they are the ones who have come out of Great Tribulation. The tribulation that will happen at this time, for the saints of God, will be worse that any tribulation up until this time. It will even be worse than the holocaust at the hands of Nazi Germany perpetrated upon the Jews. It is amazing what man can do to man. Even the beasts of the field are less atrocious to their own.

The elder tells John that these are the ones who have washed their robes and made them white in the blood of the Lamb. They have been saved by the precious blood of Christ who died for their sins. They have been changed into their eternal bodies and are clothed in the righteousness of Christ.

Therefore are they before the throne of God, and serve him day and night in the temple; and he that sitteth on the throne shall dwell among them.

Rev. 7:15

They are before the throne of God because they have been washed in the blood of the Lamb. Because God has bestowed his grace upon them, they will serve him day and night. There doesn't seem to be any need for rest in the presence of God. The God of all glory, who is sitting upon his throne, will dwell among them for all eternity. What an experience it will be to be in God's presence and have him dwell with us!

> *And shall hunger no more, neither thirst anymore; neither shall the sun light on them, nor any heat.*
>
> Rev. 7:16

These people have just been through a time of famine and they know what it is to go to bed hungry. They will never again have to experience such misery. If they had not been taken out of the world at this time they would be going through a time when the water is turned to blood, the sun doesn't shine for a third of the day and then the sun shines hotter than normal and scorches every one under the sun. They have been spared the torment of being thirsty, and have the sun scorch them with its excess heat. God is gracious in removing his people prior to the plagues that are to come upon the earth.

> *For the Lamb who is in the midst of the throne shall feed them, and shall lead them unto living fountains of waters; and God shall wipe away all tears from their eyes.*
>
> Rev 7:17

The Lamb that is in the midst of the throne shall feed them for he is the bread of life. They will forever be filled with any spiritual nourishment that their souls may desire. The Lamb will lead them unto fountains of living waters because he is the living water and anyone who comes to him shall never thirst again. During the last several years, these people have suffered like no others before them. They have experienced wars, famines, pestilence, and the death of loved ones, earthquakes, persecution, tribulation and martyrdom. No wonder that they have tears in their eyes. When they are in the presence of a loving God all tears will go away and their sorrow will turn to gladness.

It is hard to even imagine the heartaches and sadness that will be experienced by the people on earth at this time of tribulation at the hands of evil men. Our God is so gracious to take care of his own in such a time of need.

God's people have been redeemed and in his presence so let the show begin. Set the angels loose that are holding back the four wind of the earth and let the wind blow to avenge the blood of God's martyrs.

CHAPTER 8

The Trumpet Judgments Upon The Final Stage of The Sixth Kingdom

The Seventh Seal (Silence in Heaven)

In chapter 7 we have seen the gospel of the kingdom preached in every corner of the world. There has been no man that has not heard the gospel. All the kings and rich men of the earth have heard that the Lord is about to return and set up his kingdom. Their hearts have been hardened and they have refused to believe the words of the 144,000 witnesses. God has already planned his approach on how to get the attention he deserves and he is about to proceed with his plan of desolation upon this kingdom that is ruled by ten kings, "The New World Order."

> *And when he had opened the seventh seal, there was silence in heaven about the space of half an hour.*
>
> Rev. 8:1

When the Lamb opens the seventh and final seal there is silence in heaven for the length of half an hour. The silence is an indication that something dramatic is about to happen. A storm is brewing and this is the quietness that often comes before the winds arrive that sometimes causes total devastation.

Since this is the final seal to be opened, it is apparent that the total remainder of the scroll can be looked upon and revealed to John. The Lamb, that is worthy, has prevailed to reveal to the world all of the things that must happen from the time of the rapture of the church until the time of the end. The scenes that are to follow are not going to be pleasant to look upon; however, a holy, righteous God must judge all of his creation for their ungodliness and unrighteousness.

> *And I saw the seven angels who stood before God, and to them were given seven trumpets.*
>
> Rev. 8:2

John looks around and he sees seven angels standing before God. These seven angels each have a trumpet in their hand, but before they can blow their trumpets something else must happen.

> *And another angel came and stood at the altar, having a golden censer; and there was given unto him much incense, that he should offer it with the prayers of all saints upon the golden altar which was before the throne.*
>
> Rev. 8:3

Before the angels with the seven trumpets can begin to blow, another angel is seen standing before the altar. The angel has a golden censer, or bowl, in his hand and he is given much incense. He is to offer the incense along with the prayers of the saints that are in the bowl upon the golden altar.

When we study the tabernacle in the wilderness, we find a golden altar before the veil in the Holy Place. This altar is the altar of incense and represents the Lord Jesus Christ as the mediator between the priest and God. This is the place that the priest went to offer prayers for the congregation to God through the mediator Jesus Christ. It was made of gold because it represented his deity.

Here we see the same golden altar before the throne of God. The altar is the place that the angel offers the prayers of all the saints. The Lord Jesus Christ is seated at the right hand of God and is the mediator between the saints of God and the Father. This, therefore, must represent our Great High Priest accepting the prayers of the saints and presenting them to his Father. The prayers are from those saints that were martyred in chapter 6 that were asking God, "How long until you avenge our blood upon those evil men in this world that have shed our blood?"

And the smoke of the incense, which came with the prayers of the saints, ascended up before God out of the angel's hand.
Rev. 8:4

The prayers of the saints have reached the throne of grace and Almighty God, and he will respond in accordance with his will.

And the angel took the censer, and filled it with fire from the altar, and cast it upon the earth; and there were voices, and thunderings, and lightnings, and an earthquake.
Rev. 8:5

Once God has heard the prayers of the saints, the angel with the golden censer fills the censer with the coals of the altar and casts the embers upon the earth. When he does, there are voices, thunderclaps and lightning along with an earthquake. The voices are apparently from the hosts of heaven that are in preparation to begin the judgments of man for their evil deeds. The thunder and lightning is a sign that an ominous storm is on the horizon. This storm will be like no other that man has experienced. It will be earth shaking. The four angels that held the four winds are about to let the winds blow. The winds of judgment and devastation are about to begin.

And the seven angels who had the seven trumpets prepared themselves to sound.
Rev. 8:6

A holy, just God has heard the prayers of his children and he is about to let the angels with the seven trumpets begin to blow. Here we see that the angels are in preparation to sound. Nothing can happen on the earth until the judge of all the earth allows the things to happen. Jesus Christ is in complete control of the judgments that are to follow. The angels that held the four winds could not hurt the earth, sea or trees. We are about to see that the earth, sea, and trees are the very things that will be the recipients of God's judgments.

The First Trumpet

The first angel sounded, and there followed hail and fire mingled with blood, and they were cast upon the earth; and the third part of trees was burnt up, and all green grass was burnt up.

Rev. 8:7

The first angel blows his trumpet and there follows hail and fire mingled with blood. The hail alone can be devastating, but when it comes with fire mingled with blood it will be a total disaster. When the fire is mingled with blood it indicates that there will be death and bloodshed of animals and mankind because of this judgment. The devastation will be widespread upon the face of the earth since a third of all trees and all of the green grass will be burnt up. For a world government, that is pantheistic in nature and worships the creation rather than the Creator, this will be devastating. The rich men of the earth don't care about the people, but they sure care for the natural resourses that are the main sources of all of their riches. This and the following judgment are aimed at the ungodly government that is in control of the entire world; however the people of the world must suffer right along with these evil men.

The word does not tell us how long any of these trumpet plagues last. The original hail and fire will probably only last for a short period of time but the fires may last for months or until the fall rains put them out. The effect of this plague will be felt for many years to come. The green grass will spring up the next year but the trees will take a lifetime to grow to maturity.

The Second Trumpet

And the second angel sounded, and, as it were, a great mountain burning with fire was cast into the sea; and the third part of the sea became blood; And the third part of the creatures which were in the sea, and had life, died; and the third part of the ships were destroyed.

Rev. 8:8, 9

The second angel sounds his trumpet and there is a great mountain burning with fire cast into the sea. A mountain sometimes in the scriptures represents a kingdom. If we take that approach here, there is no end to the spiritualization that can be imagined. This is one place that a literal approach should be taken.

There is much talk today on the news of a very good possibility of an asteroid hitting the earth at some point in the near future. We are warned that if it happens there will be great devastation from its affect. It seems very possible that an asteroid, or some other heavenly body, is what God is going to use in this instance. As this heavenly body reaches the earth's atmosphere it begins to burn and it is cast into the sea. One third part of the sea is turned to blood, or has the appearance of blood, caused by this mountain of contamination. It is good for the earth that the mountain was cast into the sea rather than upon the land where there is much population.

The world's food supply will be greatly affected by the destruction of one third of the creatures of the sea being killed. Commerce will be severely disrupted by the loss of one third of the fleet of ships that transport goods throughout the world. There will undoubtedly be a tsunami that will cause severe damage to the coastlines surrounding the sea that has been struck resulting in the loss of many lives.

Again, the disaster will happen suddenly, possibly with some warning, but the effect will be far reaching and long lasting. This plague is aimed at the rich men of the earth but all of mankind will suffer from its devastating effect.

The Third Trumpet

And the third angel sounded, and there fell a great star from heaven, burning as though it were a lamp, and it fell upon the third part of the rivers, and upon the fountains of water. And the name of the star is called Wormwood; and the third part of the waters became wormwood; and many men died of the waters, because they were made bitter.

Rev. 8:10, 11

When the third angel blows on his trumpet, a great star falls from heaven. Sometimes stars represent angels, but in this case there is no indication that an angel is in mind, so we again will stick with the literal interpretation. Some heavenly body again makes its way to earth. It could be a meteor or even some space junk. Again, when it enters the earth's atmosphere it burns bright like a lamp. The star falls upon one third of the rivers and fountains of water. It has a name and it is called Wormwood because it poisons all of the rivers and springs of water that it comes in contact with. One third of the earth's population will be without fresh water to drink and many people will die because they will try to drink this poisoned water.

Thus far we have seen the winds set free to hurt, and cause much devastation to the trees, sea and earth. There are four trumpets yet to sound and the angel is ready to blow.

The Fourth Trumpet

And the fourth angel sounded, and the third part of the sun was smitten, and the third part of the moon, and the third part of the stars, so that the third part of them was darkened, and the day shone not for the third part of it, and the night likewise.

Rev. 8:12

The fourth angel blows his trumpet and this time the heavenly bodies are affected. The sun does not shine for one third of the time. If the sun doesn't shine then the moon cannot shine because it has no light of its own but can only reflect the brightness of the sun. The stars are affected and do not shine for one third of the time. The sun gives its light during the day and the moon and stars give their light at night. The light-giving effect of the sun, moon and stars will affect both day and night.

We do not know how long this plague will last, but in order for it to have much effect upon the inhabitants of the earth it must continue for an extended period of time. If these phenomena persist for very long, they will cause global cooling throughout the world. To have total darkness for eight hours out of each day will have a chilling effect upon mankind and all of the rest of God's creation. Plant life will not grow properly and this may cause widespread hunger throughout the world both to man and to beast. Men will feel helpless when these plagues fall upon them because there is nothing that they can do about them. God is in complete control of his creation and he is reminding the world of that fact.

God created the sun, moon and stars to reveal his glory and declare his handiwork. He also created them to provide warmth, light, and energy to provide all of the needs of man while he is on this earth. An Omniscient God knew, before he created this earth, just how much light and energy would be required each day to support his creation. Any interruption to that amount of light would be chaotic.

And I beheld, and heard an angel flying through the midst of heaven, saying with a loud voice, Woe, woe, woe, to the inhabiters of the earth by reason of the other voices of the trumpet of the three angels, which are yet to sound!

Rev. 8:13

John sees and hears an angel flying in the midst of heaven. In the midst of heaven is probably in the atmosphere around the earth between heaven and earth. The angel is speaking in a loud voice to the inhabitants of the earth. He is saying that there are three woes coming upon this earth that are far worse than anything that has happened up until this time. The burning of one third of all the trees and all of the green grass is pale compared to what is to follow. One third of the sea turned to blood is nothing compared to the woes that are to come. One third of the rivers and one third of the fresh water made bitter will seem a small thing compared to the next three judgments. And one third of the sun, moon, and stars smitten will appear as child play compared to the hand of God's judgments that are about to take place. These three woes will be initiated when the next three angels sound their trumpets.

What can be any worse than what has just happened? Man takes for granted the beauty of the forests and the comfort of the green grass. They both purify the air we breathe and provide for our livelihood. We forget to praise God for the oceans that provide much of our food and evaporate to create the rain that we drink and that nourishes our ground. When we get thirsty we just expect the fresh water to be there to quench our thirst. The sun, moon, and stars have always shown forth the glory of God and his creation and we forget to thank him for such beauty, warmth, and sustaining of all life. When these things that God has provided for mans comfort, beauty, and very existence are disturbed it will be very annoying to the heart of man. At this point man cannot help but know that all of these plagues are delivered upon this earth at the hand of God. Even so we will see that there is no repentance or turning from their evil ways.

Woe, woe, woe to the inhabitants of the earth for the next three voices of the trumpets are about to sound.

CHAPTER 9

Continued Trumpet Judgments
The First and Second Woes

We were just told at the close of the previous chapter that there are three woes to follow. One woe will follow the sounding of each of the next three trumpets. The first two trumpet woes are recorded in this chapter. A woe is a calamity that is coming upon the earth. Usually the calamity will come directly from the hand of God as will be the case in these three instances.

Sometimes it is very hard to describe the events that are being portrayed to John, which is the situation here. If mankind has never experienced a situation like what is about to be shown when the next two trumpets sound, it makes it very difficult to describe what is going to take place. It is even harder to interpret the meaning of the situations when we have not yet experienced anything like this in all of human history. We will endeavor to let the Word of God do the interpretation for us. We will be taking a literal approach as much as possible.

The Fifth Trumpet (The First Woe)

And the fifth angel sounded, and I saw a star fall from heaven unto the earth; and to him was given the key of the bottomless pit.

Rev. 9:1

The fifth angel sounds his trumpet and John sees a star fall from heaven unto the earth. When the third angel sounded his trumpet a great star fell from heaven. We interpreted that to be a literal star. Here there is given the fact that "to him was given the key of the bottomless pit." When a personal pronoun is ascribed to the star it must be interpreted as something other than a literal star. The star is not only described to be a person, but he is also given a key. The possession of a key indicates that the person has been given authority to open whatever the key is designed to keep locked. In this case the key fits the lock to the bottomless pit.

In chapter 1, we saw that the seven stars were declared to be the angels of the seven churches. Elsewhere in the scriptures, angels are described as stars. Even Satan himself is declared to be an angel of light, and declares himself to be the morning star. Since this angel has fallen from heaven to the earth it indicates that he must either be some other fallen angel or Satan himself. If the angel is fallen unto the earth, then the door to the bottomless pit must be accessed from someplace on the earth. It is described to be a pit or shaft that has no bottom. There is a good indication that the shaft leads to the center of the earth because if the earth is continually in rotation it would appear to have no bottom. In chapter 20, we will find that Satan will be bound and cast into the bottomless pit for one thousand years. In Jude 1:6 we read; "And the angels who kept not their first estate, but left their own habitation, he hath reserved in everlasting chains under darkness unto the judgment of the great day."

And he opened the bottomless pit, and there arose a smoke out of the pit, like the smoke of a great furnace; and the sun and the air were darkened by reason of the smoke of the pit.
Rev. 9:2

When the fallen angel takes the key and opens the bottomless pit, there is a smoke that ascends like the smoke of a great furnace. The smoke is so thick that it darkens the sun and totally pollutes the air that is surrounding the earth. It will be so thick that it will be very difficult for the people of the earth to breathe. If this bottomless pit leads to the center of the earth, it is no wonder that the smoke will arise like the smoke of a great volcano and totally pollute the air and block out the rays of the sun.

> *And there came out of the smoke locusts upon the earth, and unto them was given power, as the scorpions of the earth have power.*
>
> Rev. 9:3

With the smoke from the pit, there came also what appeared to be locusts upon the earth. One of the most dreaded disasters to fall upon man is a plague of locust. When they appear, locusts come in such large numbers that they block the light from the sun. The swarm is sometimes four or five miles long and two or three miles across. They eat everything green that is in their path. They even eat the bark off the trees. They are everywhere, in the fields, in the cities, and in every home. Man can not flee from their presence. The effect is long lasting since all greenery is consumed, famine is soon to follow.

These locusts are different in that they have been given power, as the scorpion of the earth has power.

> *And it was commanded them that they should not hurt the grass of the earth, neither any green thing, neither any tree, but only those men who have not the seal of God in their foreheads.*
>
> Rev. 9:4

What appeared to be locust are not locust at all, because they are commanded to not hurt any grass, green thing, or any trees. These creatures are commanded to hurt only those men that do not have the mark of God in their foreheads. Anyone with the *mark of God* will be exempt from their torment. The 144,000 who are preaching the gospel of the kingdom, and all of their followers who have not yet been martyred, will be under the protection of God, their protector, and will not be affected by the torture that these creatures will bring upon the earth.

If these are not locusts, then the logical conclusion is that they are fallen angels, or demons that have been locked in chains of darkness waiting for this time to be loosed. As we shall see, this will certainly be a calamity of gigantic proportion sent forth upon the earth by the hand of Almighty God.

And to them it was given that they should not kill them, but that they should be tormented five months; and their torment was like the torment of a scorpion, when it striketh a man.

Rev. 9:5

The power that was given unto them was to torment, but they did not have the power to kill. This torment upon the ungodly people of the world is stated to last for five months. There is no reason to believe that this duration is not a literal five month period of time. The torment will be excruciating. It will be like the torment of a scorpion's sting. When a scorpion strikes a man the poison that is injected into the body is very painful and lasts for some time, but is very seldom fatal.

And in those days shall men seek death, and shall not find it; and shall desire to die, and death shall flee from them.

Rev. 9:6

The torment from these demons will be so terrible that men would rather die than suffer from the agony of their afflictions. They will seek to die, but death will flee from them. At this time even suicide will not be a possible means of escape from the torture that has engulfed their lives. When this group of evil demons is set free without any restraint, their true character will be revealed and they will be seen for what they really are. No wonder that God has had them chained in darkness where they cannot manifest their true nature and do harm to mankind.

> *And the shapes of the locusts were like horses prepared unto battle; and on their heads were, as it were, crowns like gold, and their faces were like the faces of men.*
>
> Rev. 9:7

These demons will be well armored and protected. They will be covered all over with armor like a horse prepared to go into the battlefield. A horse was used in battle because it was strong, swift, and mobile. These creatures will, no doubt, be like the horse as far as their power, swiftness, and mobility is concerned.

The crown like gold, not of gold, indicates that they have been given power and authority to control the men of the earth. They have free reign to do as they will whenever they will. These demons will take on the appearance of men and will have faces that look like men.

> *And they had hair like the hair of women, and their teeth were like the teeth of lions.*
>
> Rev. 9:8

Even though these demons look like a man, they have long hair like a woman. Long hair on a man is a form of rebellion, which indicates their rebellion against the God of heaven and earth. I Cor. 11:14 informs us that long hair on a man is a shame. We see this form of rebellion manifest in our young men today and especially among the rock music crowd.

A lion has exceedingly strong teeth and can rip its prey to pieces. For these demons to have teeth like a lion is a good indication that they are powerful and can slash and terrorize their prey at will.

> *And they had breastplates, as it were breastplates of iron; and the sound of their wings was like the sound of chariots of many horses running to battle.*
>
> Rev. 9:9

They not only had armor like a horse going into battle, but they also had breastplates of iron. These creatures were totally protected and were indestructible. No matter what man tries to do to get rid of the torment, there will be nothing that can be done to penetrate their armor and ward off their attacks.

The sound of a swarm of locusts is very noisy and frightening. Likewise the noise of these demons as they move from place to place will be like the sound of many horse-drawn chariots going into battle. This will be a terrifying sound. The men will know that they are coming but there will be no place to hide. The wings indicate that they are extremely mobile and that they can move around at will. There will be no restrictions upon them. They will be as free as a bird.

And they had tails like scorpions, and there were stings in their tails; and their power was to hurt men five months.

Rev. 9:10

The means whereby the demons can torment man is stated that they had tails like a scorpion. In their tails was the power to sting men as oft as they willed. As mentioned above, this torment will produce excruciating pain.

We are reminded again that this torment will last for a five month period of time. That is a very long time to be subjected to such pain and suffering.

And they had a king over them, who is the angel of the bottomless pit, whose name in the Hebrew tongue is Abaddon, but in the Greek tongue hath his name Apollyon.

Rev. 9:11

The final indication that these creatures out of the pit are not ordinary locusts is that they have a king over them. This king is declared to be the angel of the bottomless pit. If this king is an angel, then it can only be assumed that the ones over whom he is king are also angels. To be the angel of the bottomless pit declares that these are all fallen angels that have been chained in darkness waiting for their day of reign and terror.

The king is said to have a name. The name is given in both Hebrew and Greek so everyone reading about him will have no doubt in understanding who he is. In both languages his name means *Destroyer*. He has been let loose with his entire kingdom of followers to raise havoc upon the earth and torment the men of the earth. We have seen that in both the good and bad angels there seems to be an order of authority among them. Here we have a king, and in other places there are strong angels and angels used for a specific purpose. In all cases, it is shown that they are all under the control of their Creator and the God of the universe. Not one of them can act alone, or do anything aside from the authority of either the Lamb or the one sitting on the throne.

> *One woe is past and, behold, there come two woes more hereafter.*
>
> Rev. 9:12

One calamity is past. The whole world has been invaded by demons out of the bottomless pit. They are instructed by Almighty God to torment the men who do not have the mark of God on their foreheads, and for a period of five months. Five months will seem like an eternity when all the people of the world are under this demonic control, and the demons can hurt and bring torment as oft as they will and upon as many as they choose without any restraint.

There are two more calamities to follow in the near future. The sixth angel is about to sound his trumpet.

The Sixth Trumpet (The Second Woe)

Before we start the discussion on this calamity, we should look at the traditional interpretation. It is traditionally taught that the angels at the river Euphrates are loosed to make way for the hordes of soldiers that will invade the Holy Land from the Orient. Since there are to be two hundred million soldiers, it is believed that the Orient is the only area of the world that can produce such an enormous army. China already boasts of an army of this magnitude. If they are to enter the Holy Land, it is not possible to kill one and one half billion people for there are not that many people that exist in that part of the world. If there are problems with the traditional interpretation then there must be another explanation or at least some modification to it.

There are more things not said in this passage than those things that are declared. We will look at the things that are declared and then try to make an intelligent decision as to their meanings. There are descriptions that apparently describe modern warfare, and since technology in warfare is changing every day it is hard to understand the meaning of some of the descriptions.

What appeared, a few years ago, to be fire coming from the tail-gun of an aircraft does not make much sense with the invention of jet airplanes that no longer have tail-guns. By the time these events will take place the technology in warfare will have advanced to something that we can't even imagine today. For this reason, this is probably one of the most difficult calamities to understand.

And the sixth angel sounded, and I heard a voice from the four horns of the golden altar which is before God, Saying to the sixth angel who had the trumpet, Loose the four angels who are bound in the great river, Euphrates.
Rev. 9:13, 14

The sixth angel sounds his trumpet and immediately there is a voice coming from the horns of the golden altar that is before God. The golden altar is the altar of incense that represents our Lord Jesus Christ in his place of being the mediator between man and God. This is where the prayers of the saints ascend into the presence of God. The voice is probably in response to the prayers of the saints asking, "How long until you avenge our blood?" Jesus Christ is probably the one that utters his voice and directs the sixth angel that has just blown his trumpet to respond to his command. The horns of the altar remind us of his strength and authority to give instructions to the angel.

The angel is instructed to loose the four angels that are in the river Euphrates. The four angels that are bound are fallen angels since the good angels are never bound. Neither the good nor the bad angels can do what they are created to do without direct authority from their Creator. The four angels that are to be loosed are said to be in the river. They are not by or near the river but in the river. There is no indication that they are there to protect the entrance of the hordes of soldiers that are about to appear. We will see that they do have a specific purpose for being there.

> *And the four angels were loosed, who were prepared for an hour, and a day, and a month, and a year, to slay the third part of men.*
>
> Rev. 9:15

The angel that has sounded the sixth trumpet is obedient to the Lord and turns the four angels loose. The four angels that were bound were prepared for this particular hour. They were also prepared for a specific day, and month, and year. It was impossible for them to do their dirty deed until the very hour that God had prepared for them to act. There are many plans that man has contrived to perform but he is unable to act upon his plans until a sovereign God allows him to act. The angels of God's creation are also restrained from performing the things that they have been created to perform until their God allows them to perform. We see that their plans are carried out to the very hour that God declares.

In this case the duty of these four angels is to kill one third of the population left on the earth. At the time of the opening of the seals it is declared that one fourth of the population was killed when the second, third, and fourth seals were opened. If there are six billion people on the earth, a fourth of them being killed would result in one and one half billion people killed at the opening of the seals. If you subtract one and one-half billion from six billion there are only four and one-half billion left at this time. One third of four and one-half billion is one and one-half billion. Two times three will be one and one-half billion people killed, resulting in one half of the original population. What a calamity this will be!

> *And the number of the army of the horsemen were two hundred thousand thousand; and I heard the number of them.*
>
> Rev. 9:16

In the previous verse we were told that the four angels in the river Euphrates were loosed to kill one third of all men. Now all of a sudden there appears an army consisting of two hundred million horsemen. Nowhere does the Word tell us who this army is, or where they come from, or where they are going. The only clue to the connection between the two is verse 18, which tells us that the third of all men are killed by this army. From this we can deduct that the angels must be in charge of this army and lead them in the destruction of mankind.

In Rev.16:12 we are told that the angel pours out his vial in order to dry up the river Euphrates to make way for the kings of the east. It is impractical to think that the trumpet plague and the vial plague are speaking of the same situation. And it is unlikely that the same plague will happen twice in such a short period of time. With this information in mind we must consider this plague to be something different than what is traditionally taught. As we study the next few verses we may be able to get a clue to help us understand what is going on at this time.

The numbers of the horsemen should be accurate because John heard the number of them.

And thus I saw the horses in the vision, and them that sat on them, having breastplates of fire, and of jacinth, and brimstone; and the heads of the horses were like the heads of lions, and out of their mouths issued fire and smoke and brimstone.

Rev. 9:17

John sees the horses with riders upon them. They have breastplates of fire, jacinth, and brimstone. These riders are mounted upon horses, which symbolically represent a means of strong, swift, and mobile warfare. They have breastplates that indicate that they are indestructible, but at the same time issue forth fire, jacinth and brimstone. We know what fire is, but what about the jacinth and brimstone? Many scholars believe that the jacinth is really amethyst as described in the stones on the breastplate of the High Priest and in the foundations of the New Jerusalem. If this is the case, then the color would be a beautiful blue. There is, however, no indication here that it is anything other than jacinth which would make it a yellow or brownish yellow color. Brimstone represents a very destructive force that annihilates everything in its path. We have read about its affect upon the cities of Sodom and Gomorrah and the turning of Lot's wife into a pillar of salt. "Fire and brimstone" is an expression used many times in the scriptures to represent total destruction, and the two words are usually used together.

The heads of the horses are like the heads of lions. The lion is the king of beasts and is victorious in his power to destroy his prey. Out of their mouths issued fire, smoke, and brimstone. Here we see that smoke is used instead of jacinth which would indicate that the color of smoke might be a dirty yellow color. This would give more credence to the fact that the jacinth is really jacinth and not amethyst.

By these three was the third part of men killed, by the fire, and by the smoke, and by the brimstone, which issued out of their mouths.

Rev. 9:18

We learn from this verse that it is the fire, smoke, and brimstone that kills one third of the human race. There is no mention of any other conventional weapons being employed in this destruction of mankind. If there is to be other weaponry used I am sure that God would have told us exactly what they would be, as he has done in every other description of battles that he has forewarned elsewhere in his word.

For their power is in their mouth, and in their tails; for their tails were like serpents, and had heads, and with them they do hurt.

Rev. 9:19

The members of this army have power in both their head and in their tail. Their tails are like the heads of serpents and when they turn around they can strike, when least expected, and cause hurt.

Sometimes the information that is lacking is more important than the information given, and that may be the case here. What do we know about the situation in the world at this time that may help us understand the meaning of this calamity? We know that the Arab Nations are all descendents of Abraham through his first born son Ishmael. They believe that since they are of the first born that all of the blessings and promises of Abraham should fall upon them. They will not be satisfied until they can usher in their own kingdom and rule this earth.

We know that the members of the Muslim faith want to kill between fifty and eighty percent of the infidels in the world. We know that there are sleeper cells of Muslim terrorists scattered in almost every nation of the world. The number of radical Muslims could be as many as two hundred million. We know that their theme is jihad. We know that they want to have a world government ruled by a constitution in accordance with their Koran.

We know that they are looking for the twelfth Imam, the *Mahdi* to appear on the scene and lead them into world dominion. We know that they think that they can hasten the appearance of their Mahdi by creating violence for he is to appear out of a chaotic situation. We know that they want sharia law to be the law of the land. We know that their religion is the fastest growing religion in the world. We know that many of the Muslim countries are developing nuclear power and have the ability to produce a nuclear bomb. We know that many of the other nations of the world are concerned about their ability to produce the bomb, but are unable, or at least unwilling, to do anything about the situation. We see the unrest in the entire Muslim world today, and we know that they will not be satisfied until all of their desires to have an International Islamic State are fulfilled.

With these things in mind, let us come up with a scenario that may be, or may not be, exactly what is described in this passage.

The Euphrates River is in the land of Iraq, in the geographical center of the Muslim nations and of the entire world. Near this river was built the tower of Babel, and on both sides of the river was constructed the ancient city of Babylon. Both the tower and the city represent wickedness and the basis for all of the false religions of the world originated here. We see that God has four angels bound here, and they are to be loosed on a specific hour, day, week, month and year. They have been in bondage at this site waiting until God allows them to be free and perform their evil deed of killing one third of the human race. There are four of them because from this point they can proceed in all four directions, to the four corners of the world, which is north, south, east, and west.

The next thing we know is that an army of two hundred million horsemen appear out of nowhere. When God provides a vision of some invasion such as described in Ezekiel 38 and 39, he shows that he is the one who puts a hook into the mouth of the coalition of nations that are to go against Israel and he does it to prove who he is and to show the nations that he is God. He reveals the names of the nations that will be involved, the weaponry to be used and the destination of the army. He tells why they are coming and what the outcome will be. We are told that

God will send rain and hail, and an earthquake to confound the invading army and that God will defend his people of Israel. Here there is no indication of where the army comes from, because they are already in their own countries and in sleeper cells scattered throughout the world. He only mentions the weaponry of fire, smoke, and brimstone because the only lethal force used in this destruction will be nuclear power. When we consider that this army is under the control of demonic angels it is not difficult to imagine that many nuclear bombs could be set off simultaneously in many of our large cities throughout the world at the precise hour that an omniscient God has predicted. The fire will be the initial blast of the nuclear bombs, the smoke will be the mushroom cloud produced by the nuclear bombs, and the brimstone will be the radioactive fallout from the bombs. By these three things a third of mankind will be killed. We are not told how the army is defeated because their goal is to perform jihad through terrorism and suicide bombing. Those that remain will reside in their own countries and there will be no real army remaining to deal with.

Many expositors believe that a new city of Babylon will be constructed at the original site of the old city of Babylon along the banks of the Euphrates River. This is a very good possibility considering the description of the destruction of Babylon that will be discussed later on in our studies. It is easy to understand how a new modern city can appear out of nowhere when we look at the beautiful city of Dubai in the United Arab Emirates. This city has emerged out of nowhere in a very short period of time. The city of Babylon could do likewise and become the economic center, the political center, and the commercial center of the world in a very short number of years considering the great wealth of the Arab nations because of their oil reserves.

With this in mind let us consider the rest of the scenario that may or may not be exactly correct, but could answer many of the unanswered questions that we have concerning end time prophecy. By this time in history, the world will be divided into ten regions and will be governed by ten kings.

Things are not going very well with these kings. There have been wars, famines, pestilences, and earthquakes. The 144,000 Jews have preached that the King is coming and have converted multitudes of people and the kings have had to kill their converts in order to prevent an uprising against their authority. They have been meeting on a regular basis by means of their satellite communication system, trying to solve the problems that they have encountered, but to no avail. What they desperately need is someone to take control and lead them out of their dilemma. The problem is, there is a great difference of opinion on who this person should be and which king should have such control over the rest of them.

In the newly constructed city of Babylon there is one who has been very active in its construction and has shown a great bit of ability for leadership. He surveys the situation in the world and decides that he can solve the world's problems by the use of his own great abilities. He devises a scheme whereby he can convince multitudes of his followers to aid him in the destruction of three of the kings who have been using their power and influence to control the other seven kings. This can be accomplished by placing nuclear bombs in strategic cities throughout the regions of these domineering kings. There are bombs that can be detonated in the air that will disrupt all electrical energy for hundreds of miles around. One such bomb set off in the middle of the United States could shut down all electricity in the entire country. There would be no computers to operate our defense mechanism. The nation would be completely helpless and would have to yield to the wishes of this individual who wants to be elevated to the position of Supreme Commander of the entire world. Billions of people would be killed throughout the world.

The Mahdi has arrived. He has been hastened into authority by creating chaos in the world. He has brought all of the ten kings under his control and he is worshiped by his followers. Israel has been untouched by his escapades at this time because he is in fear of annihilating his own people in Palestine, Syria, Egypt, and Jordan. The holy mosque on the temple mount must not be damaged and the city of Jerusalem is to be their secondary capital city. Israel will be no problem and he will take care of them at a later time. The country is completely surrounded by the Muslim nations and they will use conventional weaponry to bring them under control. The newly constructed city of Babylon will be his headquarters and he will rule the world from there. He signs a treaty with Israel and lets them build their temple and resume their sacrifices.

The coalition of nations goes against Israel to destroy them but their God protects them. The dictator is unhappy with the situation and breaks the treaty with Israel. He enters the temple and declares that he is God. He sets up his image in the temple and demands that the whole world is to worship him. Satan is kicked out of heaven and he and this evil dictator persecute Israel until the Lord returns to protect them again.

This is one scenario that may or may not be true. There are volumes that could be written on what may or may not happen at this time, but we do know that there are certain prophecies that must be fulfilled. How this actually will happen will probably not be known until the events unfold in a real life drama.

This army is described to be like horses, lions, and serpents. All three represent swift, powerful, and deadly destruction. The crowns like gold on their heads show that they will be victorious in their endeavors.

The radical Muslim Imams appear to be peace-loving people when they present themselves to the world, but to their own people they are preaching jihad and destruction of the infidels. There can be no peace for a nation of people who are in great bondage to their false god. The time will finally come when they will turn around and expose their backside and they will reveal that they have, in their tails, a head like a serpent and it will strike like lightning and with lethal force. Their true nature will be revealed but it will be too late to prevent their jihad and destruction of one and one half billion infidels on this earth.

The Muslim people will not be satisfied until the little Satan and big Satan are both destroyed and they can set up their evil form of government on this earth. It is no wonder that the kings of the earth are seen in chapter 17 to burn and destroy all forms of organized religion.

And the rest of men who were not killed by these plagues yet repented not of the works of their hands, that they should not worship devils, and idols of gold, and silver, and brass, and stone, and wood, which neither can see, nor hear, nor walk.

Rev. 9:20

There will be nearly one half of the people left on this earth after these disasters that have come upon them. You would think that by this time they would realize that these calamities were initiated by the hand of Almighty God, and that he is bringing his judgment upon sinful men. There is no disaster or calamity in this world that will be great enough to cause man to repent; the only thing that will bring repentance is the knowledge of sin in our lives and that the grace of God will forgive us of our sins. The remaining people on this earth will hang on to and continue to worship the things that they have accumulated and the things that they have made.

They would rather worship devils, or demons, that they can see than to worship the one who created them. They will continue to worship the riches of gold and silver that they have gained by their own devices than to experience the riches of a God who owns the entire universe. "What shall it profit a man if he shall gain the whole world and lose his own soul, or what can he give in exchange for his soul?" (Mark 8:36)

The many things that man has constructed with his own hands, and have become his idol, can neither see, nor hear, nor walk. What a shame that man will embrace the things of this world and have nothing to do with a God who sees everything that is going on in his life, and hears the cries of him that is suffering from the calamities around him, and the one that has a desire to walk with him, and have fellowship with him, and comfort him in these trying times!

Neither repented they of their murders, nor of their sorceries, nor of their fornication, nor of their thefts.

Rev. 9:21

Man has just gone through one of the most terrifying times in the history of mankind. One and one-half billion people have just been murdered right before their eyes. This should have a sobering effect upon their own hearts and cause them to seek forgiveness for the hatred and murder that is in their own hearts, but it seems to have the opposite affect and only increases the hardness of their own hearts.

Sorcery is a form of witchcraft whereby man can conger up visions and interprets the dreams of others. This is all accomplished through the enhancement due to the use of drugs. The very word comes from a root word from which we get the word *pharmacy*.

The use of drugs is already at an alarming level among the people of the world. It no doubt will get much worse by the time of the end. There is no repentance over the use of drugs at this time. The fact is that the use of drugs will probably help the people cope with their predicament.

Fornication is sexual perversion in and out of marriage. It can include premarital sex (free love among our youth), adultery (infidelity among the married people), and homosexuality of all kinds. Fornication will play a major role in the lifestyle of many, right up to the time of the end. The scripture declares that they will be *marrying and giving in marriage* right up to the time that the Lord returns to establish his kingdom. There will be no repentance from their fornication.

There will probably be lootings and robberies going on like no other time in history. The people remaining will rejoice over the bounty that can be gained from all of the murdered victims of this catastrophe. There will be no repentance on the part of man for any of the sins in their lives.

What kind of a god would command his people to perform such atrocities upon other members of the human race? Only the god of this world, that old serpent, the deceiver, the devil, and Satan could do such a terrible thing. As we shall see, in the next chapter, a just and loving God will warn the people of the earth that the time is short and he will give those who are left time to repent before it is too late.

CHAPTER 10

The Mighty Angel with the Little Book

We have so far seen the destruction of over one half the population of the earth at the hands of an evil government and by a despicable group of people. The people of the world have been tormented for five months by demons out of the bottomless pit. In chapter 6 we saw the destruction of one fourth of the world's population by wars, famine and pestilence. These disasters could not happen until Almighty God allowed the Lamb to open the seals. Even though God allowed the disasters to happen, he did not cause them to happen. They happened because an evil government wanted to reduce the population of the earth. They happened because of the sin in the hearts of wicked mankind. God only allowed these things to happen so man can see what is in the heart of man. We know that a loving God provided a witness so people could know the truth and accept his salvation, because there were said to be many souls under the altar that came out of this terrible time of tribulation.

In chapter 9 we saw the torture caused by the demons when they were loosed. Again, they could not perform their evil deeds until God allowed an angel to open the bottomless pit. These wicked angels had been locked up and waiting for the day when they could be set free to perform the wickedness that was in their hearts. A loving God did not perform the wickedness, he just allowed the fallen angels to show the world what they are really like. God provided the 144,000 to preach the gospel of the kingdom so people could hear, and repent, and receive God's mark upon their forehead and be exempt from the demon's torment.

Also in chapter 9 we saw the destruction of one third of the population of mankind at the hand of a two-hundred-million man army. This disaster could not happen until God allowed the four fallen angels to come out of the river Euphrates. Again God did not cause this disaster; he only allowed it to happen to reveal to the world the wickedness that is in man's heart.

In chapter 10, we will see that the second woe is coming to an end and God will warn the entire world of the third woe before it is allowed to begin. God gives every person in the world time to repent of their sins before the greatest time of tribulation that has ever come upon this world can begin.

And I saw another mighty angel come down from heaven, clothed with a cloud; and a rainbow was upon his head, and his face was as though it were the sun, and his feet like pillars of fire.

Rev. 10:1

John sees another mighty angel come down from heaven. Some authors believe that this is the angel of the Lord, or none other than the Lord Jesus Christ himself. There is, however, no indication that this is anything except another angel from heaven. Ever since the beginning of chapter 4, angels have had an important part to play in the affairs of man here on planet earth. There is, however, a conspicuous absence of angels and their influence during the church age. This angel is declared to be another mighty angel. He is no doubt a different angel than the ones blowing the trumpets.

The appearance of this angel is awesome in his description. He appears to be clothed in a cloud, which may indicate that he is above the earth, but in the clouds of the air around the earth. There is a rainbow upon his head. The rainbow was given by

God as a promise that he would never again destroy the earth by water, or a great flood. His face was as bright as the sun. Since he just descended from heaven, where he was in the presence of God, his face no doubt still shone from being in the presence and glory of the Father. (Remember how Moses' face shone when he came down from the mountain where he only saw the backside of God.) And his feet are like pillars of fire. To have something under one's foot is to have that thing under complete control and trodden down. The pillars of fire indicate that there is a destructive force involved in the power of the feet of this angel.

And he had in his hand a little book open; and he set his right foot upon the sea, and his left foot on the earth, And cried with a loud voice, as when a lion roareth; and when he had cried, seven thunders uttered their voices.

Rev. 10:2, 3

The angel had a little book that was open in his hand. This little book is different than the seven-sealed book of chapter 5. The sealed book was not open and could not be looked upon until the Lamb removed each seal. Here the book is open and can be seen and read by whoever looked upon it.

The mighty angel that is clothed in a cloud also stands with his right foot upon the sea and his left foot upon the earth. He is mighty and has been given authority over the entire earth including both land and sea. He opens his mouth like a lion when he roars and cries with a loud voice. When he stops speaking there are seven thunders that begin to speak. There are seven thunders because there is a storm brewing and this time it will be complete and result in a perfect storm.

And when the seven thunders had uttered their voices, I was about to write; and I heard a voice from heaven saying unto me, Seal up those things which the seven thunders uttered, and write them not.

Rev. 10:4

When the seven thunders began to speak, John was about to write and record what they are saying. He was instructed to not write what was being said. There are some things that God is not ready for us to hear about until it is in his timing. We will have to wait until God decides to reveal what is being spoken by the seven thunders.

> *And the angel whom I saw standing upon the sea and upon the earth lifted up his hand to heaven, And swore by him that liveth forever and ever, who created heaven and the things that are in it, and the earth and the things that are in it, and the sea and the things which are in it, that there should be time no longer.*
>
> Rev. 10:5, 6

The angel is again identified as being the angel that is standing upon the sea and upon the earth. He lifts up his voice and swears by one greater than himself. This is a good indication that this is not the Lord himself for he would not be swearing by himself. The Lord Jesus is, however, the one who is being sworn by, because he is the one who lives forever and ever, who created the heaven, the earth and the sea. This is his creation and he is about to reclaim it for himself and set up a kingdom where he will rule with a rod of iron and with righteousness.

Since he is the Creator of heaven, earth and sea then he alone has the authority to declare that there shall be time no longer. This does not mean that this will be the end of time; but it means that there will be no delay in bringing the judgment of this world to a fast conclusion.

> *But in the days of the voice of the seventh angel, when he shall begin to sound, the mystery of God should be finished, as he hath declared to his servants, the prophets.*
>
> Rev. 10:7

The seventh angel is preparing to sound his trumpet and when he begins to sound, the mysteries of God shall be finished. The mysteries of God are those things that God has spoken of by his servants the prophets. Mysteries are things that God has not yet revealed all that is to be known about a subject. God has declared to his prophets that there will be a time of Great Tribulation like no other time on earth. He has declared that he will send his Son back to earth to set up his millennial kingdom. He has declared that there will be an eternity where all of his children shall be with him in his presence and glory. These things will all begin when the seventh angel sounds his trumpet.

The entire world will hear the angel standing upon the sea and earth when he declares that time is running out and that God is about to bring an end to the world as they know it. It is time to repent and get your life right with God for that chance is fast running out.

So far in the book of Revelation we have learned very little about Israel and God's dealings with her during these last days. The only thing that has been declared is that 144,000 Jews will be sealed by God and go forth preaching the gospel of the kingdom. Since the object of the Great Tribulation is to bring the nation of Israel back to God you would think that there would be much said about his dealings with her. The objects of God's dealings so far have been with the nations and peoples of the world. There are many prophecies in the Old Testament given by the prophets that have yet to be fulfilled concerning the people of Israel. A few of these prophecies are as follows:

The world ruler will confirm a covenant with Israel that is to last for seven years. He will break that covenant in three and one half years. He will commit the abomination of desolation that will cause the children of Israel to flee into the wilderness.

Dan. 9:27

The world ruler will subdue three of the ten kings and have power over Israel for a period of three and one half years.

Dan. 7:25

The end time shall last for a period of three and one half years.

Dan. 12:5-7

Israel to be judged and two thirds of the people killed.

Zech. 13:8, 9

There are a few prophecies in the Old Testament that have to do with the nations of the world that have not yet been addressed in the Book of Revelation. Some of them are as follows:

The little horn subdues three of the ten kings.

Dan. 7:8

The willful king will exalt himself and will have much trouble on his hands.

Dan. 11:36-45

There will be a judgment of the nations around Jerusalem.

Joel 3:9-17

In the New Testament we find in Matt 24, Mark 13, and Luke 21 the Olivet discourse which gives an account of the end time events. 2 Thes. 2:3, 4 we are informed that the man of sin will be exalted and worshiped as God.

There are more prophecies about the Great Tribulation in the Old Testament and elsewhere in the Word of God than in this book of Revelation, and many of these prophecies must be fulfilled prior to the beginning of the next chapter.

And the voice which I heard from heaven spoke unto me again, and said, Go and take the little book which is open in the hand of the angel who standeth upon the sea and upon the earth.

Rev. 10:8

John hears a familiar voice from heaven, the one that he heard before, at the beginning of chapter 4, and the voice is directing him to take the little book that is open from the hand of the angel that is standing upon the sea and the earth.

And I went unto the angel, and said unto him, Give me the little book. And he said unto me, Take it, and eat it up; and it shall make thy belly bitter, but it shall be in thy mouth sweet as honey.

Rev. 10:9

John is obedient to the voice that he hears and he goes and speaks to the angel with the little book. He asks the angel for the little book and the angel replies that he should take the book and that he should eat up the little book. John is informed that when he eats the book that it will make his stomach ache and become bitter, but when he tastes the book in his mouth it will be as sweet as honey.

The little book that is open is the Word of God. Whether it is the written word as we know it today, or a new revelation that God is revealing to John at this time about the things that are going to happen in the future, we are not informed. In either case, the word of God is sweet in our mouths when we read of God's grace and salvation that he has extended to all those that put their trust in his Son, and accept the fact that he is the one who has given his life for the ones whom he loves. The word is sweet when we read of the kingdom that is coming and of the eternal state of the believers in the presence and glory of Almighty God.

When God asks us to share the word with others and tell the world of the judgments that are to come, the word becomes bitter to us and makes our stomachs ache because it is very difficult to tell people of the doom that lies ahead.

> *And I took the little book out of the angels hand, and ate it up; and it was in my mouth sweet as honey, and as soon as I had eaten it my belly was bitter.*
>
> Rev. 10:10

John takes the little book and does as he is instructed to do by the angel, and as predicted, the book was sweet as honey in his mouth but was bitter in his stomach.

> *And he said unto me, Thou must prophecy again before many peoples, and nations, and tongues, and kings.*
>
> Rev. 10:11

It is no wonder that John's stomach hurts. He is informed that it is his responsibility to reveal to many people, and nations, and tongues, and kings, the things that were written in the little book. He must inform the people of the world that a time of trouble like never before is about to come upon this world. He is to inform the nations of the world that their time to rule this world is coming to a drastic and final conclusion. He is to inform the different ethnic groups that there will be turmoil in their midst. And he is to inform the ten kings in control of the world at this time that their kingdom is coming to a close, and that a final world dictator is about to emerge on the scene, and that he too will be destroyed upon the return of the Lord Jesus Christ.

God's message of grace and salvation through faith in his Son has been extended to the whole world prior to the beginning of the seven years of tribulation as spoken by the prophets of old.

CHAPTER 11

The Measuring Of the Temple, the Two Witnesses, and the Third Woe

The final seven years of the "times of the Gentiles" is about to begin. But it cannot begin until several prophesies have been fulfilled. The authority of the ten kings has been usurped by the final world dictator as he has subdued three of the kings and placed himself in position of supreme commander of the world. The world dictator has confirmed a covenant with Israel that is to last for seven years. The signing of the covenant will start the beginning of the last week, or seven years, of Daniel's "seventy weeks." These activities have been going on behind the scene and are not recorded in the book of Revelation by John the Apostle.

As we begin the eleventh chapter we see that the temple of God on this earth is mentioned for the first time in this book. The temple is to be a place of worship for the nation of Israel. The children of Israel have returned to their land as predicted by the prophet Ezekiel.

> *And there was given to me a reed like a rod; and the angel stood, saying, Rise, and measure the temple of God, and the altar, and them that worship in it.*
>
> Rev. 11:1

John is given a reed that looks like a rod. The reed, or rod, is predetermined to be a certain length and is used in surveying as a means of measurement. The angel stands and tells John to measure the temple of God. When we buy a piece of property the first thing that we want done is to have it surveyed so that we know the exact measurement of our possession Since this is the temple of God, he too wants to establish the exact measurements of his property. It should be noted here that this is another prophecy that is being fulfilled behind the scene; the building of the temple of God.

Not only the temple is surveyed but also the altar is measured. The altar is the place where sin is covered by the substitution of the death of an animal in our stead. The forgiveness of sins is the sole responsibility of a just God who knows the thoughts and intents of mans hearts. He alone has the right to own his altar of forgiveness.

The people who worship at this temple and the altar are also God's possession and he measurers them to let them know that they are his prize possession.

> But the court, which is without the temple, leave out, and measure it not; for it is given unto the Gentiles, and the holy city shall they tread under foot forty and two months.
>
> Rev. 11:2

The covenant that will be signed by the dictator and Israel will only allow for the construction of the temple and the altar as a place for God's children to worship him. The courtyard around the temple is not measured because it is not yet God's possession. The city of Jerusalem will belong to the Gentile nations and they will tread it under foot for three and one half years. This is the first three and one half years of Daniel's "seventieth week." This should be a time of peace for Israel since they have a treaty with the dictator that assures them protection and a place for worship.

Ezekiel 38 and 39 tells of a time when a confederacy of Muslim nations will come against Israel to destroy them. This is to be when Israel has unwalled cities, or at least has some semblance of peace and security. This is the only time in the scriptures that describes such a situation. If this is the time for the fulfillment of this prophecy then it will surely not be a very peaceful time for the people of Israel. No matter when it does happen we know that Israel's God will save them from their enemy.

> *And I will give power unto my two witnesses, and they shall prophecy a thousand two hundred and threescore days, clothed in sackcloth.*
>
> Rev. 11:3

God always raises up a witness for himself to declare to the world who he is and that he is Almighty. At this time in history he is faithful to raise up two special witnesses and gives them extraordinary powers. These two witnesses will prophecy for a period of one thousand two-hundred and sixty days. If we use the Jewish calendar consisting of twelve months of thirty days each, or 360 days in a year then this time will be exactly three and one half years. These two witnesses will live during the first three and one half years of the seventieth week of Daniel. They will appear as true Old Testament prophets for they will be clothed in sackcloth. Sackcloth indicates that these are "prophets of doom," and is a symbol of mourning and lowliness of spirit. This will be a time for the nation of Israel to repent and turn their trust back to their God. Their God is the only one who can protect them and assure that they will survive this terrible time in the history of mankind.

> *These are the two olive trees, and the two candlesticks standing before the God of the earth.*
>
> Rev. 11:4

We are immediately reminded of the two olive trees and two lampstands as described in Zechariah chapter 4. There they represent two witnesses who will be raised up to declare the power or

Almighty God. Here they are declared to be two olive trees and two candlesticks. An olive tree produces olives, which produces olive oil, which produces light for the lamps. The lamps cannot shine without the oil to give it power to shine. They are to be two shining lights in an evil world. Their strength does not come from within, but from the abiding Spirit of God. These two witnesses will be filled with the Spirit of God and will be a shining light throughout the entire world. They have an unlimited supply of oil because they are an entire tree of olives. They are standing before, but under total control of, the God of this earth. It is their delight to serve the one who is the Creator of this world.

> *And if any man will hurt them, fire procedeth out of their mouth, and devoureth their enemies; and if any man will hurt them, he must in this manner be killed.*
>
> Rev. 11:5

These two witnesses are indestructible. They have been given power to spew fire out of their mouth to devour any enemy that tries to harm them. There will be many who try to hurt them or even kill them but they will not succeed. If someone does succeed in doing harm to one of the witnesses, then that person will be put to death by the same method that he used to do the harm. If he used stones then he would be stoned to death. If he used clubs then he would be clubbed to death. If one is shot then the one who did the shooting would be shot to death.

> *These have power to shut heaven, that it rain not in the days of their prophecy; and have power over waters to turn them to blood, and to smite the earth with all plagues, as often as they will.*
>
> Rev. 11:6

These two men have power to shut the heavens so it does not rain upon the earth for any duration that they shall choose during the time of their prophecy. They will have power to turn water into blood just as Moses did. They will have power to send any plague imaginable upon the earth as oft as they choose.

Some people believe that since these two witnesses have the same powers that were extended to Moses and Elijah, that they will come back to earth at this time and be these two witnesses. There is no indication here that this will be the case. God can just as well raise up two new witnesses at this time to do his will.

And when they shall have finished their testimony, the beast that ascendeth out of the bottomless pit shall make war against them, and shall overcome them, and kill them.

Rev. 11:7

After three and one half years of testimony for the God of heaven and earth, their testimony will come to a tragic end. The beast (world dictator) who is demonic controlled (he ascends out of the bottomless pit), will make war with the two witnesses and kill them. It will take the strong army of the dictator to defeat the two men that can spew fire from their mouths and smite the earth with all kinds of plagues at their will. The dictator finally has had enough of their testimony and irritations and says enough is enough and kills them both.

And their dead bodies shall lie in the street of the great city, which spiritually is called Sodom and Egypt, where also our Lord was crucified.

Rev. 11:8

These two great men of God were not even given a descent burial. This shows the hardness and cruelty that will be in the hearts of men at the time of the end. They will just let their dead bodies lie on display in the street of the great city of Jerusalem. This will be an example to any others who resist this kingdom in any way. The city is called (spiritually) Sodom because of its total depravity and sin sickness. It is called Egypt because everything about it has become worldly. Egypt represents the world. We know that this is the city of Jerusalem because that is where our Lord was crucified. What a reminder that this is the city where the Son of God was crucified! This city will always be remembered that this is the place that Jesus Christ gave his life for the sins of the world.

> *And they of the peoples and kindreds and tongues and nations shall see their dead bodies three days and a half, and shall not suffer their dead bodies to be put in graves.*
>
> Rev. 11:9

All people, nationalities, tongues and nations will observe their dead bodies as they are displayed on television throughout the world. They will lie in the street for three and one half days and no one will allow anyone to bury their dead bodies.

> *And they that dwell upon the earth shall rejoice over them, and make merry, and shall send gifts one to another, because these two prophets tormented them that dwelt on the earth.*
>
> Rev. 11:10

All those who dwell upon this earth shall rejoice over the death of these two witnesses. The statement (they that dwell upon the earth) means that the earth is the place where they abide and it is the center of their affection. They are worldly in nature and there is no hope for them for anything beyond the pleasures of this world. These two men are dead and the whole world is merry, and has a great celebration, and they send gifts to one another.

Those who "dwell on the earth" have been tormented by these two prophets and they will be very happy to see them dead. The prophets have turned their precious water into blood. They have withheld the rain that was needed for their crops and their very survival. They have brought every conceivable plague upon them, which have disrupted every aspect of their lives. The world that they love and worship so much has been turned upside down. The torment is finally over, after three and one half years of misery, and they can celebrate with one another and get on with their lives.

> *And after three days and a half the spirit of life from God entered into them, and they stood upon their feet, and great fear fell upon them who saw them.*
>
> Rev. 11:11

As the whole world celebrates the death of the two prophets, all at once, after three and one half days, as everyone is watching, these men come to life. The spirit of life from God enters into them and they stand on their feet. The celebration comes to a sudden halt as the people stand in amazement and with great fear because their tormentors are once again alive.

> *And they heard a great voice from heaven saying unto them, Come up here. And they ascended up to heaven in a cloud, and their enemies beheld them.*
>
> Rev. 11:12

The two prophets of God hear a great voice coming from heaven. The voice says to them, "Come up here." They immediately are resurrected and ascend up to heaven to be with their Lord and savior. As they ascend through the clouds, their enemies look on with astonishment at what is happening right before their eyes.

> *And the same hour was there a great earthquake, and the tenth part of the city fell, and in the earthquake were slain of men seven thousand; and the remnant were affrighted, and gave glory to the God of heaven.*
>
> Rev. 11:13

Within the same hour of the resurrection of the two prophets there is a great earthquake in the city of Jerusalem. One tenth of the city is destroyed by this earthquake and seven thousand men are killed.

All those who remain are frightened and give glory to the God of heaven. They are thrilled to see their tormentors gone, but they certainly understand where the two witnesses have gone and understand the source of the great earthquake.

The second woe is past and, behold, the third woe cometh quickly.

Rev. 11:14

The second calamity is finally over and there is one more to come. The third woe will be coming quickly. The angel has just informed us that there will be no delay in the completion of the judgment of this world.

We have just reached the middle of the last week. Three and one half years of the "covenant of peace" has expired. The Israelites have been worshiping in their temple for a few years. The final world dictator, along with his ten kings, is in control of the entire world. The world seems to be on the road to recovery and to a time of prosperity. But wait, there is one more *woe* yet to come.

Before the second half of the last week can proceed there are some more prophecies that must be fulfilled. The dictator must break his covenant. He must exalt himself to be God. He will set himself, along with his image, in the temple to be worshiped. The sacrifices of the Jews will cease. Satan will be kicked out of heaven and will begin to take his fury out on Israel. The Children of Israel will flee into the wilderness where God will care for them for three and one half years. The seventh trumpet is about to sound and the next three and one half years of *Great Tribulation* will begin.

The rest of this chapter is hard to understand because it does not seem to fit into the order of events that must happen. The best way to understand this passage is to visualize yourself at the great Indy 500 motor speedway on race day. The race is about over; there is only one lap left. The lead cars are approaching the finish line to begin the last lap. As the first car crosses the finish line the judge raises a white flag, indicating that the last lap has officially begun. The crowd of spectators immediately rises to their feet, and they begin cheering in anticipation of the finish of this great race. They continue cheering until the winning car crosses the finish line.

When the seventh trumpet sounds the crowd of spectators in heaven begins to cheer because they know that the race for control of this earth is coming to a rapid conclusion. The race is beginning its last lap and they know who the winner is going to be.

The Seventh Trumpet

And the seventh angel sounded; and there were great voices in heaven, saying, The kingdoms of this world is become the kingdom of our Lord, and of his Christ, and he shall reign forever and ever.

Rev 11:15

As the seventh and last trumpet sound there is heard many voices in heaven. The crowd of spectators is anticipating the time when the struggles on this earth will end and a kingdom of righteousness will begin. They know that the seventh trumpet will initiate the final calamity on earth and then such a kingdom will begin.

At the sound of this trumpet the struggle for supremacy by the nation of this world will begin. All of the nations of the world will be defeated and *the times of the Gentiles* shall be no more. We know from the book of Daniel that the Lord Jesus will smite the great image on its feet and it will come crashing down. In its place will grow a great kingdom that shall last forever and ever. The Lord Jesus Christ, the Messiah, shall rule this kingdom with a rod of iron. Righteousness and justice shall prevail in this kingdom that shall last for one thousand years.

> *And the four and twenty elders, who sat before God on their seats, fell upon their faces, and worshiped God, Saying, we give thee thanks, O Lord God Almighty, who art, and wast, and art to come, because thou hast taken to thee thy great power, and hast reigned.*
>
> Rev. 11:16-17

In anticipation of the kingdom age, the twenty four elders that are sitting before the throne of God fall on their face to worship God. These elders are representatives of the church in heaven while all of this tribulation is going on down on planet earth. They worship God because he is going to show his power and might and begin to reign over the affairs of the world. They give thanks and worship him because he is omnipotent, and eternal.

> *And the nations were angry, and thy wrath is come, and the time of the dead, that they should be judged, and that thou shouldest give reward unto thy servants, the prophets, and to the saints, and them that fear thy name, small and great, and shouldest destroy them who destroy the earth.*
>
> Rev. 11:18

When the seventh trumpet sounds, the nations of the earth become angry because they know that their time on this earth is limited. The wrath of God is going to be poured out upon this earth like never before. The last three and one half years of man's rule over this world, called the Great Tribulation, will be most unbearable. "It is a fearful thing to fall into the hands of an angry God."

At the end of the tribulation period there will be a resurrection of the Old Testament saints and also all of the believers in Christ who have died since the rapture of the church. There will be a time of judging at this time because only those who fear the name of God, and trust in him, will be resurrected. All of these will receive their rewards at this time. The crowd of onlookers is looking forward to this day.

Also at the end of the tribulation God will destroy all those who have had a part in trying to destroy the earth. This will include all those who are alive when Christ returns in power and glory. There will be a separation of the sheep from the goats and only those who have been kind to his people during this time of trouble will be considered sheep. The sheep will continue on into the kingdom and all the rest will be destroyed.

> *And the temple of God was opened in heaven, and there was seen in his temple the ark of his testament; and there were lightnings, and voices, and thunderings, and an earthquake, and great hail.*
>
> Rev. 11:19

At the end of the heavenly scene, and the rejoicing over the sounding of the last trumpet, we see the temple of God opened in heaven. The temple is the dwelling place of Almighty God. He has in his temple the Ark of the Covenant. This is a continual reminder of the covenant that he made with the children of Israel during their wilderness journey. In the Ark are three articles. The tablets of stone of his commandments, Aaron's rod that budded, and a bowl of manna were in the Ark. His commandments are a reminder that all those who keep his commandment shall have eternal life. God knew that no man could keep his commandments, so he sent his Son to fulfill the Law and all those who put their trust in the Son would be saved.

The law was given to show us that we need a savior and it became a school master to lead us to Christ. Aaron's rod that budded is a constant reminder that those that trust in God's Son will be resurrected in the last day. The manna is a reminder that God provided for the children of Israel for forty years in the wilderness, and he will take care of them during this most terrifying time in their history.

There is a terrific storm approaching. The lightning is flashing, the thunder is rolling, and there are many anxious voices in anticipation of the mighty storm. There is an earthquake that rattles the earth and when the storm hits, it is tremendous and pours out much hail.

The purpose of the seventh trumpet is twofold. First and foremost, it is to make the Israeli people repent and return back to the God of their fathers. It will accomplish this purpose. Secondly, it will do away with the evil, perverse governments that Satan—with man's help—has contrived to rule the people of this earth. This, too, will be accomplished by the destruction of all of the Gentile nations of this world.

CHAPTER 12

The Characters of the Tribulation

Starting with this chapter and continuing through chapter 14 we will not see much movement in the chronological events of the end time. What we will be seeing is a series of visions that are seen by John that reveal the main characters involved in the end time events. We will get a little glimpse of what part they play and a description of the things they are doing behind the scene.

Israel the Woman

And there appeared a great wonder in heaven; a woman clothed with the sun, and the moon under her feet, and upon her head a crown of twelve stars. And she, being with child, cried, travailing in birth, and pained to be delivered.

Rev. 12:1-2

And he dreamed yet another dream, and told it to his brethren, and said, Behold, I have dreamed a dream more; and, behold, the sun and the moon and eleven stars made obeisance to me.

Gen 37:9

The first vision that John sees is a great wonder in heaven. The wonder is a sign that is seen in heaven but the activity of this wonder will be here on this earth. There is seen a woman clothed with the sun and she has a moon under her feet. From the passage in Genesis we learn that the sun represents Jacob, and the moon represents his wives. The eleven stars represent their eleven sons, minus Joseph, which are to be a crown on the parent's head. This is the beginning of the children of Israel. A religious organization is depicted as a woman in the scriptures. This woman will eventually be the wife of Jehovah. Israel is the first character to be described and she will have a major part to play in the end time events. Even though she will be a main character during the tribulation period and millennial kingdom, there is not much mention of her in the book of Revelation. The book of Revelation has more to do with God's dealing with the Gentile nations during the end time.

She is seen here to be with child. God told Abraham and some of his descendents, including the prophets, that he is going to send a Savior into the world to deliver them out of their bondage to sin and to deliver them from the control that other Gentile nations have over them. God will send the Messiah who will establish his kingdom on earth and rule over his people Israel. They have been crying and travailing for the birth of their Messiah to be born and deliver them from their enemies and to establish his kingdom.

Satan the Great Red Dragon

And there appeared another wonder in heaven; and, behold, a great red dragon, having seven heads and ten horns, and seven crowns upon his heads. And his tail drew the third part of the stars of heaven and did cast them to the earth; and the dragon stood before the woman who was ready to be delivered, to devour her child as soon as it was born.

Rev. 12:3, 4

There is another sign in heaven and this time it is a great red dragon with seven heads, ten horns and seven crowns upon their heads. The great red dragon is Satan. The seven heads are the seven great Gentile nations that will be doing the will of Satan here on the earth. Satan will use these Gentile nations to accomplish his goal to have all mankind worship him. He must have a means of promoting himself, and he has chosen to use the existing political systems that man has established. The ten horns will be the ten kings that shall rule in the last days. The seven heads each are wearing crowns which indicate that they have been given authority to rule. There will be more discussion on this subject when we study chapter 17.

When Satan rebelled against God he had one third of the angels in heaven believe in him and they followed him. They were cast unto the earth where they became demons that tempt and torment mankind. Some of them have been chained in darkness waiting for their release as studied in chapter 9.

The dragon is seen standing before Israel waiting for the Messiah to be delivered so he can kill him as soon as he is born. When King Herod heard that The King of Israel had been born he sent out the decree that every male child under the age of two should be killed. God warned Joseph and Mary that they should take their child and flee to Egypt where he would take care of them. They were obedient and spared the attempt on Jesus' life when he was born. The nations of the world have done their best to destroy Israel so the Messiah could not come into the world. Satan tempted Jesus to follow him so his work on the cross could not happen. The great dragon is red from the blood of the saints who have been killed because of their faith in Jesus Christ. Satan thought that he could defeat Jesus if he could have him put to death on the cross. Again he was foiled because Jesus arose from the grave and ascended to heaven to be with his Father until the appointed time for him to return and put his enemies under his footstool.

We see that Satan is actively trying to defeat Israel clear up to the time of the end. Satan and his angels, along with the nations of the earth, have a major role to play in the end time events.

Christ the Male Child

And she brought forth a man child, who was to rule all nations with a rod of iron; and her child was caught up unto God, and to his throne. And the woman fled into the wilderness, where she hath a place prepared by God, that they should feed her there a thousand two hundred and threescore days.

Rev. 12:5, 6

In due time, the King of the Jews was born into the family of Israel. God's promise to Israel was that he would send a king who would bear the scepter of David and he would rule all nations with a rod of iron. When Jesus was born, the nation of Israel expected him to become their Messiah and immediately establish his kingdom of righteousness and bring peace to this world. When Jesus was resurrected and caught up by God and set upon his throne in heaven, the nation of Israel rejected him. He is, today, on his throne at the right hand of God interceding for those who come to him in prayer. He will be there until he returns for his church in the air.

The vision immediately jumps ahead over two thousand years until the last three and one half years of Great Tribulation. At the beginning of the 1260 days in time, the world dictator will sit in the temple of God in Jerusalem and declare that he is God. This will be recognized as the "abomination that causes desolation" that is spoken by the prophet Daniel. When this happens the children of Israel are instructed to flee into the wilderness where God has prepared a place for her.

Israel will be fed and provided for by them. Both the Father and the Son will feed them for 1260 days or three and one half years.

War in Heaven

And there was war in heaven; Michael and his angels fought against the dragon, and the dragon fought and his angels, And prevailed not, neither was their place found any more in heaven.

Rev. 12:7, 8

Up until the time of the middle of Daniel's seventieth week, Satan is seen in heaven before the throne of God accusing the brethren. Jesus is there as our attorney and pleading our case. We are found not guilty because we have been washed in the blood of Christ. At the appropriate time Michael the archangel, and his angels, wage war on Satan and his angels. This is no contest and the devil and his angels are cast out of heaven. They are not ever allowed to appear in heaven again.

And the great dragon was cast out, that old serpent, called the Devil and Satan, who deceiveth the whole world; he was cast out into the earth, and his angels were cast out with him.

Rev. 12:9

We learn from this verse that the great dragon really is that old serpent called the devil and Satan. When he is called that old serpent, we are reminded that he is the one who appeared as a serpent when he deceived Eve in the Garden of Eden. Since that time he has been called the devil or Satan. He not only deceived Eve, but he has deceived the entire world. He is the greatest deceiver that ever existed. If the very elect are not careful he will deceive even them. One of his greatest deceptions is yet to come when he deceives the world into believing a lie about the rapture of the church. He will deceive the entire world in making them believe that he is God and the whole world will worship him.

The devil and his angels have no place to go except to be cast out into the earth. They are not persuaded to leave on their own accord but they were cast out like a bucket of bath water.

And I heard a loud voice saying in heaven, Now is come salvation, and strength, and the kingdom of our God, and the power of his Christ; for the accuser of our brethren is cast down, who accused them before our God day and night.

Rev. 12:10

When the devil is cast out of heaven there is heard a loud voice. The voice is declaring that now the time is short and the world will witness the salvation of Israel. The world shall witness the strong arm of God as he pours out his wrath upon a sinful world. It won't be long now until the kingdom that was promised so long ago will finally come to pass. Christ, the Messiah, will show his power when he rules during his kingdom that shall last for one thousand years.

These things are about to happen because the accuser of the brethren is cast down to earth. While Satan was in heaven he never ceased accusing the brethren. He continued around the clock, both day and night. All those in heaven feel the excitement knowing that the time is short.

And they overcame him by the blood of the Lamb, and by the word of their testimony; and they loved not their lives unto the death.

Rev. 12:11

The accused overcame the accuser because they were covered with the blood of Christ. His blood was shed to take away the sins of the world. Their very own testimony before their advocate was sufficient to overcome the accuser. The accused loved the Lord Jesus so much that they were willing to lay down their own lives rather than to deny the one who died for them.

Therefore rejoice, ye heavens, and ye that dwell in them. Woe to the inhabiters of the earth and of the sea! For the devil is come down unto you, having great wrath, because he knoweth that he hath but a short time.

Rev. 12:12

All those who dwell in heaven can rejoice because the accuser is cast down to the earth. But woe to the inhabitants of the earth and sea for the devil is now going to be dwelling in their midst. The devil has been cast out of heaven, never again allowed to return, and he is very angry. He has just lost another battle. Because of his anger he will begin to show his wrath and take out his fury upon the people of this earth. In particular he will be angry at the Israelites because they are the ones who brought the male child into this world. He believes that it is because of the male child that he is in this predicament. He will never admit that the fault lies in his own pride and disobedience. He now knows that he has but a short time to accomplish his goal of becoming the most high, and requiring all of creation to worship him.

Israel Persecuted By the Devil

And when the dragon saw that he was cast unto the earth, he persecuted the woman who brought forth the man child.

Rev. 12:13

The devil will not only be angry at the woman but he will begin to persecute her like she has never before been persecuted. This time for Israel will be a worse time than when they suffered at the holocaust at the hands of Hitler. All those who do not flee into the wilderness will suffer great persecution. The city will be ravaged, the women will be raped, and the men will be beheaded. There will be no escaping the fury of an angry devil. Matthew 24 tells us that when they see the desecration of desolation that they shall immediately flee into the wilderness. Do not go back into your house, and woe to those that are with child or nurse in those days, and pray that it is not in the winter. At this time two thirds of the population of Jerusalem shall fall at the hand of Satan. Those who endure until the end shall be saved and enter into the kingdom.

> *And unto the woman were given two wings of a great eagle, that she might fly into the wilderness, into her place, where she is nourished for a time, and times, and half a time, from the face of the serpent.*
>
> Rev. 12:14

Israel shall be given supernatural help from her God to help her escape into the wilderness. She will escape into the special place that God has already prepared for her. She will be able to flee rapidly like flying on the wings of an eagle. God will take care of her there and nourish her there just like he did for her in the wilderness as they fled from Egypt. This supernatural protection and provision will last for three and one half years. That will be the entire duration of the Great Tribulation. During this entire time they will be at the mercy and grace of their Father in heaven and the Lamb of God who died for them. They have just been saved from the coalition of Muslims who tried to annihilate them and now they have been delivered to a place of protection and nourishment. Israel now knows that the God of heaven is their God and they are his people. They will never again fall into the worship of money and idols.

> *And the serpent cast out of his mouth water like a flood after the woman, that he might cause her to be carried away by the flood.*
>
> Rev. 12:15

The devil has apparently found out where the children of Israel have been taken and protected. He has the power to cast a flood of water out of his mouth in order to annihilate, once and for all, the remainder of the Israelites. He thinks that the water is sufficient to totally destroy them.

> *And the earth helped the woman, and the earth opened up her mouth and swallowed up the flood which the dragon cast out of his mouth.*
>
> Rev. 12:16

Again their God uses his power over the elements of his creation and thwarts the effort of the devil to harm his children. The earth that Almighty God has created, responds to his control and it swallows up all the flood of water that has been sent to destroy his people. Remember how God dried up the Red Sea so the children of Israel could cross over on dry ground? He did this by sending a strong wind that separated the waters. When the Egyptians tried to follow, God stopped the wind and the water returned to drown them. Once again his people shall see the mighty hand of their God at work in their lives.

> *And the dragon was angry with the woman, and went to make war with the remnant of her seed, who keep the commandments of God, and have the testimony of Jesus Christ.*
>
> Rev. 12:17

Once again the devil is very angry with God's children because he has not been able to totally destroy them. He leaves them in the wilderness and continues to persecute the remnant that did not make it out of the city of Jerusalem and into a place of safety. The ones that are left have turned from their idolatry and are worshiping their God and keeping his commandments. They have realized that Jesus Christ is the one whom they pierced and he is the one who gave his life on the cross of Calvary that they might have eternal life. They too will be faithful to their new-found Messiah and be willing to suffer death because of their testimony.

We will continue to look at the cast of characters in the next few chapters.

CHAPTER 13

The Beast Out of the Sea and the Beast Out of the Earth

In chapter 12 we studied the cast of characters that have a part to play in the end time. The traditional teaching of chapter 13 has been that the "beast out of the sea" is the antichrist and the "beast out of the earth" is the false prophet. There are some problems with this interpretation that we must consider and we should therefore examine another alternative. The scriptures do not identify these two beasts as the antichrist and false prophet, so the identification is left to subjection. In chapter 19 we see that the beast and the false prophet are cast alive into the lake of fire so we know that they shall exist.

In the book of Daniel the beasts represent kingdoms. It may be that we should be consistent with Daniel in our interpretation. If the first beast is the antichrist then why does he have seven heads and ten horns, and upon his horns ten crowns? It is commonly taught that the antichrist will be mortally wounded and supernaturally come back to life. If this is true then which one of the seven heads is wounded? Horns are identified in scripture as kings and heads represent kingdoms. This does not fit the description and identification of the antichrist (world dictator) as described elsewhere in the scriptures. Why does the second beast have two horns like a lamb, and speak like a dragon?

In our study we will be consistent with other scriptures and let the beast with seven heads represent kingdoms and the horns represent kings or rulers of kingdoms. We will coordinate our interpretation with the 17th chapter where there is to be eight kingdoms but seven heads. There is also to be ten horns. The seventh head or kingdom is stated to "remain for a short space." The beast that was, and is not, even he is the eighth, and is of the seven, and goeth into perdition. With this information in mind we will consider the beast out of the sea to be the "*new world order*," the revived Roman Empire and the eighth kingdom.

The beast out of the earth will be considered to be the antichrist and false prophet or seventh head. This chapter will be looking at more of the characters that have a part in the end time. In the twelfth chapter there is no mention of two of the leading characters. These characters are the Gentile nations of the world and the final world dictator. These two characters are described in detail in chapter 13.

The Beast Out Of the Sea

And I stood upon the sand of the sea, and saw a beast rise up out of the sea, having seven heads and ten horns, and upon his horns ten crowns, and upon his head the name of blasphemy.

Rev. 13:1

After this I saw in the night visions, and, behold, a fourth beast, dreadful and terrible, and strong exceedingly, and it had great iron teeth; it devoured and broke in pieces, and stamped the residue with its feet; and it was diverse from all the beasts that were before it, and it had ten horns.

Dan. 7:7

In John's vision, he is standing on the sand of the sea and sees a beast rise out of the sea. In chapter 2 of Daniel, Nebuchadnezzar saw a vision of a great image with a head of gold, a breast and arms of silver, belly and thighs of bronze, legs of iron, and feet of iron and clay. This image is revealed to represent the four kingdoms that are to rule the world in the future. They are Babylon, Medo-Persia, Greece, and Rome. This vision is from man's viewpoint and man sees this image as a beautiful creation.

In the seventh chapter, Daniel has a vision and sees the same four kingdoms as beasts. This vision is from God's viewpoint and He sees them as wild beasts devouring one another. If they do indeed represent the same kingdoms, then the fourth beast must represent the Roman Empire. This beast is the only beast to have ten horns. There has never been a time in history when the Roman Empire was comprised of ten kings. This vision then must represent the revived Roman Empire as seen in the ten toes of iron and clay.

The beast rises out of the sea.
And he saith to me, the waters which thou saweth, where the harlot sitteth, are peoples, and multitudes, and nations, and tongues.

Rev. 17:15

This beast will be comprised of the masses of humanity from all corners of the world. The ungodly men of this world have been trying to form a world government ever since the time of Nimrod and the tower of Babel. They will finally succeed, in the time of the end, under the leadership and formation of the new world order led by ten kings, who have had no kingdom as yet, and eventually under the leadership of the world dictator.

The beast has seven heads. This beast represents all of Gentile domination imposed upon the world since the time of Egyptian rule until the time of the end. According to Daniel 2:42, 43, this kingdom shall remain until God sets up his eternal Kingdom. This final beast will go into perdition (destruction) at the return of Jesus Christ in power and glory. It must have a major role to play in the end time scenario.

The *horns* have crowns. It should be noted that in chapter 12, the *heads* have crowns. The difference being that in chapter 12 the kingdoms are in view, and in chapter 13 the kings have come into power and are in control of world affairs. The crowns represent the fact that the kings have complete authority to rule. They also have the name of blasphemy upon their heads. There is one thing in common with all of these kingdoms, and that is the fact that every one of them thought that they had the right to rule through man's wisdom with a total disregard to the God of Heaven. They all "counted God as nothing" when it came time for them to rule their kingdom. God eventually showed every one of them that He had ultimate control upon whom and when they should have authority. He "puts up whom He will and puts down whom He will" whenever He wills.

And the beast which I saw was like a leopard, and his feet were like the feet of a bear, and his mouth like the mouth of a lion; and the dragon gave him his power, and his throne, and great authority.

Rev. 13:2

No wonder Daniel described this beast as "dreadful and terrible, and strong exceedingly." It will act swiftly like a leopard. A bear is noted for its strength and it "will stamp the residue with his feet." And the lion will have "great iron teeth; it will devour and break in pieces." When a lion opens its mouth and roars it puts fear into all of its prey. This beast will have all of the attributes of all of the kingdoms before it. Greece was swift as a leopard, Media-Persia was strong like a bear and Babylon was majestic and powerful like a lion.

The dragon (Satan), will give him all of his power. His power is limited; however, he will give everything he has to accomplish his purpose in ruling the world and have every man worship him. He will give a throne or seat from which he will have the right to rule. This kingdom will have great authority over all of the people of this world.

And I saw one of the heads as though it were wounded to death; and its deadly wound was healed, and all the world wondered after the beast.

Rev 13:3

There are seven heads on this beast and one of them is wounded to death. If the seven heads represent seven kingdoms, then they represent the seven Gentile kingdoms that have existed, or will exist, throughout history. They consist of Egypt, Assyria, Babylon, Media-Persia, Greece, Rome, and the final world dictator. According to Daniel, the only one of these that is not in existence, but will return into power, is the Roman Empire. The Roman Empire must be revived and consist of ten horns, or ten kings that will rule over the entire world. A little horn will come up after them and subdue three of the kings and emerge into becoming the world leader. When the Roman Empire is revived the entire world will be surprised and "wonder after the beast."

And they worshiped the dragon who gave power unto the beast; and they worshiped the beast, saying, who is like the beast? Who is able to make war with him?

Rev.13:4

The world will wonder after the beast and they will worship the dragon that has given the beast his power. The world will worship this new world order because of its majesty, power, and might. There has never been a kingdom like it since the world began. With the modern technology, conveniences, and warfare, the masses of humanity will think that they are in utopia. Who would think of warring against, or who would even want to fight against, such knowledge and power? There may be some that will resist this new kingdom; however, they will be in complete subjection to its authority so they will have no way to resist. They will have been made slaves to society and treated as "human cattle." By this time there will only be two classes of society; the rich and powerful and the poor and enslaved.

And there was given unto him a mouth speaking great things and blasphemies, and power was given unto him to continue forty and two months.

Rev. 13:5

Satan is the great deceiver and he is the one giving the power to this kingdom. There will be many lies and promises made to the people of the world so that they will think that there is nothing like the situation in which they find themselves. This will be a kingdom that disregards any existence of a God or any authority above themselves. The ten kings ruling this kingdom will declare themselves to be gods and demand ultimate allegiance to their authority. The people will be deceived into believing them.

This ten-king kingdom will be allowed to remain in existence after the world dictator takes control of the world. The dictator will use the existing kingdom as his foundation for rule and authority, and he will be more than happy to build upon it. Since this kingdom will be in existence when the Lord comes back in power and glory, it will join forces with the dictator and the dragon in persecuting the people of Israel during the final three and one half years of the tribulation. However the Lord will protect Israel during this "time of Jacob's trouble." After this, the kingdom will go into perdition.

And he opened his mouth in blasphemy against God, to blaspheme his name, and his tabernacle, and them that dwell in heaven.

Rev. 13:6

Blasphemy is the written, spoken, or implied statement that a person of honor does not deserve the honor bestowed upon him. It implies that a person does not count for anything. To blaspheme God deems that He does not exist and he is without authority. God's moral and spiritual laws do not exist if one says that God does not exist. Without moral laws there is anarchy, lawlessness, and total depravity in the lives of mankind. Without spiritual laws there is no need of the Savior and the forgiveness of our sins. In the last days "everyone will do what is right in his own eyes." This is anarchy!

When man blasphemes God's name, he declares that He is not who He says He is. He is not the Great I Am. He is not the Creator of our universe. He is not the redeemer of His people. He is not the final judge of all mankind. He is not the sustainer of life. He is not eternal, omnipotent, omniscient, and immutable. To believe these things leaves man without hope and without meaning to life.

To blaspheme His tabernacle one denies that Jesus Christ is "the way the truth and the life"; Jesus is the "door" into the tabernacle courtyard. He is the Lamb who was slain on the altar. He is the brazen altar where sin is dealt with. He is the laver where we are cleansed. He is the light of the world, the bread of life, and our intercessor as seen in the lampstand, table of showbread and altar of incense.

Blasphemy states that he is not our propitiation as seen in the mercy seat; nor our law, bread from heaven, or our resurrection as seen in the Ark of the Covenant. Without the figure of the tabernacle there is no way to know how sinful man can come into the presence of a Holy God. The tabernacle is the place that the living God chose to live among, and commune with, His people. This government has chosen to disregard the true and living God of the universe.

To blaspheme those who dwell in heaven is to deny the resurrection, and that the redeemed have a home in heaven, or even that there is the existence of heaven. To believe this, once again, leaves one without any hope or meaning to life.

This kingdom will declare that there is no God; that he is not who he says he is and denies the need of salvation for man and that there is a reward waiting for those who trust in God. It is no wonder that it can destroy over half the population on earth through wars, famine, and diseases without any remorse. It will be plagued with anarchy and violence throughout its dominion. Without a belief in God there is no love, compassion, morality, or justice. There will be genocide, murder, all kinds of immorality, and lawlessness on every hand. The kings will only be concerned on how they can control the people and use them for their own gratification and monetary gain.

And it was given unto him to make war with the saints, and to overcome them; and power was given him over all kindreds, and tongues, and nations.

Rev. 13:7

This kingdom, with the aid and direction of the final dictator and Satan himself, will make war with the saints (Israel and other believers). They will overpower them and kill them, or drive them into the wilderness where their God will protect them. Satan will give power to this kingdom to have ultimate control over every individual on the face of the earth. This Satanic trinity will eventually set up the long awaited kingdom where all peoples of the world will be in subjection to Satan and will be forced to worship and serve him.

And all that dwell upon the earth shall worship him, whose names are not written in the book of life of the Lamb slain from the foundation of the world.

Rev. 13:8

The great deceiver will finally accomplish the fulfillment of his pride and desire, to have all mankind worship him. This will be accomplished through Gentile kingdoms and world domination where all peoples of the world cannot exist without the provisions provided by a world government. The people will be dependent upon the government for their protection, food, raiment, health and well being. No one can exist without government support, provision, and protection. Because of the control and perceived provisions provided by this government the people will worship the one that gives his authority to the kingdom. Satan has finally usurped the authority of God (our sustainer), and since man must worship something, they have chosen to worship the new provider of life itself.

There will be a remnant that will not worship Satan and his kingdom. These are those who have their names written in the book of life of the Lamb. It is those who have received the Lamb as their Lord and Savior. God determined to provide a savior before the world was created because He knew that man would sin and fail to obey Him. He also keeps record of those that have chosen to follow him and worship Him. This record is recorded in the book of life, the names of those that have received eternal life.

If any man have an ear, let him hear.
Rev. 13:9

Do you have an ear? Are you interested in hearing the truth? Then open your ear and hear what has just been revealed about the total depravity of man and complete control of man by Satan to the extent that the whole world will worship him. Our only hope is to put our trust in the Lord Jesus Christ who died for our sins and set us free from the powers of darkness of this world. Do not be deceived!

He that leadeth into captivity shall go into captivity; he that killeth with the sword must be killed with the sword. Here is the patience and the faith of the saints.
Rev. 13:10

This is the law of *divine retribution*. Our Heavenly Father knows the hearts and actions of all of His creation. He alone will be the final judge for their affairs.

Ever since the fall of Satan, he has had the desire to conquer and bring his subjects into captivity. He first deceived a third of the angels of heaven to follow him. He then deceived Adam to follow him resulting in every man to be born with a sin nature and a desire to have dominion over others. There has been a desire by all men to bring others into captivity or subjection. This total dominion will be accomplished by the rich men of the earth through the influence of Satan in the form of a new world order.

Satan will receive for his efforts to bring every one into captivity, a just reward where he himself will be locked in the bottomless pit for one thousand years, and eventually cast into the lake of fire. The rich men and rulers of the final evil kingdom will be held in a place of torment until the final judgment, and eventually cast in the lake of fire with Satan, the beast and the false prophet.

There will be many billions of people killed by the sword when the evil leaders take control during the end time. These same men will be slain by the sword (the Word of God) when the Lord appears from heaven riding upon His white horse.

The Beast Out Of the Earth

And I beheld another beast coming up out of the earth; and he had two horns like a lamb, and he spoke like a dragon.
Rev. 13:11

The first beast comes out of the sea (the masses of humanity). This second beast comes out of the earth, is earthly, worships the earth, and is pantheistic in nature. The first kingdom has blasphemed the God of heaven and has removed any allegiance to Him from their form of government.

Pantheism is the worship of Gaia (mother earth) and is the fundamental belief of all pagan religions. It has been the basis of the belief system of all ungodly religions and is the worship of the creation rather than the Creator.

The beast out of the sea consists of seven heads and ten horns. It represents the power of all the Gentile kingdom preceding it, and the ten kings that have had no kingdom as yet. This is the revived Roman Empire, the new world order, the eighth kingdom mentioned in Rev. 17:11.

There is one more kingdom to emerge on the scene, and this is the final dictator, the man of sin, or the antichrist kingdom. Again, Rev. 17:10 states that it "must continue for a short space." This kingdom must emerge out of the ten-king kingdom since three of the ten kings must be subdued, and then it can arise greater than them all.

This kingdom will have two horns or two people in authority. The two that come to mind are the antichrist and the false prophet. These two, combined with Satan himself, make up the Satanic Trinity—Satan being God, the antichrist representing Jesus Christ; and the false prophet portraying the Holy Spirit. They will appear to be gentle like a lamb, but will speak and act like the devil. Satan will have achieved his long-time sought after kingdom where he can proclaim himself to be god and have the world worship him.

And he exerciseth all the power of the first beast before him, and causeth the earth and them who dwell on it to worship the first beast, whose deadly wound was healed.

Rev. 13:12

This kingdom exercises all the power that the first kingdom had developed. It owes all of its existence to the division of the world into ten regions and total world domination by the ten-king kingdom, the revised Roman Empire. Because the world has been brought under subjection of a totalitarian government, this kingdom causes the entire world to worship (show worth-ship), to the ones who brought it about. Without the first kingdom's power and control, the second kingdom could not exist.

The deadly wound that was healed has reference to the Roman Empire that ceased to exist and then miraculously reappears.

And he doeth great wonders, so that he maketh fire come down from heaven on the earth in the sight of men…

Rev. 13:13

The leaders of this kingdom will have extraordinary powers through the aid of Satan and technical aids available to them. With the space industry and space stations available at their disposal, it will be very easy to give the illusion of fire coming down from heaven. This and other illusions will deceive many.

And deceiveth them that dwell on the earth by the means of those miracles which he had power to do in the sight of the beast, saying to them that dwell on the earth, that they should make an image to the beast, that had the wound by the sword, and did live.

Rev. 13:14

The great deceiver and illusionist was able to deceive those who dwell on the earth with the miracles he had power to perform. He received his power from the master deceiver, the dragon. He instructed the inhabitants of the earth that they should make an image to the beast. This image was in honor of the great society created by the ten kings.

And he hath power to give life unto the image of the beast, that the image of the beast should both speak, and cause that as many as would not worship the image of the beast should be killed.

Rev. 13:15

In chapter 3 of Daniel, Nebuchadnezzar, king of Babylon, made a golden image of the vision he saw in his dream. He instructed the people of Babylon that anyone who did not bow down and worship the image, would be cast into the fiery furnace. We find here in the last days a similar situation where the person that does not bow down and worship Satan's image will be killed.

The leaders of this last kingdom seem to have power to make the image have life and to speak. With today's technology and animation it should be easy to make the image to appear to have life and speak, thus deceiving the people.

And he causeth all, both small and great, rich and poor, free and enslaved, to receive a mark in their right hand, or in their foreheads...

Rev. 13:16

This final kingdom will require every person on the earth to take a mark, either in their right hand, or in their forehead. This mark will probably be in the form of a microchip implanted under the skin. This chip will contain the identity of the person and every known thing about the person. Their health record, bank account, residence, age, sex, height, weight, eye color, hair color, drivers license number, social security number (if still in effect), and any other pertinent information. To many this will appear to be a good thing. It will be difficult to steal another's identification. Mentally ill and those who get lost can be immediately identified and returned to their residence or hospital. This chip will give complete control of the people by the government.

The problem with this mark is that it will identify the person belonging to and worshiping this new government. It will signify that the person receiving the mark is in total agreement with, and in subjection to, the government's control. For those believers in that day, the taking of the mark will be in total disobedience to the word of God. God expects his children to be controlled by Him and accept Him as their God and sustainer of all life.

And that no man might buy or sell, except he that had the mark, or the name of the beast, or the number of his name.

Rev. 13:17

The mark will be the identification required for buying and selling. Without it there will be no other means to transfer money. There will be no cash, checks, or credit cards, available to make transactions. It will be a total cashless society. There will be no more stealing of money, or bank robberies. Once the mark passes over a scanner the amount of purchase will be withdrawn from the person's account. The only way around this situation will be through bartering and this will be illegal and punishable by death if caught. For those who refuse to take the mark this will be their only alternative.

By taking the mark, one identifies oneself with the beast or the number of his name. That person will be in complete control of this diabolical system. This is the plan that Satan has had since his fall whereby he can control every aspect of every life on this earth. He now will be in a position where he must be worshiped or the people will perish.

> *Here is wisdom. Let him that hath understanding count the number of the beast; for it is the number of a man; and his number is six hundred threescore and six.*
>
> Rev. 13:18

It will require wisdom and understanding to count the number of the beast and identify who this man is. This wisdom and understanding may not be revealed to man until the man of sin appears on the scene. We do know that it is the number of a man, and his number will be 666.

There may be significance in the number 6, and the sequence of three sixes. The number for God is 3 and the number of man is 6. Seven is the number of perfection, and six does not quite measure up to that number neither can man attain perfection. The final dictator will be a man who sets himself up to be God and to be worshiped as God. He will enter the temple of God and sit upon his throne in the temple declaring himself to be God. This will be the abomination of desolation spoken of by Daniel the prophet.

Chapter 17 has the key to understanding the characters that have a major role to play in the end time events. We will look in more detail to the eight kingdoms and the seven heads with ten horns when we get there. The two beasts or kingdoms discussed in this chapter will be diabolical in nature. During the last seven years they will rule together as one kingdom with ten kings over the ten regions of the world and with one dictator over the entire world. This kingdom will have "great iron teeth and stomp the residue with his feet." There will be no one who can escape the tyranny of this Satan-controlled system.

It is not too late to trust Jesus Christ as your Lord and Savior today while there is still time. If you make this decision you will be changed in a moment, in the twinkling of an eye at the rapture of the church, when Jesus comes in the clouds for His Church. You can spend these last days in heaven with the Lord and avoid the cruel unjust tyrannical governments that are to follow the rapture.

Behold, I Come Quickly.
Even So, Come, Lord Jesus.

CHAPTER 14

The Victory of the Saints and Judgment of the World

In this chapter we will see the continuation of the series of visions that are being revealed to John. The first two visions will reveal the victory of the saints and the preaching of the everlasting gospel. The next two will reveal the fall of Babylon and the doom of those who take the mark of the beast. The fifth vision is a beatitude about the holy dead, and the final vision will show John that there will be a great harvest of the armies of the earth in the end time.

The Lamb with the 144,000 on Mount Zion

And I looked and, lo, a Lamb stood on Mount Zion, and with him an hundred forty and four thousand, having his Father's name written in their foreheads.

Rev 14:1

John looks and, behold, the Lamb of God is standing upon Mount Zion. Mount Zion is the place that has been foretold by the prophets to be the place from which Jesus Christ shall rule during the kingdom age. The mount is in Jerusalem and is known today as the Temple Mount. The only time that the Lamb shall stand on this mount is at the beginning of the Millennium and for the next one thousand years. Therefore, we know that the vision is at the time of the beginning of Christ's kingdom here on earth.

With the Lamb is seen 144,000 who have the name of the Lamb's Father (the God of Heaven) written in their foreheads. These have to be the same 144,000 that were told about in chapter 7. It is very unlikely that there would be another group of the exact same number with a mark in their foreheads in such a short period of time. It is amazing that they could be preaching the gospel of the kingdom for the past twenty or thirty years and they are still alive and appear with their Lord on the mount at the beginning of his kingdom. There is not one missing because their God has put his mark on them and preserved every one of them, even through the time of the Great Tribulation.

These men have been in the jungles, in the cities, in the deserts, and to every corner of the earth warning everyone alive that the King is coming, make your ways straight and repent. Oh, the stories that they can tell of how their God fed them, clothed them, and protected them from all of their enemies. There is no end to the hardships that they must have endured because of their zeal and love of their Lord. They can now begin to enjoy the comfort and fellowship that they experience with the Lord for the next one thousand years as they help him rule and reign over his earth.

And I heard a voice from heaven, like the voice of many waters, and like the voice of a great thunder; and I heard the voice of harpers harping with their harps.

Rev. 14:2

John has just seen a vision of the Lamb with his 144,000 preachers here on earth, on Mount Zion. Now all of a sudden his attention is drawn to a great choir and harpers who are singing and playing their harps in heaven. Their number is so great that they sound like many waterfalls and the sound of thunder. This must have been something to behold!

And they sang, as it were, a new song before the throne, and before the four beasts and the elders; and no man could learn that song but the hundred and forty and four thousand, who were redeemed from the earth.

Rev. 14:3

The choir is standing before the throne and they are singing a new song to the one sitting on the throne. The four living creatures and the twenty four elders are around the throne, and they are listening to this new song being sung to the God of heaven. No man could sing this song because it must have been praising God for his protection and preservation of the preachers for their faithfulness these last several years. There is no way that any man could understand the terrible time that these preachers have endured. Only they could appreciate the praise that is being declared to God on their behalf.

The 144,000 have been redeemed from the earth. This means that they have been purchased with a price, and given salvation through the shed blood of Jesus Christ. Because they have been purchased they shall enter the kingdom with their Lord and Savior. What a song of redemption and grace is being sung unto their God.

These are they who were not defiled with women; for they are virgins. These are they who follow the Lamb wherever he goeth. These were redeemed from among men, the first fruits unto God and to the Lamb.

Rev. 14:4

These preachers are said to be virgins; they have never been distracted from their responsibility of preaching the gospel by taking a woman as their wife. If they had, it would have been a burden to them to care for their loved one, and it would have hindered them from being a full-time minister of God's message that so desperately needed to be proclaimed at such a time as this.

Their undivided attention was to follow the Lamb wherever he led them, even to the end of the world.

They have been redeemed from among the men of this earth and have become the first ones to enter the kingdom with the Lamb. By so doing they have become the first fruits of the many that shall follow in the very near future. They have been gathered unto God and to the Lamb where they shall remain forever and ever.

> *And in their mouth was found no guile; for they are without fault before the throne of God.*
>
> Rev. 14:5

In their mouth was no guile; they did not portray a lie in any way during their ministry. They preached the truth of the word of God. They were not deceived in any way by the lies that were being perpetrated upon the world by the dictator and his kingdom. They did not join, in any way, into their deceit and deception.

These men were without a blemish on their record as they were presented before the throne of God. They were declared to be righteous because they were clothed in the righteousness of Christ. This is the same way that we will be seen as we stand before God for the first time. It will not be because of our goodness, but only because of the grace of God that we will even be able to stand.

The Everlasting Gospel

> *And I saw another angel fly in the midst of heaven, having the everlasting gospel to preach unto them that dwell on the earth, and to every nation, and kindred, and tongue, and people, Saying with a loud voice, Fear God, and give glory to him; for the hour of his judgment is come; and worship him that made heaven, and the earth, and the sea, and the fountains of waters.*
>
> Rev. 14:6, 7

The angels are very busy during these last days and John sees another one fly in the midst of heaven. He is flying around the world in the atmosphere above the earth. He has the everlasting gospel to preach to everyone on the earth. The everlasting gospel is the good news that everyone should fear God. The fear of God is the beginning of wisdom. Everyone who has put his trust and worship into the things of this earth should begin to fear God before the final judgment of the things they love begins to happen.

Again we are reminded that the people of this world love their world and love where they dwell. The gospel will reach the ears of every person that is still remaining on this earth. What a God who will warn the people of the doom that is coming before the disaster comes! All will be given a chance to repent and fear God prior to the plagues that are to fall upon the earth. The message of the angel is to fear God and give glory to him for the judgment is coming. Worship the one who made the heaven, earth, sea, and springs of water that flow from the earth. All of these things will be affected when God has the angels pour out their vials on the earth at the time of the last plagues.

If you have your love and trust upon the creation of God then you will be most miserable when you see his judgment fall upon His creation. If you have your affections on the Creator instead of his creation, the devastation will not seem so bad.

Babylon is Fallen

And there followed another angel, saying, Babylon is fallen, is fallen, that great city, because she made all nations drink of the wine of the wrath of her fornication.

Rev. 14:8

John sees another angel and he hears the angel say that Babylon is fallen. He repeats "is fallen" to emphasize the importance of this statement. Babylon has been the epitome of evil since her founding by Nimrod at the tower of Babel. The belief that man could form a universal government and rule himself was the basis of all the evil that followed this false religion. From this belief came the worship of the mother and child, the goddess worship, the belief that man can reach heaven by his own works, the worship of one man (Nimrod) above all others, and that the people of the world should be united under one world system.

Out of these beliefs Satan began to build his kingdom here on earth. He would use the nations of the world to form a foundation of control and dominance over the people of the world. Through this political and commercial system, he could take control of the entire world through the world dictator that he would promote, indwell, and control. Satan is seen as the beast, or dragon, throughout this entire book. He has seven heads that are the nations of the world that do his bidding and pave the way for Satan to rule the world and be worshiped by all mankind. The nations of the world have been deceived into thinking that this is a wonderful plan. They have been drunk from the wine and the wrath that will come because of Satan's fornication.

Doom For Those who Worship the Beast and Take His Mark

And the third angel followed them, saying with a loud voice, If any man worship the beast and his image, and receive his mark in his forehead, or in his hand, The same shall drink of the wine of the wrath of God, which is poured out without mixture into the cup of his indignation; and he shall be tormented with fire and brimstone in the presence of the holy angels, and in the presence of the Lamb; And the smoke of their torment ascendeth up forever and ever; and they have no rest day nor night, who worship the beast and his image, and whosoever receiveth the mark of his name.

Rev. 14:9-11

The third angel appears on the scene and John hears him speak with a loud voice. The voice of the angel is loud so everyone can hear him. The world dictator has set up himself to be god and to be worshiped as god. He has constructed an image of himself and requires that everyone bow down and worship his image. He has demanded that everyone receive a mark, either in their forehead or on their right hand. If they do not receive the mark they can neither buy nor sell which would eventually lead to their death.

The angel informs the earth-dwellers that if they worship the beast or his image or take his mark that God is going to pour out his wrath upon them. God's wrath will be poured out without being diluted. God has become indignant over the situation in the world and he will fill his cup of wrath to the brim, and his full judgment will be experienced by the whole world. What a predicament these people are in. If they do not take the mark they will die, and if they do take the mark then God's wrath will fall upon them.

The results of his wrath will be fire and brimstone that will torment the people in the presence of the angels and the Lamb. The smoke of their torment will ascend forever and ever, or for all eternity. At the great white throne judgment the unsaved of the world will be judged according to their works, but if their name is not written in the book of life they will be cast into the lake of fire that shall burn forever and ever. The Lamb and the angels will be the ones who are judging the people. There will be no rest from their torment day or night for the rest of eternity if they choose to worship the beast.

> *Here is the patience of the saints; here are they that keep the commandments of God, and the faith of Jesus.*
>
> Rev. 14:12

The saints of God who keep his commandments and have put their faith in the Lord Jesus Christ are waiting for the day when God says enough is enough; he will punish those who have disobeyed his commandments and not put their faith in Jesus. God will someday set the record straight and punish those that have gotten away with murder, lies, fornication, fraud, injustices in our judicial systems and governments, and any wrongdoing that they have committed upon one of their fellow men. For the saints to wait for that day takes patience, but we know that a just God must do what is right and punish those that do wrong.

The Holy Dead Shall Be Blessed

And I heard a voice from heaven saying unto me, Write, Blessed are the dead who die in the Lord from henceforth, Yea, saith the Spirit, that they may rest from their labors, and their works do follow them.

Rev. 14:13

John hears a voice from heaven telling him to write. The Great Tribulation is looming over the world. The Jews will be driven into the wilderness and those who do not make it will be killed. The mark of the beast will be required for everyone, and those that do not take it will be killed. The battle of Armageddon is coming where many will be killed. John is instructed to write that those who are in the Lord or those who have received him as their Lord will be blessed if they die before all of this tribulation comes upon them.

The Spirit informs them that they shall rest from their labors. They will not have to run into the wilderness. They will not have to hunt for their food in the garbage barrels because they have not taken the mark of the beast. They will not have to worry about the war that is threatening their very existence. They shall rest.

What a contrast from them that shall never rest from their torment for taking the mark of the beast. God will not forget the works that they have performed in his name and they will be rewarded for them.

The Harvest of The Earth

In order to understand this vision we must look at Matthew 25:31, and beyond, for a description of the separation of the sheep and the goats at the end of the tribulation period. We also need to look at Matthew 13:39-42 to understand that Jesus is the one who has the authority to judge the earth, but the angels are the ones who actually help with the reaping.

> *And I looked and, behold, a white cloud, and upon the cloud one sat, like the Son of man, having on his head a golden crown, and in his hand a sharp sickle.*
>
> Rev. 14:14

Again John looks and this time he sees a white cloud. When he looks a little closer he sees someone sitting upon the cloud. The appearance of the one sitting is like the "Son of Man." He has a golden crown upon his head which gives him the regal authority to rule over his creation. The sickle in his hand is an indication that there is going to be a harvest of some kind and it will be in the form of judgment. The sickle is used to cut the grapes from their vines, and to cut the grains from their roots to prepare them for the threshing floor. In both cases the fruit and seeds are removed from their parent plant and they no longer have life within themselves.

The world has heard that Jesus Christ will return someday and that he will come in the clouds. They do not believe this and he will come as a thief in the night when they least expect him to come. When he does come he will appear in the clouds and every eye shall see him. This will strike terror in the hearts of all those who dwell upon this earth. At the time of his coming all of the armies of the nations will be gathered around Jerusalem with the intent to overthrow the dictator. When they see The Son of Man in the heavens they will turn all of their attention and power toward him. There will be more discussion on this subject when we get to chapter 19.

And another angel came out of the temple, crying with a loud voice to him that sat on the cloud, Thrust in thy sickle, and reap; for the time is come for thee to reap; for the harvest of the earth is ripe.

Rev. 14:15

Another angel comes out of the temple. This is the dwelling place of God the Father. The Father has given the angel instruction that he needs to pass on to the Son. The angel cries with a loud voice unto the one sitting on the cloud and informs him that the Father has declared that it is time to beginning reaping. It is important to understand that it is the Father, and the Father only, who can determine when the harvest is to begin.

The harvest that is going to take place is the harvest of the earth. The Father declares that the fruit is ripe. The indication here is that the fruit is overripe, it is beginning to shrivel. God in his mercy and grace has allowed man every opportunity imaginable and all the time needed to repent of their sins and accept his Son's sacrifice on the cross for them, but they have refused to accept his free gift to them.

And he that sat on the cloud thrust in his sickle on the earth, and the earth was reaped.

Rev. 14:16

When the Son receives the word from his Father that it is time to start the harvest, he immediately is obedient to his Father and casts in his sickle on the earth. Jesus has the authority to harvest the earth and when he casts his sickle on the earth, the earth is harvested. Remember that in Matthew 13 we learn that Jesus has the authority to begin the harvest, but the angels are the ones who do the work of the harvest. Jesus has the authority because he is the owner of this field that is to be harvested. The remainder of this chapter will give some of the details on how the angels perform their work of harvesting.

And another angel came out of the temple which is in heaven, he also having a sharp sickle.

Rev. 14:17

There is seen another angel with a sharp sickle in his hand. He has come out of the very presence of God the Father in his temple in heaven. This angel has also been given the authority to harvest a crop.

And another angel came out from the altar, who had power over fire, and cried with a loud cry to him that had the sharp sickle, saying, Thrust in thy sharp sickle, and gather the clusters of the vine of the earth; for her grapes are fully ripe.

Rev. 14:18

Yet another angel comes out from the altar, no doubt from the golden altar of incense. This would be in direct response to the prayers of the saints who have suffered at the hand of the new world system. A holy, just God will answer their prayers and shed the blood of those who have shed the blood of his people. This angel has power over the fire of judgment of the wicked. The fire will remove all of the dross from the works of the wicked and there will be nothing left after their judgment.

The angel with the fire cries to the angel with the sharp sickle that he should start the harvest of the earth. It is time to gather the clusters of grapes from the vine of the earth because they are fully ripe. The meaning of ripe here is that the grapes are ready to burst from the juice within.

And the angel thrust in his sickle into the earth, and gathered the vine of the earth, and cast it into the great winepress of the wrath of God.

Rev. 14:19

The angel is obedient to thrust his sickle into the earth and begins to harvest. The grapes of the vine are fully ripe and they are thrown into the winepress where God's wrath will crush the blood out of them.

> *And the winepress was trodden without the city, and the blood came out of the winepress, even unto the horse bridles, by the space of a thousand six hundred furlongs.*
>
> Rev. 14:20

The winepress of God's wrath will be located outside the city of Jerusalem. A winepress was in the form of a vat and the grapes would be thrown into the vat and then the workers would get into the vat, barefooted, and begin to stomp on the grapes until they were all crushed and the juice squeezed out of them. When the Lord comes to the earth in power and glory, he will be greeted by the armies of the world gathered around Jerusalem for the battle of Armageddon. The angels of the Lord will stomp on them and their blood will be squeezed out of them. The blood will spurt as high as the bridles on a horse or about four feet high. The carnage will be spread over a distance of just under one hundred and eighty two miles. This distance is approximately the length of the entire land of Israel.

What a tragic end to the armies of this world! This will be no contest for the mighty angels of God.

CHAPTER 15

The Seven Last Plagues:

Judgment upon the Seventh Kingdom

The narrative picks up where it left off at the end of chapter 11. It will start with a heavenly scene in preparation for the final seven vial plagues that will contain the fullness of the wrath of God.

Before we begin, we must look at all of the activities that are going on here on the earth. We have reached the middle of the last "week of Daniel." The last three and one half years before the return of Jesus Christ in power and glory. The dictator has broken his treaty with Israel. He has declared himself to be god and desecrated the temple.

The children of Israel have been driven into the wilderness where their God will protect them for these three and one half years. Satan has been thrown out of heaven and cast a flood of water after Israel. God's earth has swallowed up the flood of water. Satan is angry and is in the land of Israel persecuting the Jews that did not make it into the wilderness. The cities are being ravaged, the women raped, and the men are being beheaded. The people of the earth have been required to worship the beast and take his mark in their foreheads or in their right hand or they cannot buy or sell. The dictator is in full control of the ten kings and they give all of their authority to him.

The earth is not a very nice place in which to be right now, and God is going to make it even worse as he prepares to pour out the fullness of his wrath upon the kingdom of the world dictator (The Antichrist). The trumpet plagues were directed at the "ten king kingdom" and the vial plagues, which are very similar but more severe, will be directed at the "dictator kingdom."

> *And I saw another sign in heaven, great and marvelous, seven angels having the seven last plagues; for in them is filled up the wrath of God.*
>
> Rev. 15:1

John sees a great and marvelous sign in heaven. He sees seven angels with the seven last plagues. In these plagues will be the wrath of God filled to overflowing. Almighty God has been very patiently waiting for man to repent and turn from his wicked ways, but instead of repenting he has become more wicked and disobedient to him. Man has cursed God and has blamed him for all of the difficulties that he is encountering at this time and is worshiping one of his created beings. The wrath of God has been kindled against man and he is about to send some terrible plagues to show the world that he is God and that all of the things that man enjoys were created by him.

> *And I saw, as it were, a sea of glass mingled with fire, and them that had gotten the victory over the beast, and over his image, and over his mark, and over the number of his name, standing on the sea of glass, having the harps of God.*
>
> Rev. 15:2

We are reminded of the heavenly scene in chapter 4 where the sea of glass is before the throne of God. Here John sees a sea of glass mingled with fire. In chapter 4 it was clear as crystal. The sea is as smooth as glass signifying the tranquility surrounding the throne and the glass will reflect the glory of God. The fire signifies that there will be judgment proceeding from the "Judge of All the Earth."

All those who have refused to bow down and worship the dictator are seen standing on the sea of glass. They have been victorious over his demands to worship him and his image, to take the mark in their foreheads, or to receive the number of his name. Their victory has resulted in their martyrdom, and now they are in the presence of God and are receiving the blessings that he promised for all those who die in the Lord at this time. They are seen with harps which indicate that they are worshiping the one who has redeemed them from their torment here on earth.

And they sing the song of Moses, the servant of God, and the song of the Lamb, saying, Great and marvelous are thy works, Lord God Almighty; just and true are thy ways, thou King of saints.

Rev. 15:3

Moses was a great servant of God and he sang songs unto his God. He sang a song in Exodus 15 thanking God for the deliverance through the Red Sea. Again in Deuteronomy 32 he sings a song praising God, because he is just and true and thanking him for his deliverance, salvation, and faithfulness. It is probably the latter song that is in mind here, for this song that the martyred saints are singing is to praise God for his justice and truth. The song of the Lamb is sung to thank him for being their redeemer.

Lord God Almighty, you are all powerful and you are wonderful and your works manifest who you are. Your ways are just, you must punish evil and reward good. There is no truth besides you, your Word is truth and it shall abide forever. Lord God Almighty, you are the King of all those who know you and we shall worship you forever and ever for the great and marvelous thing that you have provided for us.

Who shall not fear thee, O Lord, and glorify thy name? For thou only art holy; and all nations shall come and worship before thee; for thy judgments are made manifest.

Rev. 15:4

Our God is a Holy God. By being Holy he is set apart to perform those things that are only just and only true. Every individual should fear him and glorify his name because he is Holy. His righteousness, justice, and truth will be manifest on this earth as it is in heaven. The judgments that he extends to both the saved and unsaved alike will be performed with mercy, justice, truth and righteousness because he is Holy.

During the millennial kingdom, all nations will come and worship before him because they will then know that he is Holy. If they do not come and worship, God will withhold the rain from their land.

The judgments of God manifest that he is holy, just, true, and righteous. Sinful man always gets what he deserves when it comes from the hand of a Holy God.

And after that I looked and, behold, the temple of the tabernacle of the testimony in heaven was opened.

Rev. 15:5

There is seen a temple in heaven. Moses was given specific instructions on how to build the temple here on earth. It was to be built after the pattern that God would show him. The real temple is in heaven and the one that Moses built was to be patterned after the true temple. In the temple was the Holy of Holies where there was the Ark of the Covenant with the mercy seat over it. This is where the High Priest could commune with God once a year, and then only after certain conditions were met, to atone for the sins of the people.

In the ark were the tablets of stone which had engraved into them the commandments of God. His commandments give instructions on how man should conduct himself in every aspect of his life. This is God's testimony to man, and man will be judged in accordance to how he keeps God's commandments. If he breaks even one of them he is guilty of breaking them all. Man cannot live up to God's standard and that is the reason that God sent a Savior into the world, to rescue man from his sins.

The temple in heaven is opened. This is the place where the testimony of God's covenant and God himself are located.

And the seven angels came out of the temple, having the seven plagues, clothed in pure and white linen, and having their breasts girded with golden girdles.

Rev. 15:6

When the veil is opened from the entrance into the Holy of Holies, there are seen seven angels coming out of the temple, having the seven last plagues. Notice the use of seven as the number of seals, trumpets, and now the last plagues. The number seven signifies the indication of "completeness." These angels have the seven *last* plagues. These seven plagues will demonstrate the complete wrath of God and they will be the last ones that will come before the Son of God is revealed in the clouds at his second coming back to earth.

The angels are coming from the very presence of Almighty God. The pure white linen in which the angels are clothed, is a reassurance that God is righteous in sending the plagues. Their golden girdles will reflect the deity and glory of God.

And one of the four beasts gave unto the seven angels seven golden vials full of the wrath of God, who liveth forever and ever.

Rev.15:7

As the seven angels come out of the temple, they are approached by one of the four living creatures and he gives to the seven angels, seven golden bowls filled with the wrath of God. God is eternal, he lives forever and ever. He has also given man an eternal soul and what he has done with the Son of God will determine where the soul will spend eternity. It will either be in the presence of a loving God or in the lake of fire with the devil and his angels.

> *And the temple was filled with smoke from the glory of God, and from his power; and no man was able to enter into the temple till the seven plagues of the seven angels were fulfilled.*

The sea of glass is mingled with fire and its smoke fills the temple, because God is about to show his glory and power when the seven angels begin to pour out the bowls of his wrath upon the earth. No man is allowed into the presence of an angry God until all of the seven last plagues have been fulfilled. This is not a joyous time for a God who loved the world so much that he sent his only begotten Son to die for their sins. All man has to do is believe God, and repent of his sins, and accept the sacrifice that his Son had made on the cross of Calvary, and he could be saved and spend eternity with the one that loved him so much. Because of their unbelief, God is required by his holiness, righteousness, and justice to send judgment on all of them who have spurned such a wonderful plan of salvation.

The last seven terrible plagues are about to be poured out on a sinful world to show the people of this world that God is in control of his creation. He must judge the people, nations, kings, and dictator, for the evil that they have committed on his earth. It is not too late to repent and accept Jesus Christ as your Savior and Lord and escape the plagues that are to immediately come.

CHAPTER 16

The Vials of the Wrath of God Upon the Earth

Chapter 16 is a continuation of the events described in chapter 15. Keep in mind that these events will take place in the last three and one half years of the Great Tribulation.

And I heard a great voice out of the temple saying to the seven angels, Go your ways, and pour out the vials of the wrath of God upon the earth.

Rev. 16:1

The time has come for the four angels with the last plagues to pour out their bowls of God's wrath upon the earth. There is heard a great voice coming from the temple proclaiming to the angels that they should proceed with their plagues.

As we examine these plagues we should take special notice of the objects of the plagues. They are all poured out on the things that man worships. They are the things that are God's creation and God wants the people to know who he is and to worship him.

The First Bowl of Wrath

And the first went, and poured out his vial upon the earth, and there fell a noisome and grievous sore upon the men

233

who had the mark of the beast, and upon them who worshiped his image.

Rev. 16:2

The angel is obedient to the voice from the temple and he pours out his bowl of wrath upon the earth. We see that the dictator has already built an image of himself and has required that all people should take his mark and worship him. This plague is targeted directly to all of the men who have taken his mark and worship him. Terrible and painful sores will break out on the bodies of those who worship the beast.

When Moses brought the plagues upon the Egyptians, Pharaoh would entreat Moses to remove the plague and it would be removed. Here there is no indication that these boil-like sores will ever be removed prior to the return of Christ. The worshipers of the beast could be in torment for several years.

The Second Bowl of Wrath

And the second angel poured out his vial upon the sea, and it became like the blood of a dead man; and every living soul died in the sea.

Rev. 16:3

When the second angel pours out his bowl of wrath, he causes the sea to become like the blood of a dead man. The oceans become congealed and everything in them dies. Every living creature in the sea will die which will have a devastating effect upon the food supply of the world. Shipping will grind to a sudden halt because the ships will be unable to maneuver in the gooey mess. Unlike the trumpet plague in chapter 8 where only one third of the sea is turned to blood we see here that the entire sea is made like blood. The entire earth will be affected because there will not be the proper evaporation from the oceans to produce the much needed rain. Again there is no indication as to how long this plague will last.

The Third Bowl of Wrath

And the third angel poured out his vial upon the rivers and fountains of waters, and they became blood.

Rev. 16:4

When the third angel pours out his bowl of wrath, it falls upon all of the fresh water of the earth and it is turned to blood. All those who have been able to enjoy the beauty and recreation that the beautiful rivers and lakes, will have only blood to swim in and drink. It is a good possibility that the fish and other creatures of the fresh water will die. Every man, woman and child will be affected by this terrible disaster. Again, there is no indication how long this plague will last.

And I heard the angel of the waters say, Thou art righteous, O Lord, who art, and wast, and shalt be, because thou hast judged thus.

Rev. 16:5

We learn here that the angels of God have control over the elements of his creation. Here we see there is an angel of the waters. We have seen angels in control of the winds. The angels seem to have a responsibility to watch over the things that God has created. When the water is turned to blood, the angel of the waters is in total agreement with God in his judgment. The angel declares that God is righteous because he has judged in such a manner. The eternal God who is, and was, and will be forever, is the Lord over his creation and can do as he chooses with his creation.

For they have shed the blood of saints and prophets, and thou hast given them blood to drink; for they are worthy.

Rev. 16:6

The angel of the waters continues to give the reason why God is righteous in turning the waters into blood. The ungodly men

235

of this world have, down through the centuries, killed and shed innocent blood of the saints because of their faith in the living God of Heaven. When God would send a prophet to warn the world that he was going to judge them for their ungodliness, they would kill the messenger and shed his blood because they did not want to hear nor believe what he had to say. They thought that if the messenger was killed then his message would not come to pass. They refused to believe that there is a God in heaven who was the source of their message. Now God's divine retribution is poured out on them and they will have blood to drink because they have shed the blood of God's children. God is righteous and they are worthy to receive such a judgment.

> *And I heard another out of the altar say, Even so, Lord God Almighty, true and righteous are thy judgments.*
>
> Rev. 16:7

Another voice is heard coming from the altar. Apparently from the altar of incense in answer to the prayers of those who have shed their blood for the testimony of their Savior. The voice is saying that it agrees with the voice from the temple, and declares that Lord God Almighty is true and righteous in judging the world for their deaths.

The Fourth Bowl of Wrath

> *And the fourth angel poured out his vial upon the sun, and power was given unto him to scorch men with fire. And men were scorched with great heat, and blasphemed the name of God, who hath power over these plagues; and they repented not to give him glory.*
>
> Rev. 16:8, 9

The fourth angel pours out his bowl upon the sun. In the trumpet plague, the sun did not shine for one third of the day. The angel has been given power to scorch men with fire. The bowl plague makes the sun hotter and it scorches men with heat. The sun is so hot that if anyone is out in it for any length of time he will be severely sunburned. The global warming that man thinks is going on today will be nothing compared to the warming of the earth caused by this plague. Once more there is no indication given for the length of time that this plague will last.

The men who have been tormented by the extreme heat blaspheme the name of God. To blaspheme means that he is counted as nothing, that he has no influence in the affairs of man. They take his name in vain, and curse him, and refuse to acknowledge that he has the power to start or stop these plagues as he wills. They refuse to recognize Almighty God and do not repent of their sins and fall on their faces before him and do not give him the glory that he deserves. Isn't it interesting that man can curse and take God's name in vain but will not believe that he even exists?

The Fifth Bowl of Wrath

And the fifth angel poured out his vial upon the seat of the beast, and his kingdom was full of darkness; and they gnawed their tongues for pain, And blasphemed the God of heaven because of their pains and their sores, and repented not of their deeds.

Rev. 16:10, 11

The fifth angel pours out his bowl of wrath upon the seat, or throne, of the world dictator. Almighty God, who made this world, is able to make his kingdom full of darkness. When we experience pain, there is no time like the night when we are trying to sleep, for the pain always seems more intense.

At this time the beast and his worshipers will have boils like sores and have become severely sun burned. They have no water to drink and now they are engulfed in darkness. They gnaw their tongues because of the pain that they are suffering. They blame the God of heaven and blaspheme his name because of the pains and sores but refuse to repent of the evil deeds that they are performing on this earth.

The Sixth Bowl of Wrath

And the sixth angel poured out his vial upon the great river, Euphrates, and its water was dried up, that the way of the kings of the east might be prepared.

Rev. 16:12

When the sixth angel pours out his bowl of wrath, it falls on the great river Euphrates. The angel has power over the water of the river to dry it up to prepare for the kings of the east. There are two more events that must take place before Jesus can come back to earth and claim it for himself. The seventh bowl must be poured out and the battle of Armageddon must be ready to start. The drying up of the river makes way for the kings of the east to begin mobilizing for the last great battle of the Gentile nations.

The next few verses give a description of how the kings of the earth will be gathered together for this battle.

And I saw three unclean spirits, like frogs, come out of the mouth of the dragon, and out of the mouth of the beast, and out of the mouth of the false prophet.

Rev. 16:13

As John looks, he sees three unclean spirits come out of the mouths of the dragon, beast, and false prophet. We know that the dragon is Satan because he has been positively identified at previous times. The beast can either be a kingdom or the leader of that kingdom. In this case a kingdom doesn't fit the situation so we will consider him to be the leader of the final world kingdom, the world dictator, or as some call him the antichrist. This is the first mention of the false prophet so we need to look elsewhere for any information about him. The only clue is given in the description of the beast out of the earth in chapter 13.

That beast (kingdom) is said to have two horns like a lamb and he spoke like a dragon. There are going to be two leaders of this last kingdom and one is like a lamb (the false prophet) and the other will speak like a dragon (the dictator). The false prophet will be the religious leader and the dragon will be the political leader of this satanic kingdom. The dragon, beast, and false prophet make up the unholy trinity that will be ruling the entire world in the last days. They will require every living soul to worship them.

They are like frogs. They are not frogs but like frogs. A frog lives in the slime pools of the world and crawls out at night and begins to croak. These unclean spirits are like frogs, because they too are associated with the slime bags that are ruling this world. They go about croaking, obeying, and praising the unholy trinity.

For they are spirits of devils, working miracles, that go forth unto the kings of the earth and of the whole world, to gather them to the battle of that great day of God Almighty.
                                                          Rev. 16:14

We are told that the unclean spirits are actually spirits of demons and they have power to work all kinds of miracles and deceive the kings and all of the people of the world. The two horns of the beast in chapter 13 have the same abilities to work all kinds of miracles and deceive the entire world.

The great deception here is to convince the ten kings and their people to gather together their armies for that great battle of the day of God Almighty. The implication here is that Satan has been thrown out of heaven and he knows that his time is short. He knows that there must be a showdown between him and God Almighty so he is gathering all of his reinforcements to back him up in this final battle for control of this earth. We know from Dan. 11:36-45 that there will be several skirmishes going on in the Middle East. The king from the north and the king from the east will come against the willful king. Several countries will be overrun but Jordan will be spared. Egypt will be conquered, and Libya and Ethiopia will be next in line. Tidings from the east and out of the north will trouble him and he will go forth with much fury to utterly destroy many. The kings have grown tired of the dictator and are going to try to get him under control.

The plan of the unholy trinity will turn into chaos, but a sovereign God has accomplished his purpose in having all of the kings of the earth gathered in one place where he can deal with them once and forever.

> *Behold, I come as a thief. Blessed is he that watcheth, and keepeth his garments, lest he walk naked, and they see his shame.*
>
> Rev. 16:15

Jesus has warned that when he comes back to earth that he will come when the world least expects him, like a thief in the night. They will be eating, drinking, and giving in marriage right up to the end just like they did at the time of the flood.

Those that are watching for their Lord to return and those who have not defiled their garments with the lies and filth of the unholy trinity, will be blessed. They will not be found naked and spiritually destitute when their Lord appears. What a shame for those who have been deceived to worship the beast and his image. They will have nothing to show for their lives and there will be nothing worth saving.

> *And he gathered them together into a place called in the Hebrew tongue Armageddon.*
>
> Rev. 16:16

We do not know who the "he" is speaking about here. It could be the one who is coming as a thief in the night. Or it could be Almighty God himself. Another possibility is the angel who poured out the sixth vial. Some believe it to be the unholy trinity acting in unison. No matter who it is, he is acting in accordance with the will of an omniscient sovereign God.

He gathers the armies of the world together in a place called Armageddon. This is the only place that the word Armageddon is used in the scriptures; however, it is alluded to in many places in the Old Testament. The word is actually a compound Hebrew word *Har* which means mountain, and *Megiddo* which is a mount in Northwest Israel. Mount Megiddo is situated in the very fertile valley or Plain of Esdraelon.

The Seventh Bowl of Wrath

And the seventh angel poured out his vial into the air, and there came a great voice out of the temple of heaven, from the throne, saying, It is done.

Rev. 16:17

The seventh and last angel pours out his bowl of wrath into the air. The seven last plagues have affected the bodies of those who worshiped the beast, the sea as it is turned into blood, the fresh water as it is also turned into blood, the sun as it became hot and scorches man, the kingdom of the beast was filled with darkness, and the Euphrates River is dried up to prepare the way for the king from the east. Now finally, this one affects the air. Jerusalem is being ravaged, the children of Israel are being persecuted, and the world dictator has his hands full with battles all around. Planet earth is not a very pleasant place to be. Satan's plan for a utopia on his earth has failed miserably.

When the angel poured out the last bowl of wrath, there is heard a great voice out of the temple and from the one sitting on the throne. The voice proclaims that "It is done." God's wrath is complete and now it is time to bring the judgment that a wicked world deserves. The completion of the seventh bowl, the final battle of the nations, and the return of the Lord will bring a fitting climax to the time of Gentile rule over the nations of the world.

And there were voices, and thunders, and lightnings; and there was a great earthquake, such as was not since men were upon the earth, so mighty an earthquake, and so great.

Rev. 16:18

When the angel pours out his bowl upon the air there are heard voices in heaven in anticipation of the wrath it will cause. The voices were followed by thunder and lightning preceding the mighty storm that is on its way. There is a mighty earthquake that causes the whole earth to shake. There has never been such a mighty and great earthquake since man has been on the earth. This will be a terrifying time with much death and destruction for the inhabitants of the earth.

And the great city was divided into three parts, and the cities of the nations fell; and great Babylon came in remembrance before God, to give unto her the cup of the wine of the fierceness of his wrath.

Rev. 16:19

The earthquake is so great that the city of Jerusalem is divided into three parts. The great cities of the world are devastated and their great buildings fall to the ground. God remembers the great city of Babylon and the wickedness that originated in her. The religion, commercial, and political system that has brought chaos into the world has been a result of the materialistic philosophy that originated in Babylon. The cup of God's indignation and the fierceness of his wrath will be poured out on her.

And every island fled away, and the mountains were not found.

Rev. 16:20

The earthquake is so severe that every island disappears. Islands sometimes mean coastlines and if that is the case here then the coastlines will slide into the sea and disappear. Most of the large cities of the world are located on the coastline so this would be most devastating. Even if the meaning is not coastlines we know that islands are just mountains in the midst of the sea and all the mountains will not exist. Many of the large cities are located between the mountains and the sea and when the mountains are leveled the cities will be destroyed.

And there fell upon men a great hail out of heaven, every stone about the weight of a talent; and men blasphemed God because of the plague of the hail, for the plague was exceedingly great.

Rev. 16:21

The final plague caused by the angel pouring out his bowl into the air, is great hailstones falling from heaven upon mankind. Every stone weighs about one hundred pounds. That is equivalent to about twelve gallons of frozen water. The earthquake is devastating and then men are pounded with giant hail stones. It is very hard to imagine such a disaster.

Instead of man falling on his knees and repenting of his sins and asking for God's forgiveness, man curses God and takes his name in vain and blasphemes God because the plague is exceedingly great. Man refuses to acknowledge that God is omnipotent or that he is sovereign over the affairs of man.

"It is done." The last and final plague is poured out on the world causing much loss of life and physical changes to the earth's landscape. Man's heart is only hardened to the point that there is no hope for mankind. The only thing left is for the Lord Jesus Christ to appear in the clouds and judge all of the people on this earth and then establish his kingdom of peace and comfort for his people. When we study chapter 19 we will see him do just that.

CHAPTER 17

The Judgment of the Great Whore

Chapter 17 should answer some of the questions that are frequently asked concerning the identity of the woman on the beast, the beast with seven heads, the seven heads, and the ten horns. When we try to interpret scriptures we must be very careful to let the scriptures interpret themselves as much as possible. There has been much speculation by many authors as to who these characters must represent. In this study we will try not to speculate but let the scriptures do the interpreting. We must start in the book of Daniel since it is the key to understanding prophecy.

Nebuchadnezzar, king of Babylon, had a dream that revealed the nations that will come to be known to rule during *the times of the Gentiles.* All of these nations will have a great influence on the nation of Israel. The final or fourth kingdom will not only have influence on Israel but also on the entire world. We will concentrate our attention on this fourth kingdom since it is the only kingdom that has a part to play in the end time.

The Dream Revealed

Thou, O king, sawest, and behold a great image. This great image, whose brightness was excellent, stood before thee, and the form of it was terrible. This image's head was of fine gold, its breast and its arms of silver, its belly and its thighs of bronze, Its legs of iron, its feet part of iron and part of clay. Thou sawest until a stone was cut out without hands, which smote the image upon its feet that were of iron and clay, and broke them to pieces. Then were the iron, the clay, the bronze, the silver, and the gold broken to pieces together, and became like the chaff of the summer threshing floors; and the wind carried them away, that no place was found for them; and the stone that smote the image became a great mountain, and filled the whole earth.

Dan. 2:31-35

The Interpretation of the Dream

This is the dream, and we will tell its interpretation before the king.

Dan. 2:36

And the fourth kingdom shall be strong as iron, forasmuch as iron breaketh in pieces and subdueth all things; and, as iron that breaketh all these, shall it break in pieces and bruise. And whereas thou sawest the feet and toes, part of potters' clay and part of iron, the kingdom shall be divided; but there shall be in it of the strength of the iron, forasmuch as thou sawest the iron mixed with miry clay. And as the toes of the feet were part iron and part clay, so the kingdom shall be partly strong and partly broken. And whereas thou sawest iron mixed with miry clay, they shall mingle themselves with the seed of men; but they shall not adhere one to another, even as iron is not mixed with clay. And in the days of these kings shall the God of heaven set up a kingdom, which shall never be destroyed; and the kingdom shall not be left to other people, but it shall break in pieces and consume all these kingdoms, and it shall stand forever. Forasmuch as

thou sawest that the stone was cut out of the mountain with-
out hands, and that it broke in pieces the iron, the bronze,
the clay, the silver, and the gold, the great God hath made
known to the king what shall come to pass hereafter; and the
dream is certain, and the interpretation of it sure.

Dan. 2:40-45

Over 2500 years ago, an all-knowing God caused an ungodly king of Babylon to have a dream. He could not reveal the dream, nor could he reveal the meaning of the dream. He called his magicians to interpret the dream but they could not. In desperation, he called Daniel to reveal the dream and interpret it. God revealed to Daniel that there would be four kingdoms to appear upon the earth and then He would send His Son to establish His kingdom. These kingdoms were revealed to be Babylon, Medo-Persia, Greece, and Rome. The fourth kingdom, Rome, has some things revealed about it that needs to be examined. These things are listed as follows:

1. Its legs were of iron.
2. Its feet were part iron and part clay.
3. A stone was cut out without hands and smote the feet of the image and broke them to pieces.
4. The entire image became like chaff on the threshing floor.
5. The stone became a mountain and filled the entire earth.
6. The fourth kingdom will be strong as iron and will break in pieces and subdue all things.
7. It shall break in pieces and bruise.
8. The kingdom that is part iron and part clay will be divided but it will be strong as iron.
9. The **ten** toes shall be part iron and part clay and will be part strong and part broken.

10 They shall mingle themselves with the seed of man but will not adhere.

11. In the days of these kings God will set up a kingdom that shall never be destroyed.

12. The kingdom will not be left to other people.

13. God has revealed to the king what shall be hereafter.

14. The dream is certain and the interpretation of it sure.

God gave Daniel a vision of the same four kingdoms. They were represented as wild beasts. There are more interesting things revealed about the fourth kingdom in Daniel's vision recorded in chapter 7 of the book of Daniel.

The Vision

After this I saw in the night visions, and, behold, a fourth beast, dreadful and terrible, and strong exceedingly, and it had great iron teeth; it devoured and broke in pieces, and stamped the residue with his feet; and it was diverse from all the beasts that were before it, and it had ten horns. I considered the horns, and behold, there came up among them another little horn, before which there were three of the first horns plucked up by the roots; and, behold, in this horn were eyes like the eyes of man, and a mouth speaking great things.

Dan. 7:7, 8

Daniel's Questions

Then I would know the truth of the fourth beast, which was diverse from all the others, exceedingly dreadful, whose teeth were of iron, and its nails of bronze, which devoured, broke in pieces, and stamped the residue with his feet; And of the ten horns that were in its head, and of the other which came up, and before whom three fell; even of that horn that had eyes, and a mouth that spoke very great things, whose look was more stout than its fellows. I beheld, and the same horn made war with the saints, and prevailed against them, Until the Ancient of days came, and judgment was given to the saints of the Most High; and the time came that the saints possessed the kingdom.

Dan. 7:19-22

The Interpretation

Thus he said, The fourth beast shall be the fourth kingdom upon earth, which shall be diverse from all kingdoms, and shall devour the whole earth, and shall tread it down, and break it in pieces. And the ten horns out of this kingdom are ten kings that shall arise; and another shall rise after them, and he shall be diverse from the first, and he shall subdue three kings. And he shall speak great words against the Most High, and shall wear out the saints of the Most High, and think to change the times and the laws; and they shall be given into his hand until a time and times and the dividing of time. But the judgment shall sit; and they shall take away his dominion, to consume and to destroy it unto the end. And the kingdom and dominion, and the greatness of the kingdom under the whole heaven, shall be given to the people of the saints of the Most High, whose kingdom is an everlasting kingdom, and all dominions shall serve and obey him.

Dan. 7:23-27

In Daniel's vision several things of importance are revealed and are listed as follows:

1. The fourth beast is dreadful and terrible.
2. It is exceedingly strong with great iron teeth.
3. It broke in pieces and stamped the residue with its feet.

4. It was diverse from all of the other beasts.
5. It had **ten** horns in its head.
6. There was another little horn to come up after the ten horns.
7. Three of the first horns were subdued and plucked up by the roots.
8. It had eyes like the eyes of a man.
9. It had a mouth speaking great things.
10. It was diverse from all the others.
11. It had nails of bronze.
12. His look was stouter than its fellows.
13. The little horn made war with the saints and prevailed against them.
14. It will be in existence when the Lord Jesus comes back to set up His kingdom.
15. The fourth beast shall be the fourth kingdom upon the earth.
16. He will be diverse from all kingdoms.
17. He shall devour the whole world.
18. He will tread down and break the world into pieces.
19. The ten horns are ten kings that shall arise.
20. Another king shall arise after the ten kings.
21. He shall be diverse from the first ten kings.
22. He will speak great words (blaspheme) against the Most High.
23. He will wear out the saints of the Most High.
24. He will think to change the times and the laws.
25. The saints will be given into his hands for three and one half years.
26. His kingdom and dominion shall be taken away to be consumed and destroyed.

With this information in mind we should be able to rightly divide the truth presented in chapter seventeen. We have already discussed many of these things in chapter 13.

> *And there came one of the seven angels who had the seven bowls, and talked with me, saying unto me, Come here; I will show unto thee the judgement of the great whore that sitteth upon many waters...*
>
> Rev. 17:1

The seven bowls of God's wrath were just discussed in chapter 16 and one of the angels that poured out these bowls said to John to come and see the judgment of the great whore that sits upon many waters. Verse 18 indicates that the woman is that great city that reigns over the kings of the earth. This great city most assuredly is the city of Babylon. It will be discussed in great detail in the next chapter.

Verse 15 indicates that the waters where the whore sits are peoples, and multitudes, and nations, and tongues. This woman has had a great influence upon the masses of humanity upon this earth. Because of her devastating influence upon the masses, a righteous God will bring her to judgment.

According to Webster's dictionary, a whore is "A woman who practices unlawful sexual commerce with men, especially one who prostitutes her body for hire." When a woman decides to prostitute herself she plaits her hair, paints her face, and dresses in skimpy attire. She does everything that will attract herself to the fleshly desires of her prey. In so doing, many become very wealthy from their enterprise at the cost of the breakdown of the family structure and their own morality.

In the scriptures, religious organizations are commonly referred to as women. The church is called *the bride of Christ,* while the nation of Israel is called "the wife of Jehovah." Organized rebellion against God is represented by the woman in the ephah in Zech 5. In this study we will also consider the woman to be a religious organization. Here she is represented as an evil woman who has sold herself for worldly gain and therefore must represent the false religions of the world.

With whom the kings of the earth have committed fornication, and the inhabitants of the earth have been made drunk with the wine of her fornication.

Rev. 17:2

Throughout history the kings of the earth have been led astray by false religions, and in so doing have committed spiritual fornication by leaving and ignoring the true and living God of the universe. All nations of the world have been governed by the religious beliefs and teachings of their false gods. All of their laws and moral standards have been predicated upon their belief in false religions.

The inhabitants of the earth have been made drunk by the intoxication and the satisfaction of the flesh through faith in salvation through works of the flesh, and ignoring the Grace of God that brings eternal life through His Son Jesus Christ. False religions have separated mankind from a life of faithfulness toward a loving and righteous God. False religions operate in the same manner that a prostitute does in that they are appealing to the flesh and are attractive to the natural man. They lurk in dark places with skimpy attire and look very attractive to the world. It is easy to be led astray when the basis of salvation is predicated upon good works or the satisfaction of the flesh.

So he carried me away in the Spirit into the wilderness and I saw a woman sit upon a scarlet-colored beast, full of names of blasphemy, having seven heads and ten horns.

Rev. 17:3

John is carried away in the Spirit into the wilderness where he sees a woman sitting upon a scarlet-colored beast. Zech.

5:5-11 describes a woman called *wickedness* placed into an ephah and carried to the land of Shinar and set upon her own base. This woman represents false religions, rebellion against the living God, and a belief that mankind can attain acceptance into God's presence through self righteousness and good works. This belief system was originated in the land of Shinar shortly after the flood by the person of Nimrod, accompanied by his wife, Semiramis, and their son, Tammus. Nimrod made the first attempt toward establishing a world government in the construction of the tower of Babel. He was a mighty hunter (of men's souls) with a total disregard to God. He endeavored to build a tower that would reach to heaven. This was a futile attempt at reaching God by one's own efforts. Semiramis added to his belief the idea of the mystery religions and of goddess worship. Tammus was believed to be supernaturally conceived and led to the worship of the woman and the child. All false religions have sprung from this beginning in the land of Babylon and God will deliver them back to their origin where they will be finally judged and destroyed.

The woman was riding upon the beast which indicates that she was supported by the beast. It is no wonder that the beast was full of names of blasphemy when he is the one who upholds all wickedness and is in control of and supports her every movement. This woman, under the control of the beast, has been in control of the seven heads of the beast and has influenced them through her false religious system. Every ruler has relied upon the sorcerers and magicians for answers to their questions and to make their laws.

This beast has seven heads and ten horns. Verse 9 states that the seven heads are seven mountains. The ten horns are described in verse 12 as ten kings. We will discuss them in more detail as we look at each of these two verses.

And the woman was arrayed in purple and scarlet color, and decked with gold and precious stones and pearls, having a golden cup in her hand, full of abominations and filthiness of her fornication...

Rev. 17:4

Sorcerers and magicians were used to make very important decisions concerning laws, interpretation of dreams, war strategy and, many other subjects. Often times these false leaders would be elevated to a place of authority in the kingdom as indicated by their purple attire. Sometimes they were considered the savior or redeemer of the people thus the color scarlet, and they were declared to be gods. They would be lavished with all kinds of wealth such as gold, precious stones, and pearls.

In spite of all the glamour and riches bestowed upon them by mankind, they were seen by God as full of abominations and filthiness because of their fornication (rebellion against God). It has always been God's desire that mankind should place Him supreme and at the head of their government. Unfortunately this has not happened and He has been left out of all recognition and decision-making in the affairs of man.

And upon her forehead was a name written, MYSTERY, BABYLON THE GREAT, THE MOTHER OF HAR-LOTS AND ABOMINATIONS OF YHE EARTH.

Rev.17:5

This woman is identified by her name being placed upon her forehead. The word *mystery* signifies that there is something about this woman that has never been revealed before in scripture. We all know that Babylon is great. She is represented by the head of gold in the vision described in the book of Daniel. The hanging gardens of Babylon were one of the seven wonders of the ancient world. The Babylonian kingdom was one of the most spectacular and magnificent kingdoms that has ever existed. So what is there about Babylon that has never been revealed? She is the *mother of harlots*. It was in Babylon that all of the false religions of the world originated. She is the *mother*, the one who brought them all into being and gave life to them. This woman was a harlot because she entered into an illicit affair with the world and worshiped the creation rather than of the Creator.

Babylon is also the *mother of abominations of the earth*. Our God is a jealous God, and it is an abomination to Him for his creation to worship anything other than Himself. If He is all-powerful, all-knowing, everywhere present, and never changing, is He not worthy of our worship (worth ship), praise, and adoration? Babylon chose to worship the things of this world which is known as *pantheism*. The belief that man is good enough to work his way into God's presence was shown in the building of the tower of Babel.

The worship of the woman and child was established in Babylon. The goddess worship and the worship of false gods were conceived in Babylon. These and many other abominations have been carried down to other nations throughout history.

The Medes and the Persians worshiped their false gods and they became the basis for all legal authority in the land. The Greeks had a god for everything that they could think of, and even had an unknown god for fear that they might have missed one. The goddess worship and the sexual orgies committed in their temples was an abomination.

The Roman emperors advanced their belief system to the point that they declared themselves to be a god. We have seen all of these atrocities carried on into the many governments of modern times. They will be exaggerated in the *New World Order* and the final dictator's authority. This wickedness was in charge of the seven-headed beast and will be in charge of the ten horn kingdom. No wonder it was named THE ABOMINATION OF THE EARTH!

> *And I saw the woman drunk with the blood of the saints, and with the blood of the martyrs of Jesus; and when I saw her, I wondered with great admiration.*
>
> Rev. 17:6

The greatest enemy of God and his saints has been the men controlled by the false religions of the world. This woman (wickedness) has been responsible for the destruction of God's people since its conception at the tower of Babel. The Israelites have been attacked by ungodly nations throughout their history. The prophets were killed by Jezebel and other wicked people in the name of their gods. Hitler killed four million Jews in the name of his god. Stalin killed many million believers because of his atheistic views. The Muslims have killed hundreds of thousands of Jews and Christians in the name of their god before the Roman Catholic Church retaliated through the crusades and quelled their carnage.

The carnage is not over. There will be multitudes of believers killed in the end times because of the atheistic and pantheistic views of the world leaders. What an abomination! No wonder God in his righteous judgment will carry this woman back to the plains of Shinar and judge her there.

And the angel said unto me, Why didst thou marvel? I will tell thee the mystery of the woman, and of the beast that carrieth her, which hath the seven heads and ten horns.

Rev. 17:7

The angel tells John that he does not need to wonder for he is going to reveal the mystery of the woman on the beast, the beast itself, the seven heads and the ten horns.

We have been told in chapter 12 that the red dragon is the one who has seven heads and ten horns. He was identified to be Satan so we do not need to wonder about this beast for he is the only one who is described to have seven heads and ten horns.

The beast that thou sawest was, and is not, and shall ascend out of the bottomless pit, and go into perdition; and they that dwell upon the earth shall wonder, whose names were not written in the book of life from the foundation of the world, when they behold the beast that was, and is not, and yet is.

Rev. 17:8

Verse 11 tells us that the *beast that was, and is not, even he is the eighth, and is of the seven, and goeth into perdition.* This is the same beast spoken of in verse 8 and we will discuss it in more detail when we get to verse 11. This beast will ascend out of the bottomless pit, and go into perdition. The bottomless pit is the abode of the demons that will be let loose to torment men when the fifth trumpet is sounded in chapter 9. There is a king over these demons and he has the name *destroyer.* This beast will be controlled by demonic power and will exist until the Lord comes back and sets up his kingdom as described in the book of Daniel. This beast must be in control of the entire world in the last days.

The people upon the world at this time will wonder with great amazement when they behold this beast that was, and is not, and yet is. These are the people who have not received the Lord Jesus Christ as their savior and have not had their names written in the book of life. They have not received God's Spirit so they cannot understand or know what is taking place on the earth.

> *And here is the mind which hath wisdom. The seven heads are seven mountains, on which the woman sitteth.*
>
> Rev. 17:9

The word tells us that it takes wisdom to understand the meaning of the seven heads. We are first informed that the seven heads are seven mountains. In the book of Daniel we are told that there will *be a stone made without hands and it will become a great mountain.* This stone will smite the great image; it will be destroyed and the stone will become a great mountain. We know that this stone is The Lord Jesus Christ and he will destroy the four kingdoms that are represented by the four metals, of gold, silver, brass, and iron, and He will set up His Kingdom upon the earth. In the scriptures, kingdoms are often represented by mountains.

It has long been believed by many that the seven mountains represent Rome since it was built upon seven hills. It should be noted here that a mountain is not a hill and therefore does not need to represent anything except a kingdom. It is not very likely that the woman sitting upon the beast is in control of seven hills, but she could surely be in control of the Gentile Kingdoms of the world. The next verse ties this all together when it states that *there are seven kings.*

> *And there are seven kings: five are fallen, and one is, and the other is not yet come; and when he cometh, he must continue a short space.*
>
> Rev. 17:10

The understanding of this verse, and the next three verses that follow, is the key to understanding the meaning of the seven heads and ten horns of the beast upon whom the woman is riding and of whom she is in control. This verse states that there are seven kings or kingdoms. When we look at scripture and the history of Israel we find that there has been, or will be, only seven kingdoms that have had, or will have, any influence upon her. These kingdoms consist of Egypt, Assyria, Babylon, Mede-Persia, Greece, Rome and the final antichrist kingdom. There are seven kingdoms, no more and no less. When this book was written the first five had fallen. One was in existence, Rome. There is one yet to come, the final antichrist kingdom, and when it comes it will remain for a short time, only a little more than seven years.

> *And the beast that was, and is not, even he is the eighth, and is of the seven, and goeth into perdition.*
>
> Rev. 17:11

We have come to the verse that explains the meaning of the beast that was, is not, and is. He is declared to be the eighth head and he will go into perdition. The beast that the woman was riding had only seven heads. Now it declares that it has eight. Why is there a difference? This beast is said to be of the seven. He must, therefore, be another phase of one of the kingdoms mentioned in the explanation of the seven kings in verse 10. But which one is he? Again Daniel comes to the rescue in the description of the image and the fourth beast. The last kingdom described by the legs and toes of the image is Rome. It will be in existence when Christ comes back to setup His Kingdom. He smites the image on the feet and it crumbles and goes into perdition. The fourth beast of Daniel's vision is a description of Rome. It has ten horns and is dreadful and terrible. The late Roman Empire does not fit this description so there must be a future Roman empire that does fit this picture.

We can now list the eight heads as follows: Egypt, Assyria, Babylon, Medo-Persia, Greece, Rome, the *revived Roman Empire (the new world order),* and the antichrist kingdom. The revised Roman Empire is the only one of the seven that can meet the description of Daniel. It is the one that was in existence when the book of Revelation was written. It is not in existence today. It will again be in power at the time of Christ's return in power and glory. And it will go into perdition (destruction). The final kingdom will not only encompass Europe, but will control the entire world.

Go back to the beginning of this chapter and re-read the requirements of the vision of the fourth beast. This kingdom will meet all of those requirements.

And the ten horns which thou sawest are ten kings, who have received no kingdom as yet, but receive power as kings one hour with the beast.

Rev. 17:12

This verse tells us that the ten horns will be ten kings. These ten kings have not had a kingdom as yet. This cannot be a description of ten kings of Europe because they have all had a kingdom for many centuries. The entire world will be divided into ten regions and a king will be assigned to rule over each region. These kings will declare themselves to be gods and will rule with a heavy hand. They will have great iron teeth and will stomp the residue with their feet. Read again the requirements of the image and its toes at the beginning of this chapter. These kings will meet all the requirements described there.

They will receive power as kings to rule for a short time in conjunction with the antichrist. They must be in power for a time prior to the rule of the final world dictator, for that dictator will subdue three of these kings and will become greater than them all and rule the entire world. There must be a time when ten kings are in control of this world, three of them are subdued, and then the antichrist can emerge into his position of power. The tribulation cannot happen until the antichrist is in power and he signs a peace treaty with Israel for seven years. In the middle of the seven years he breaks the treaty and takes his fury out on the nation of Israel. The signing of the peace treaty will start the seven year period of tribulation.

> *These have one mind, and shall give their power and strength unto the beast.*
>
> Rev. 17:13

These ten kings shall have one mind. They will be controlled by Satan and will give all of their power and strength to him to accomplish his world dominance and to establish his kingdom through which all of the world will worship him. This will be known as the *New World Order.*

> *These shall make war with the Lamb, and the Lamb shall overcome them; for he is Lord of lords, and King of kings, and they that are with him are called, and chosen, and faithful.*
>
> Rev. 17:14

This verse is a reminder of what Daniel declared in the vision of the great image. The stone that was made without hands will smite the ten toes of the image and it will crumble and become rubble, never again to come back into existence. Jesus Christ, the Lamb of God is that stone and he will overcome the ten kings, for he is Lord of all the world and King over all of his creation. We are again reminded that he will bring with him all those who have been called, chosen, and faithful.

> *And he saith unto me, The waters which thou sawest, where the whore sitteth, are peoples, and multitudes, and nations, and tongues.*
>
> Rev. 17:15

The angel who is speaking to John now explains that the waters that he saw where the whore is sitting are the masses of humanity consisting of peoples, multitudes, nations, and tongues. These represent the people from every corner of the world. They will all be under the influence of the whore as she is in control of the Gentile nations that are ruling the world.

> *And the ten horns which thou sawest upon the beast, these shall hate the whore, and shall make her desolate and naked, and shall eat her flesh, and burn her with fire.*
>
> Rev. 17:16

The ten kings shall declare themselves to be gods and pave the way for the antichrist to be worshiped as a god, so there will be no need or desire for any other religions to exist among the multitudes. They will hate all religions so much that they will completely destroy any form of an organized religion to the point of extinction. This whore that has lied to, beguiled, and deceived the masses of society throughout the centuries, will finally be done away with so all peoples, tongues, and nations will only worship Satan through his incarnation into the final world dictator. Organized rebellion against Almighty God will be sent back to the plains of Shinar, the place of her origin and be destroyed.

> *For God hath put in their hearts to fulfill his will, and to agree, and give their kingdom unto the beast, until the words of God shall be fulfilled.*
>
> Rev. 17:17

An all-knowing, all-powerful God can influence the hearts of sinful man to accomplish his will. The ten kings agree among themselves to give their kingdom and control of the entire world unto Satan and his world dictator. These things must be, for God had predicted the end results thousands of years prior to this time and his word must be fulfilled.

> *And the woman whom thou sawest is that great city, which reigneth over the kings of the earth.*
>
> Rev. 17:18

The woman (whore) who was seen sitting on the beast is that great city (Babylon). Her Satanic influence has been in control of all the Gentile nations since the time of the tower of Babel. Nimrod and his organized rebellion against a Holy, just, and righteous God, has been the controlling influence on all of the rulers of mighty nations throughout history. This evil influence has reigned over the nations of the world and will continue to reign over them until God's word is fulfilled.

In this chapter we have seen the judgment of the great whore that has dominated the kings of the earth by her wickedness. We have learned the meaning of the seven heads upon the beast controlled by this whore. We know that there have been six of the kingdoms that have come and gone. There must be one more head appear on the horizon, but before it can appear there must be the eighth head (one of the seven) reappear and dominate the entire world. This eighth head will remain throughout the reign of the seventh head until it is destroyed by the Lord Jesus Christ when he returns in power and glory to set up his kingdom. There must be a time when ten kings rule over the world. Three of them must be subdued, and one mightier than them all shall appear as the final world dictator and usher in the *Time of Jacob's Troubles*—the tribulation period of seven years.

The rapture of the church is imminent, but the tribulation is still in the future because much must happen before the antichrist can appear on the scene. Are you ready to meet your Lord and Savior in the air and ever be with him in the presence of his glory? If you have not yet accepted him as your Savior, now is the time while there is still the freedom to do so. I urge you to make that decision today and assure that your name will be written in the Book of Life and you will not be left behind to endure all of the plagues and hardships that are to follow in the near future.

CHAPTER 18

Babylon the Great is Fallen, is Fallen

The time has come for the God of heaven and earth to judge the great city of Babylon for her spiritual fornication that she has committed with the kings of the earth. The glue that holds the economy of the world together is materialism. The rich men of the world have gotten their riches from the desire of the people to have *things*. The things of this world has become the gods of the people. They worship the things they have accumulated during their lives. Things never satisfy; we just want more, and more, and more. The more things we have, the more self-sufficient we become, and less dependent upon God for our daily requirements. The world is committing spiritual fornication when it turns its affection on the things of this world and rejects the love and affection that God wants to bestow upon it.

In this chapter we will see that a Holy God is going to judge the great city of Babylon because she is the epitome of materialism and wickedness in this world.

> *And after these things I saw another angel come down from heaven, having great power, and the earth was lightened with his glory.*
>
> Rev. 18:1

We have just studied in chapters 16 and 17 about the seven last plagues, and the destruction of the woman riding upon the beast. After these things John sees another angel come down from heaven. This angel has great power and he lights up the entire earth by the glory that he resonates because he has been in the presence of Almighty God.

> *And he cried mightily with a strong voice, saying, Babylon the great is fallen, is fallen, and is become the habitation of devils, and the hold of every foul spirit, and a cage of every unclean and hateful bird.*
>
> Rev. 18:2

The powerful angel announces with a very strong voice that the great city of Babylon is fallen, is fallen. *Is fallen* is repeated to emphasize the importance of the fact that she has fallen. Isaiah 13:19-22 predicts the fall of Babylon and this will be the fulfillment of that prophecy. There is no prophecy that precludes the fact that the city of Babylon will be rebuilt in the last days and then come to an end as predicted by an all-knowing God.

The city of Babylon will become the dwelling place of demons and the prison of every evil spirit. Babylon has been controlled by demons for centuries and has influenced the world to believe their deceptive lies and sorceries. They will be locked up for one thousand years during the time of the Kingdom of Jesus Christ as he rules this world. Their king, Satan, will be locked in the bottomless pit for the same duration. There will be no evil influence on mankind during this time, but that will not prevent man from sinning. They just can't say "the devil made me do it." Man sins because he has a sin nature and it is his nature to sin.

The unclean and carnivorous birds will be caged in the city of Babylon during the millennium because there will be no need for the scavengers of the earth during a reign of peace and tranquility and where death does not abound.

For all nations have drunk of the wine of the wrath of her fornication, and the kings of the earth have committed fornication with her, and the merchants of the earth are waxed rich through the abundance of her delicacies.

Rev. 18:3

All of the nations of the world have been caught up into materialism as a way of life. There is nothing wrong with having things as long as they do not take away from our relationship with God. The nations that have made materialism their sole purpose for being, are in danger of the judgment of God.

The kings of the earth have been greedy and have grown rich through the corruption that is available to them because they are in control of the nation. Merchants of the earth have grown exceedingly rich through the abundance of stuff for them to entice the people to buy. The people are taken advantage of through false advertising and inflated prices.

And I heard another voice from heaven, saying, Come out of her, my people, that ye be not partakers of her sins, and that ye receive not of her plagues; For her sins have reached unto heaven, and God hath remembered her iniquities.

Rev. 18:4, 5

The Jewish people learned to be merchants, and how to make money, while they were in captivity in Babylon. They continue to practice what they learned even today. There is another voice from heaven warning God's people to come out of their materialistic way of cheating other people, or they will be guilty of the same sins as Babylon and fall under God's judgment. God has seen their sins and he remembers their evil doings and judgment is surely to come on those that do not heed his word.

Reward her even as she rewarded you, and double unto her double according to her works; in the cup which she hath filled fill to her double.

Rev. 18:6

God remembers how the Babylonians treated the Jews when they were taken into captivity. Their homes were ravaged, their women raped, the city of Jerusalem was severely damaged and the temple was destroyed. The golden goblets and instruments that were set aside and consecrated unto the Lord, were stolen and desecrated. Babylon did not spare any mercy when they filled their cup of destruction against the Jews. Now God's cup of indignation is filled to the brim and he instructs the angel to use the same cup, but to give her double what she has given to his people. This is divine retribution.

> *How much she hath glorified herself, and lived deliciously, so much torment and sorrow give her; for she saith in her heart, I sit a queen, and am no widow, and shall see no sorrow.*
>
> Rev. 18:7

The original city of Babylon was the most beautiful city in the world and it can be assured that the new city will be just as glorious and beautiful. The people of Babylon will live in luxury because of the riches from the commerce she controls. She will boast of her wealth and live like a queen and be proud that she does not have to live in poverty like a widow. She boasts that she will never see any sorrow in her life. Because of her pride God will send much torment and sorrow upon her.

> *Therefore shall her plagues come in one day, death, and mourning, and famine, and she shall be utterly burned with fire; for strong is the Lord God who judgeth her.*
>
> Rev. 18:8

God hates pride and he has a way of removing it out of the city of Babylon. In one day her plagues will come upon her. She will suffer death, mourning, famine, and she shall be utterly burned with fire and be completely destroyed. The God of heaven is almighty and he will judge her for her arrogance and past sins.

And the kings of the earth, who have committed fornication and lived deliciously with her, shall bewail her, and lament for her, when they shall see the smoke of her burning, Standing afar off for fear of her torment, saying, Alas, alas, that great city, Babylon, that mighty city! For in one hour is thy judgment come.

Rev. 18:9, 10

When the kings of the earth that have been committing fornication with her, and living in luxury because of her, when they see the smoke of her burning, they will be in great sorrow for her. Their livelihood has been destroyed and they stand afar off in fear that they will be next to receive a judgment of like manner. They praise the city for being such a great and mighty city, but stand in amazement that such a city could be judged in just one hour.

And the merchants of the earth shall weep and mourn over her; for no man buyeth their merchandise any more: The merchandise of gold, and silver, and precious stones, and pearls, and fine linen, and purple, and silk, and scarlet, and all thyine wood, and all manner of vessels of ivory, and all manner of vessels of most precious wood, and of all brass, and iron, and marble, And cinnamon, and odours, and ointments, and frankincense, and wine, and oil, and fine flour, and wheat, and beasts, and sheep, and horses, and chariots, and slaves, and souls of men.

Rev. 18:11-13

The city of Babylon will become the center of commerce for the entire world. The world traders will see her destruction and will cry out loud and mourn because their economic system has just evaporated before their eyes. There will be no more merchandise for the wealthy that have grown accustomed to living in luxury. There will be no more gold, silver, precious stones and pearls for those that have adorned themselves in such riches. The fine linen, purple, silk and scarlet for their glamorous clothing will be gone. All thyine wood for luxurious furniture will be burned up. The vessels of ivory, precious woods, and all brass, iron and marble used in the furnishing of their expensive homes will not be available.

There will be no more cinnamon, perfumes, ointments and frankincense to make their bodies soft and smell good, or their homes to have a sweet odor. The fine foods such as wine, oil, fine flour, wheat, cattle, and sheep, that only the rich can enjoy, will not exist. The horses and chariots represent all forms of transportation. The expensive automobiles, airplanes and yachts for the wealthy will not be available. And the servants that the rich posses in body and soul, will no longer exist. The rich have lived in the luxury and pleasures of this world with no regard for the God who created all things and allowed them to possess the riches that they have.

And the fruits that thy soul lusted after are departed from thee, and all things which were dainty and goodly are departed from thee, and thou shalt find them no more at all.
Rev. 18:14

The fruits of their labors and the riches that their souls lust after are all gone. All of the finer things in life, and the things that make one feel good, are departed from them. They shall never again be found in their lives.

The merchants of these things, who were made rich by her, shall stand afar off for the fear of her torment, weeping and wailing, And saying, Alas, alas, that great city, that was clothed in fine linen, and purple, and scarlet, and decked with gold, and precious stones, and pearls!
Rev. 18:15, 16

The merchants all around the world have become rich through the trading of the luxurious items found in the city of

Babylon. They will cry and mourn over her destruction and stand far away in fear that they may be the next to be judged. They all agree that there has never been a city like this great city. She was clothed in the finest of clothing such as fine linen, purple, and scarlet. She was adorned in gold, precious stones, and pearls.

> *For in one hour so great riches are come to nought. And every shipmaster, and all the company of ships, and sailors, and as many as trade by sea, stood afar off, And cried when they saw the smoke of her burning, saying, What city is like unto this great city?*
>
> Rev. 18:17, 18

It has only taken Almighty God one hour to bring an end to such riches. All of the captains of the ships, and the sailors on the ships, that have been distributing the luxury found in this city stand at a distance and can't believe what they are seeing. They cry when they see the smoke rising from the great fire burning in the city. They agree with the merchants that there has never been a city like the great city of Babylon.

> *And they cast dust on their heads, and cried, weeping and wailing, saying, Alas, alas, that great city, in which were made rich all that had ships in the sea by reason of her costliness! For in one hour is she made desolate.*
>
> Rev. 18:19

The shipping industry has just been decimated. All those who have become rich through the costly merchandise found in this city cast dust upon their heads and cry out loud and mourn over the loss of their income. It has only taken one hour for their entire industry to be made desolate.

> *Rejoice over her, thou heaven, and ye holy apostles and prophets; for God hath avenged you on her.*
>
> Rev. 18:20

Heaven and the holy apostles and prophets should rejoice over the fall of Babylon. All those who have lived holy before the God of heaven should realize that Babylon represents all that is ungodly and unholy by reason of her organized rebellion against God and his people. A just God is finally avenging the blood of those who have died at the hands of those who have followed after the ways of this evil city.

> *And a mighty angel took up a stone like a great millstone, and cast it into the sea, saying, Thus with violence shall that great city, Babylon, be thrown down, and shall be found no more at all.*
>
> Rev. 18:21

A mighty angel takes a stone like a great millstone and casts it into the sea. When a millstone is cast into the sea it sinks to the bottom and is never found again. The Angel says that the great city of Babylon will be thrown down with the same violence as symbolized by the millstone cast into the sea. She too will be found no more forever and ever. This will be the final destruction of the city of Babylon as prophesied in Isa. 13:19-22

> *And the voice of harpers, and musicians, and of pipers, and trumpeters shall be heard no more at all in thee; and no craftsman, of whatever craft he be, shall be found any more in thee; and the sound of a millstone shall be heard no more at all in thee; And the light of a candle shall shine no more at all in thee; and the voice of the bridegroom and of the bride shall be heard no more at all in thee; for thy merchants were the great men of the earth; for by thy sorceries were all nations deceived.*
>
> Rev. 18:22, 23

There will never again be heard any musical instruments in the city of Babylon. The craftsmen that have made the city so wealthy shall never be found in her again. The millstone that ground the fine flour for the rich shall never be heard again in her. The bright lights of this great city shall never be seen again. There will never be any more weddings because there shall never be any inhabitants living in her.

The final judgment of the city of Babylon has taken place because she has deceived the nations of the earth along with the merchants (the great men of the earth), that have gotten rich from her materialism. The world has been deceived into thinking that wealth and riches and the accumulation of material things is the measure of the stature of a man. Thinking that at the end of life, the one with the most possessions, wins.

And in her was found the blood of prophets, and of saints, and of all that were slain upon the earth.

Rev. 18:24

The quest for a world government, and total control of mankind by the elite, has been forefront in the minds of the rich since the time of the building of the tower of Babel in the plains of Shinar by that great hunter of men's souls, Nimrod. Satan declared that he would become the most high and he devised a scheme where he can rule the world and every man must worship him. This scheme included the nations of the world setting up a system where his *man of sin* could take control of the entire system and he could rule the whole world. This man would be controlled by Satan and he would require every living soul to worship him and the beast that empowered him.

There has been opposition to Satan's plan by those who have believed that there is a God in Heaven who also has a plan for his people. His people who will not be on this earth for they shall be in his presence in the new heaven and new earth for eternity. The prophets of old have declared God's promises to the people of the world and many of them were killed because of their message in opposition to the plan of Satan.

Many saints of God have been killed because they trusted in God's only Son for eternal life and have rejected the message of this world concerning Satan and his kingdom on this earth. Multitudes of believers will be slain during the last forty years of the world domination during the time of the ten kings' reign of terror. The blood of the prophets, saints, and all who were slain on the earth, was found in the great city of Babylon that had its beginning at the tower of Babel.

A just and righteous God has no choice other than to bring total destruction upon a city that would allow Satan to deceive them for so many centuries into following after his diabolical scheme.

CHAPTER 19

The Coming of Christ in Power And Glory

C hapter 19 opens with the hallelujahs in heaven over the destruction of the great city of Babylon as described in chapter 18.

> *And after these things I heard a great voice of much people in heaven, saying, Alleluiah! Salvation and glory, and honor, and power, unto the Lord, our God; For true and righteous are his judgments; for he hath judged the great whore, who did corrupt the earth with her fornication, and hath avenged the blood of his servants at her hand.*
>
> Rev. 19:1, 2

After God has destroyed the city of Babylon there is heard a great voice of multitudes in heaven saying, Hallelujah unto the Lord our God. You are the one who has wrought salvation to your people. All glory and honor and power belong to you. God is true and righteous for judging the great whore that corrupted the earth with her love affair with the world. The blood of God's servants has been avenged through his judgment of the murderer of the righteous.

And again they said, Hallelujah! And her smoke rose up forever and ever.

Rev. 19:3

Again they say Hallelujah to the Lord our God for the smoke of the city will rise up forever and ever. The smoke is a continual reminder that God is just in his judgments of a wicked ungodly system of rebellion.

And the four and twenty elders and the four beasts fell down and worshiped God that sat on the throne, saying, Amen. Hallelujah!

Rev. 19:4

The twenty four elders (those who represent the church), and the four living creatures (heavenly beings who forever declare the attributes of Jesus Christ), join in on the worship of God and they fall down, saying, Amen. Hallelujah. Almighty God you have had the last word and we praise you for your justice.

And a voice came out of the throne, saying, Praise our God, all ye his servants, and ye that fear him, both small and great.

Rev. 19:5

A voice comes out of the throne telling all of God's servants to praise our God. All those who fear him both small and great are to praise our God.

And I heard, as it were, the voice of a great multitude, and like the voice of many waters, and like the voice of mighty thunderings, saying, Hallelujah! For the Lord God omnipotent reigneth.

Rev. 19:6

All of God's servants and all those who fear him respond to the voice of the angel. There is a great multitude that sounds like many waters and like mighty thunders, saying, hallelujah. They praise the Lord God because he is omnipotent and he is about to begin his reign over the affairs of his creation.

The Marriage of the Lamb

In order to understand the *marriage supper of the Lamb*, we must first understand the events that take place in a typical oriental wedding. The boy meets the girl and they have a period of courtship before he proposes to her, she accepts the proposal, and they become engaged. The boy pays a dowry to the girl's father and she becomes his legal wife because she has been purchased by him. He goes away for a while and prepares a place for his new bride to live. She doesn't know when he will return, but she must be ready at all times for him to take her to their new home.

One day he shows up, just as he had promised, and takes her to his new home and the marriage is consummated. In a few days the bride prepares herself in her finest attire and the groom presents her to his father. The father prepares a great feast and invites many guests to celebrate the marriage of his son and new wife. And they live happily for ever after.

As for Christ and his bride, the church, there was a brief courtship while he was here on the earth. The engagement took place and the dowry was paid with his own blood and she was redeemed to become his wife. He went back to heaven to prepare a place for his bride and will come again to receive her unto himself. We have seen that all of these events have happened by this time in the study of the book of Revelation. The only event that has not been fulfilled is the presentation of the bride to the father and the marriage feast that is to follow. The marriage supper of the Lamb is that great event that will happen at the beginning of the millennial reign of Jesus Christ here on the earth.

Let us be glad and rejoice, and give honor to him; for the marriage of the lamb is come, and his wife hath made herself ready.

Rev. 19:7

The bride of Christ (the church) has been caught up to be with the bridegroom at the rapture and has been with him for several years and has become his wife. She has been purified and is now ready to be presented to the Father who has prepared a great feast in honor of the bride and groom. Let us be glad and rejoice, and give honor to him.

> *And to her was granted that she should be arrayed in fine linen, clean and white; for the fine linen is the righteousness of saints.*
>
> Rev. 19:8

Even though the bride has some spots and blemishes from her life here on earth, she is granted the honor of being dressed in fine linen, clean and white. The fine linen is the righteousness of the saints. She has been washed in the blood of the Lamb and made clean and dressed in the righteousness of Christ. When the Father sees her he will see the pure white linen given to her by his righteous Son.

> *And he saith unto me, Write, Blessed are they who are called unto the marriage supper of the Lamb. And he saith unto me, These are the true sayings of God.*
>
> Rev. 19:9

John is instructed by the angel who has been talking to him, to write. Blessed are those who are called to the marriage supper of the Lamb. It is a great honor to be called to such a prestigious affair. Only those who are associated with the groom will be allowed to attend. According to Matthew 25, only those with oil in their lamps (those with the Holy Spirit in their lives) will make it to the wedding. And only those who have been allowed to enter the kingdom will be invited to the marriage feast. The supper will probably be here on earth after the Son of God returns to earth in power and glory at the end of the tribulation period and after the battle of Armageddon. The Jews and Gentiles who have shown kindness to Christ, or one of his brethren, and have made it through the tribulation, will be invited to the feast. They will be blessed because God has spoken the truth concerning these things.

And I fell at his feet to worship him. And he said unto me, See thou do it not! I am thy fellow servant, and of thy brethren that have the testimony of Jesus. Worship God; for the testimony of Jesus is the spirit of prophecy.

Rev. 19:10

When John is told of these things he falls at the feet of the angel who is talking to him. He is overjoyed at the promise of the marriage feast and begins to worship the angel who revealed the truth to him. The angel instructs him to not worship him because he is just another servant just like his brethren who have the testimony of Jesus. The testimony of Jesus is what all prophecy is about. There is no one who should be worshiped aside from God.

The bride has made herself ready in anticipation of the feast, but there is one more tremendous event that must take place before the feast may begin. The Lord must return to earth and defeat his enemies and then he can begin to reign with his new bride. What a celebration this will be!

The Second Coming of Christ

And I saw heaven opened and, behold, a white horse; and he that sat upon him was called Faithful and True, and in righteousness he doth judge and make war.

Rev. 19:11

In chapter 4 we saw a door opened in heaven and John was instructed to come up hither. The vantage points for all of John's visions were from heaven. Now we see the curtains being pulled to reveal heaven and the greatest show of all time is about to begin. The Son of Man who was seen on the white cloud in chapter 15 is now revealed to be riding upon a white horse. The first time he came to earth he came to save the people from their sins. This time he has come to judge the earth and make war. He is called Faithful and True because his judgments will be performed with justice and righteousness in accordance with the truth of his word.

> *His eyes were like a flame of fire, and on his head were many crowns; and he had a name written, that no man knew, but he himself.*
>
> Rev. 19:12

The one riding upon the white horse uses his eyes to look upon the world that he is about to return to and set up his kingdom of peace and righteousness. As he looks from his lofty height upon the white cloud in heavens he sees a world in complete turmoil. The ten kings have taken control of the entire world. Another man comes along and subdues three of the ten kings and takes over dominion of the world. The ten kings give all of their authority to this new dictator. The dictator sits in the temple of God in Jerusalem and declares that he is god. He makes an image of the beast and requires that all people should take a mark in their foreheads or in their right hand and that they should worship the beast, his image, or the number of his name. All those who do not take his mark or worship him shall die from being beheaded, or die from the lack of ability to buy or sell. Israel has been driven into the wilderness where their God will protect them for three and one half years. Those who do not make it to God's safe keeping will be murdered, raped, and beheaded. If he does not return soon there will be none to save.

His eyes are like a flame of fire. As he looks at his creation his anger is welled up within him and he is going to judge all that his eyes behold that is evil. Fire consumes and destroys whatever it comes in contact with. In this case it will be the evil nations of the world that have been deceived by Satan to do his will.

He has been given complete authority as indicated by the many crowns upon his head. This is his creation and he may do with it as he chooses. Since he is holy, just, and righteous, he must judge accordingly. No man can know the name that has been given to him. He alone can know this name.

> *And he was clothed with a vesture dipped in blood; and his name is called The Word of God.*
>
> Rev. 19:13

The one riding upon the white horse has his garments dipped in blood. The blood is his own blood that he shed upon the cross of Calvary for the sins of the people that he is about to judge. The world has rejected his salvation and that is the reason that it is in such a mess.

The name that is given to him is, *The Word of God*. He spoke and the world was created. He will speak and the world will be judged. His Word is the only weapon that he needs to judge his enemies. It is by his word that man can either be redeemed or lost for eternity.

> *And the armies that were in heaven followed him upon white horses, clothed in fine linen, white and clean.*
>
> Rev. 19:14

There is a multitude of angels in heaven. One hundred million and thousands and thousands of angels were seen around about the throne. They, and all of the saints in glory, will follow him riding upon white horses. They are all clothed in his righteousness of fine linen, white and clean. The saints have been made clean and white and adorned in their finest ready for the great supper that is to follow the judgment of the nations.

And out of his mouth goeth a sharp sword, that with it he should smite the nations, and he shall rule them with a rod of iron; and he treadeth the winepress of the fierceness and wrath of Almighty God.

Rev. 19:15

The word of God is a sharp two-edged sword. This sword is in his mouth and by it he will smite the nations of the world. He will open his mouth and speak, and the evil nations shall be no more forever and ever. Those who do remain shall be under his control and he will rule them with a rod of iron. If they try to get out of control he will judge according to his word.

The nations of the world will be trodden under foot of the one who is treading in the winepress of Almighty God. God's fierceness and his wrath have reached the point of no return. He, in his long suffering, has given mankind every possible chance to repent. For those who have, there is a righteous kingdom awaiting them. For those that do no repent, there is only judgment and eventually the lake of fire awaiting them.

And he hath on his vesture and on his thigh a name written,
KING OF KINGS, AND LORD OF LORDS.

Rev. 19:16

There will be no doubt as to who he is for he will have his name written upon his vesture and on his thigh. His name is KING OF KINGS AND LORD OF LORDS. He has come back to earth to establish his kingdom that shall last for one thousand years on this earth and for all eternity in the new heaven and earth. He truly is King of kings and Lord of lords. There has never been a king who has ruled with righteousness. It will be a kingdom of peace and tranquility, where the lion will lie down by the lamb, and the child shall play with the asp.

Armageddon

The time for the destruction and annihilation of Gentile rule, and the *times of the Gentiles* has come. The God of heaven and earth has warned the world many times in his word that such a time is coming. In chapter 16 we have already seen that the three evil spirits that come out of the mouths of the dragon, beast, and false prophet are calling for the nations of the world to be gathered to the battle of that great day of God Almighty. They are to be gathered to a place called Armageddon. The nations of the world will be judged and they will never again be seen as having any influence in the governing over the affairs of the people of this world. It is time for a kingdom that will be ruled with justice and righteousness. If we want to understand more about this final battle for control of the entire world we must look at other scriptures such as the books of Daniel, Joel, and other Old Testament prophecies.

> *And I saw an angel standing in the sun; and he cried with a loud voice, saying to all the fowls that fly in the midst of heaven, Come and gather yourselves together unto the supper of the great God.*
>
> Rev. 19:17

There has never been a time of carnage since the time of the flood when all but eight people on the earth were destroyed. By this time the population of the earth will have been reduced to somewhere under three billion people. Of the remaining three billion people there will no doubt be a small remnant that will be saved and go into the kingdom. All of the others will be destroyed by the Word that proceeds out of the mouth of the Lamb of God. The stench and putrefaction will be beyond belief.

God in his wisdom has prepared a means whereby the world can be cleansed from such carnage. There is seen an angel standing in the sun, crying with a loud voice for all of the fowls of the air to gather themselves together for the great supper of the great God.

> *That ye may eat the flesh of kings, and the flesh of captains, and the flesh of mighty men, and the flesh of horses and of them that sit on them, and the flesh of all men, both free and bond, both small and great.*
>
> Rev. 19:18

There is no one, except those who have put their trust in the Lamb and those who have befriended his people, who will be exempt from the judgment that is to immediately come upon the inhabitants of this earth. All flesh eating birds will feast upon kings, captains, mighty men, animals, all men both free and bound, both small and great. A person's position in life will not assure him of victory over this judgment. The fact is that the greater position that one has will almost guarantee his destruction because he has had an influence in causing the masses to worship the beast and his image.

> *And I saw the beast, and the kings of the earth, and their armies, gathered together to make war against him that sat on the horse, and against his army.*
>
> Rev. 19:19

As John looks, he sees the beast (the world dictator, the antichrist), and the kings of the earth (the ten kings that were in control of the world and have given their authority to the dictator), and their armies gathered together to make war against the Lamb of God on his white horse and against the army of the Lamb. The birds have already been dispatched in preparation for the outcome of this futile rebellion by finite men against their Creator who has infinite power and is almighty. Who does man think that he is that he is in any way a match for the one who is omnipotent?

The Beast and False Prophet Cast into a Lake Of Fire

And the beast was taken, and with him the false prophet that wrought miracles before him, with which he deceived them that had received the mark of the beast, and them that worshiped his image. These both were cast alive into a lake of fire burning with brimstone.

Rev. 19:20

The mighty dictator of the whole world, and his sidekick the false prophet, were taken. There was no contest, they were simply taken. The false prophet had power to perform many miracles in order to deceive the people of the world into receiving the mark of the dictator and worshiping his image. Both of these evil men were taken and cast alive into a lake of fire burning with brimstone. In the next chapter, verse 10, we see that they both are still in the lake of fire after one thousand years. From this we know that the souls of man are immortal and they shall either be blessed or punished forever and ever. The choice of where our souls shall spend eternity is up to each and every one of us. We can choose to follow the Lamb of God and have eternal life or choose to follow the deceiver of this world and end up in the lake of fire that burns forever and ever.

Remnant Were Slain With the Sword

And the remnant were slain with the sword of him that sat upon the horse, which sword proceeded out of his mouth; and all the fowls were filled with their flesh.

Rev. 19:21

The remainder of the armies of the world was slain by the sword of the Lamb of God who is sitting upon the white horse. The sword that proceeds out of his mouth is the word of God. The Lamb spoke the world into existence and he will speak it out of existence. All of the birds of the air were filled with the flesh of all those who fought against the ruler of heaven and earth. The remainder of all the deceived people of the world will be judged as soon as Satan is cast into the bottomless pit and Jesus sets up his kingdom.

Satan has just been dealt another devastating defeat from which he can never recover. He has put all of his eggs in one basket. For centuries he has been influencing and manipulating the governments of the world to accomplish his purpose. The nations have finally been brought together as one governing institution under the direction of the ten kings that are completely under his control. Out of this confederacy of ten kings there has arisen a dictator who has won control of the entire world. The dictator and his right hand man, the false prophet, have established a world government that has deceived the people of the entire world to worship Satan by taking his mark and worshiping his image. This most powerful and influential kingdom has been defeated by the one riding upon his white horse with the sword in his mouth.

Satan has nowhere to turn. His only power and might has been defeated. He will be chained and bound and cast into the bottomless pit where he will remain for one thousand years. At the end of the thousand years he will be set free and he will again stir up the nations of the world to destroy the one who is ruling the world in righteousness. His efforts will fail and he will be cast into the lake of fire along with his friends the beast and false prophet.

In this chapter we have seen the end of Gentile rule. The rule of evil men over the inhabitants of the earth shall never happen again. The kingdom of peace, justice, and righteousness shall last forever and ever. The stone *made without hands* has struck the feet of the great image. The image has toppled and been broken to pieces. The stone shall become a great mountain and fill the whole earth. The Lord Jesus Christ has prevailed to reclaim the earth as his own. The world is his creation and he is the rightful owner of it.

Chapter 20

Satan in the Bottomless Pit, And the 1,000 Year Reign of Christ

Satan Bound in the Bottomless Pit

With the loss of the ten kings, dictator and the false prophet, Satan, the great deceiver, has just lost his ability to rule over the people of the world. He had deceived them into believing that they, through his power and guidance, could create a perfect world. There was one thing wrong with their plan. The world cannot be perfect when it is controlled by sinful men. Sin must be taken care of before God can create a new heaven and earth wherein shall dwell righteousness. He will start by dealing with the one who brought sin into the world through his deception of Adam and Eve in the Garden of Eden.

> *And I saw an angel come down from heaven, having the key of the bottomless pit and a great chain in his hand.*
>
> Rev. 20:1

God sends an angel down to earth from heaven to deal with the one who has deceived the world. The angel has a key in his hand that can give access to the bottomless pit. In chapter 9, we saw another angel who had been given the key to the bottomless pit and he let loose many demons that tormented man for five months. It was discussed in chapter 9 that the bottomless pit is probably in the center of the earth. This angel is different from the one in chapter 9 for he also has a great chain in his hand.

> *And he laid hold on the dragon, that old serpent, who is the devil and Satan, and bound him a thousand years, And cast him into the bottomless pit, and shut him up, and set a seal upon him, that he should deceive the nations no more, till the thousand years should be fulfilled; and after that he must be loosed a little season.*
>
> Rev. 20:2, 3

The angel from heaven lays hold on the dragon. The dragon is unable to resist the angel from heaven and he is bound with the chain in the angel's hand. The dragon will remain bound for one thousand years. He will have a long time to think about what he has done to the people of this world. Time will not change his mind on how he can become the most high and be worshiped by all of mankind. Time will only give him time to think about how he can accomplish his purpose for himself.

We are reminded that this dragon is that old serpent who appeared to Eve in the garden. He is also known as the devil and Satan, the deceiver of mankind.

After the angel lays hold on the dragon he is cast into the bottomless pit. The angel shuts him up and puts a seal upon him so he cannot escape for one thousand years. After the one thousand years, he will be loosed for a short period of time.

The time of one thousand years will be the duration of the millennial reign of Jesus Christ here on earth. The devil will not be around to deceive the nations or the people who live during these one thousand years. There will still be sin in the world because it is the nature of man to sin. Man will just not be able to say "*The devil made me do it*," for he will not be present. The kingdom will be an external kingdom. Man will be judged by what he does outwardly but not what is in his heart. Man will rebel at the one who is ruling with a rod of iron, but will not be able to resist outwardly or he will be put to death. When he is loosed for a short period of time at the end of the one thousand years, it won't be hard for Satan to find the people and nations of this world to rebel against the one who is ruling with justice and righteousness.

The First Resurrection

There have been resurrections in the past and there will resurrections in the future. There was a resurrection when Jesus rose from the grave. Another resurrection occurred at the same time when the graves were opened and many came forth and walked around the city of Jerusalem. There will be a resurrection at the time of the rapture of the church.

There will be a resurrection of the Old Testament saints prior to the millennial reign of Christ here on the earth. There will be two more resurrections yet to occur, one for the just and one for the unjust. These two resurrections discussed in this chapter are called "the first resurrection" and "the second resurrection." Since there have been several resurrections prior to these two, the indication of the first and second is to distinguish between the resurrection of the just and the resurrection of the unjust.

> *And I saw thrones, and they sat upon them, and judgment was given unto them; and I saw the souls of them that were beheaded for the witness of Jesus, and for the word of God, and who had not worshiped the beast, neither his image, neither had received his mark upon their foreheads, or in their hands; and they lived and reigned with Christ a thousand years.*
>
> Rev. 20:4

As John looks around he sees thrones (plural), and they (plural) sat upon them, and judgment was given unto them (plural). There is no identification as to who the ones sitting on the thrones might be, and there has been much supposition as to their identity. The most common beliefs are that Jesus, and his bride—the church—that has just arrived from heaven, will be given the duty of judging the tribulation saints. The ones sitting on the thrones are thought to be the Lord and his twelve apostles (Mat. 19:28) or Jesus and the twenty four elders. If the twenty four elders represent the church, and if the twelve apostles also represent the church, then the distinction between the interpretations are insignificant.

The ones to be judged are the believers who have been martyred during the tribulation period. They have been beheaded for their witness of their Lord and savior Jesus Christ. They have been faithful to the word of God as presented by the one hundred and forty four thousand, the two witnesses and the angel proclaiming the everlasting gospel. They refused to believe the lies and delusions of the world dictator and his false prophet, and have refused to worship the beast, or his image, or take his mark.

Because of their faith in Jesus they will be resurrected and live with Christ for one thousand years. They will live and reign with Christ for the entire duration of his kingdom on the earth, and will live with Him through all eternity on his new earth.

> *But the rest of the dead lived not again until the thousand years were finished. This is the first resurrection.*
> Rev. 20:5

By this time the majority of six billion people will have been killed either by the new world order or by the antichrist during his reign of terror. Only the believers in Jesus Christ will be resurrected at this time. All those who have refused to fear God and worship the Creator of this world will remain in the grave, Hades, for an additional one thousand years. This is the first of the two remaining resurrections.

Blessed and holy is he that hath part in the first resurrection;
on such the second death hath no power, but they shall be
priests of God and of Christ, and shall reign with him a
thousand years.

Rev. 20:6

Those who are resurrected in the first resurrection will be blessed and will be made holy. They shall be priests of God and of Christ and shall reign with him for one thousand years. The second death will not have any power over them. Death means separation. Physical death is separation from the body, and spiritual death is separation from God.

In order to escape the spiritual death, one must be born again by the Spirit. If one is born once he must die twice. If one is born twice he will only die once. When a person leaves this world in physical death and has not received the Lord as his savior he must die again and suffer eternal separation from God. The ones spoken of in this passage have believed in Jesus as their savior, and since they have been martyred for their belief in him, they will never again have to experience a second death. They will forever live with their Lord and savior whom they have loved.

Satan Loosed

One thousand years ago the Lord Jesus Christ came to earth and established his kingdom. The Gentile armies of the world were defeated and Satan was cast into the bottomless pit. The kingdom that was promised to Abraham and his descendants is about to come to an end. The kingdom is a major topic in the Old Testament but is conspicuously ignored in the New Testament.

And when the thousand years are expired, Satan shall be
loosed out of his prison, And shall go out to deceive the
nations which are in the four quarters of the earth, Gog
and Magog, to gather them together to battle; the number of
whom is as the sand of the sea.

Rev. 20:7, 8

After one thousand years in the bottomless pit, Satan is loosed for a short period of time. His time in prison has not diminished his desire to be worshiped; he has not forgotten that the means to accomplish his goal is through the governments of the world that he has been so gifted into deceiving and beguiling to accomplish his wicked desires. He is allowed to be set free to go into every corner of the earth and again deceive the nations of the world. It will not be difficult in finding an enormous number of people who are not happy with a kingdom of righteousness. Satan will convince the nations that they should overthrow the King of kings and Lord of lords and he will lead them into battle against the Most High. Remember, this kingdom is an external kingdom. People will be judged by their outward rebellion against a righteous king. They will be put to death for any evidence of rebellion. They will not be held accountable for their inward thoughts and hatred of righteousness, but they will be more than ready to follow anyone who will lead them into battle against the one who is keeping them under his thumb.

> *And they went up on the breadth of the earth, and compassed the camp of the saints about, and the beloved city; and fire came down from God out of heaven, and devoured them.*
> Rev. 20:9

Satan and his army have come from every part of the earth to the city of Jerusalem where the Lord has set up his headquarters for his kingdom. The entire army circles the beloved city of Jerusalem where the saints are located and are ready to destroy them. Before Satan and his army can strike, Almighty God sends down fire from heaven and devours them all. This is *Satan's last stand* and he will be defeated before he even begins to fight.

Satan Cast into The Lake Of Fire

And the devil that deceived them was cast into the lake of fire and brimstone, where the beast and the false prophet are, and shall be tormented day and night forever and ever.

Rev. 20:10

The greatest deceiver that ever existed has failed in his attempt to defeat the Lord. The devil is taken and cast into the lake of fire and brimstone. His two comrades have been there for one thousand years and are still alive. The devil, beast, and false prophet will be tormented continually forever and ever. There will be no rest from their torment day or night for all eternity.

The Second Resurrection
The Great White Throne Judgment

And I saw a great white throne, and him that sat on it, from whose face the earth and the heaven fled away, and there was found no place for them.

Rev. 20:11

John sees a great white throne with someone sitting upon it. The one sitting upon the throne is about to judge the unjust people who have lived upon the earth since the beginning of mankind. The only one worthy to judge is the Son of Man who has lived in human flesh just like they have, and was tempted in every way that they could possibly be tempted. He was tempted with the lust of the eyes, the lust of the flesh, and the pride of life, but did not yield to the temptation. Jesus alone knows their hearts and can judge them with righteousness and justice.

The Creator of heaven and earth shall cause both heaven and earth to disappear and their place will never exist again.

And I saw the dead, small and great, stand before God, and the books were opened; and another book was opened, which is the book of life. And the dead were judged out of those things which were written in the books, according to their works.

Rev. 20:12

All of the dead who ever lived upon the earth shall stand before God. Their position of importance and influence has nothing to do with who will be judged. The books that have recorded their works are opened, and also the book of life was opened. The dead are judged out of those things that were written in the books. They were judged according to their works. Satan has deceived mankind into believing that their good works will outweigh their bad works and that they can enter into God's presence because they are basically good people. God will oblige them by judging them in accordance with their desire.

And the sea gave up the dead that were in it, and death and hell delivered up the dead that were in them; and they were judged every man according to their works.

Rev. 20:13

It will not matter where the souls of the dead have been since the time of their death. If they died at sea and were never given a proper burial they will be resurrected. All those that have died and live in the grave will be resurrected. Hell (Hades) will give up the souls of those who have died and are in it. They will all be judged in accordance with their works as recorded in the books.

And death and hell were cast into the lake of fire. This is the second death.

Rev. 20:14

There will be no more death and there will be no more hell. Henceforth there will be no more death, only eternal life for those who have believed in the savior of the world. There will be no more hell for it has been emptied of all those who have been in torment throughout the centuries. They both will be cast into the lake of fire and destroyed forever and ever. This is the second death. This is eternal separation from the presence of a loving God who has done everything he could do to provide eternal life, if people would only fear him and trust him.

> *And whosoever was not found written in the book of life was cast into the lake of fire.*
>
> Rev. 20:15

God wants to be assured that there has been no mistake in the final judgment of mankind, so he looks into the book of life to see if their name is written in it. If their name is not found, they will be cast into the lake of fire along with the devil, beast, and false prophet. This will be the end to all wickedness on the part of mankind. There will be a new heaven and new earth wherein shall dwell righteousness forever and ever.

CHAPTER 21

A New Heaven and a New Earth,
And the New Jerusalem

U p until this point in the Revelation of Jesus Christ, we have seen the revelation of Jesus Christ in chapter 1 and the history of the church age and the main characteristic features of each church in chapters 2 and 3.

Chapters 4 and 5 are heavenly scenes showing that the Lamb is the only one worthy to open the seals and allow the narrative to proceed. Chapters 6 through 10 reveal what is going to happen to the nations and peoples of the world during the time between the rapture of the church and the start of the tribulation period.

There is very little to reveal how the antichrist is elevated into becoming the world dictator in this section, however, he must be in a place of authority by this time in order to sign a peace treaty with Israel and allow the temple to be rebuilt. The temple is being used by Israel to worship their God in chapter 11. This is the beginning of the tribulation period. The battle of Ezekiel 38 and 39 probably happens in the first three and one half years of a declared peace.

The main characters of the end time, and some of the events of the tribulation period, are revealed in chapters 12 through 19 where Jesus Christ appears upon a white horse to judge the nations of the world that have disregarded his existence and authority throughout the ages. The beast and false prophet are cast into the lake of fire, and the kings and nations are judged. In chapter 20 Satan is bound for one thousand years, the first resurrection allows the righteous to enter the kingdom, Satan is loosed and cast into the lake of fire, and the unrighteous are judged and cast into the lake of fire. There is very little to indicate that the millennial reign of Jesus Christ is taking place at this time. In fact, the mention of Israel is conspicuously left out of this book which indicates that the book is about God's judgment upon the Gentile nations and people of the world.

Since all of the unrighteous of the world are judged and punished by this time, the only ones left are the righteous. This means the remainder of the book is about what God has prepared for his people for all eternity. This is sometimes the most difficult part of the book to understand since no man, except John the apostle, has ever seen what is in store for those who have put their trust in the Lord Jesus Christ. Even John tries to describe the beauty and glory of the new heaven and new earth by describing them as beautiful gems and earthly things.

The New Heaven and New Earth

And I saw a new heaven and a new earth; for the first heaven and the first earth were passed away, and there was no more sea.

Rev. 21:1

God is going to create a new heaven and a new earth where his children can dwell with him in all of his majesty and glory. There will be no remembrance of the old world to remind us of the sin and unrighteousness that had such a hold on the inhabitants of that old world. Peter tells us that the old world will pass away with fervent heat and be destroyed. There will be no need of the sea to provide the water to nourish the ground to provide for the food to sustain life as required in the world as we know it. All nourishment and refreshment that will be required for the glorified body will be provided by the Lord in the new earth.

> *And I, John, saw the holy city, new Jerusalem, coming down from God out of heaven, prepared as a bride adorned for her husband.*
>
> Rev. 21:2

> *In my Father's house are many mansions; if it were not so, I would have told you. I go to prepare a place for you. And if I go to prepare a place for you, I will come again, and receive you unto myself, that where I am, there ye may be also.*
>
> John 14:2, 3

> *But as it is written, Eye hath not seen, nor ear heard, neither have entered into the heart of man, the things which God hath prepared for them that love him.*
>
> 1 Cor. 2:9

God has promised his children that he will prepare a place for them where they shall dwell with him for all eternity. As we look at the dwelling place that God has prepared, we cannot help but be amazed at the beauty and glory he has created. He will dip into his vast treasure trove and construct the most beautiful city that has ever existed. He will use some of his most precious gems, transparent gold, enormous pearls, and crystals. All of these items will be not only for his children to enjoy, but they will reflect his glory and majesty to remind us of how much he loves us. We shall inherit all things and all that God possesses shall be for us to enjoy.

The first thing that John sees is the Holy City, the New Jerusalem, coming down from God out of heaven. This beautiful city is prepared by God and is adorned as a bride adorned for her husband. Never is there a time when a woman is more beautiful than on her wedding day, the day when she is presented to the one she loves and has chosen to spend the rest of her life with. This city is most beautiful and is the place where God shall spend eternity and dwell with his children.

> *And I heard a great voice out of heaven saying, Behold, the tabernacle of God is with men, and he will dwell with them, and they shall be his people, and God himself shall be with them, and be their God.*
>
> Rev. 21:3

John not only sees the beautifully adorned city, but he also hears a voice out of heaven, saying, *Behold, (gaze upon) this city because it is going to be the tabernacle of God. The tabernacle is where God dwells and it is now going to be in the midst of his children.*

What a time this will be when man shall be God's people and he will be with them and he will be their God. There has never been a time like this since the time when Adam walked and talked with God in the cool of the evening. The relationship between God and man will again be the way God intended it to be. He will be our God and we will be his children having unbroken fellowship forever and ever.

> *And God shall wipe away all tears from their eyes; and there shall be no more death, neither sorrow, nor crying, neither shall there be any more pain; for the former things are passed away.*
>
> Rev. 21:4

In this life, and in particularly the last days of life on this earth, there will be many tears caused by the suffering and death of loved ones. All of this suffering will be done away with because the former things are passed away. There will no longer be any tears because all of the things that cause tears will be removed from the lives of God's children. There will no longer be death but everyone shall receive eternal life. There will be nothing that causes sorrow, crying, or pain for we shall be in the presence of our heavenly Father. After living in a world that is full of tears, death, sorrow, crying, and pain it is hard to imagine a world that is void of such suffering. Oh how much our Father cares and loves us!

> *And he that sat upon the throne said, Behold, I make all things new. And he said unto me, Write; for these words are true and faithful.*
>
> Rev. 21:5

The one sitting upon the throne declares that he will make all things new. There will be a new heaven, a new earth, a New Jerusalem, and a new relationship between the one on the throne and his children. John is instructed to write because the things that are about to be revealed to him are true. They are not only true but they are faithful, and will be accomplished just as he declares them to be.

> *And he said unto me, It is done. I am Alpha and Omega, the beginning and the end. I will give unto him that is athirst of the fountain of the water of life freely.*
>
> Rev. 21:6

The one who sat upon the throne informs John that his work of creating a new heaven and new earth is completed. He is the first and the last, and the beginning and the end, He is eternal. Anyone who is thirsting after knowing God, and having fellowship with him, will have all of his desires completely satisfied.

> *He that overcometh shall inherit all things, and I will be his God, and he shall be my son.*
>
> Rev. 21:7

Everyone who has overcome the penalty for sins by trusting his Son shall inherit everything that is promised to his Son, the Lord Jesus Christ. We will be joint heirs with Christ because we too have become the sons of God.

> But the fearful, and unbelieving, and the abominable, and murderers, and whoremongers, and sorcerers, and idolaters, and all liars, shall have their part in the lake which burneth with fire and brimstone, which is the second death.
>
> Rev. 21:8

Those that are fearful of trusting Jesus as their Savior, and are unbelievers in the saving grace of Jesus, have committed abominable sins such as murders, sexual perversions, witchcrafts, worshiped idols, and have habitually lied. The reward for their sins is the lake of fire which is the second death. The first death is separation from the body and loved ones. The second death is eternal separation from God.

The New Jerusalem

> And there came unto me one of the seven angels who had the seven vials full of the seven last plagues, and talked with me, saying, Come here, I will show thee the bride, the Lamb's wife.
>
> Rev. 21:9

One of the angels with the last plagues, as seen in chapter16, comes to John and begins to talk with him. The angel says to John to come with him and he will show him the bride, the Lamb's wife. Since the description that follows indicates that the bride is the New Jerusalem we must conclude that the angel is not actually speaking of the Lamb's bride, but that it is adorned and as beautiful as if it were his bride. The indication is that it has an intimate relationship with the Lamb.

And he carried me away in the Spirit to a great and high mountain, and showed me that great city, the holy Jerusalem, descending out of heaven from God, Having the glory of God; and her light was like a stone most precious, even like a jasper stone, clear as crystal; And had a wall great and high, and had twelve gates, and at the gates twelve angels, and names written on the gates, which are the names of the twelve tribes of the children of Israel: On the east three gates; on the north three gates; on the south three gates; and on the west three gates.

Rev. 21:10-13

As John is carried away in the Spirit to a great and high mountain he must have been amazed at what he sees. Right before him appears that great city. It is enormous in size and is spectacular to look upon. It is the Holy Jerusalem, not the restored old city of Jerusalem that has been a bone of contention among the nations for hundreds of years, but a new creation of God coming down out of heaven from God.

It was created as a place for God to dwell among his children and created to reveal the glory and majesty of God. The only light in the city was the glory of God and it shone like a most precious stone, jasper stone (diamond) clear as crystal. Everything in this city is designed to reflect the glory of God and reveal to his children who He is.

When the beauty of this city is revealed to us, I have always been somewhat disappointed because it appears to be very gaudy and modernistic. I have always looked forward to my mansion as being a rustic log or timber-frame home constructed of earth tone materials. I have come to realize that this city is not my mansion; it is the throne of God and it is to reveal his glory and beauty, and its construction will do just that.

God wants his children to see the riches of his majesty and share with them the inheritance of his vast treasures of gold and precious stones. God has revealed all of the riches in his city and besides that there will be many mansions (dwelling places) for his children either in the enormous city or on the new earth surrounding the city.

The city was surrounded by a great and high wall with twelve gates into the presence of God. There were twelve angels guarding the gates and the names of the twelve tribes of the children of Israel were inscribed on the gates. There were three gates on the east side, three gates on the north side, three gates on the south side, and three gates on the west side. The way into the presence of God has always been through the gate (Jesus Christ), who came through the lineage of the twelve tribes of Israel because of the faith of Abraham and his descendants.

> *And the wall of the city had twelve foundations, and in them the names of the twelve apostles of the Lamb.*
>
> Rev. 21:14

The high wall surrounding the New Jerusalem is constructed upon twelve foundations. God does not reveal whether there are twelve foundations stacked one upon another or the foundation is divided in twelve sections, one under each of the twelve gates. No matter which is correct, we are told that the names of the twelve apostles will be written in them. The words of the twelve apostles as revealed to them by their Lord when he was with them here on the earth is the very foundation upon which our belief and faith is founded upon.

> *And he that talked with me had a golden reed to measure the city, and the gates of it, and its wall.*
>
> Rev. 21:15

The angel with John has a golden reed in his hand and is instructed to measure the city, gates, and walls. God always surveys and measures what belongs to him.

And the city lieth foursquare, and the length is as large as the breadth; and he measured the city with the reed, twelve thousand furlongs. The length and the breadth and the height of it are equal.

Rev. 21:16

The city is declared to be foursquare, a perfect square with the length and breadth the same. The breadth and length are twelve thousand furlongs in length. A furlong is 600 feet long and twelve thousand furlongs is 1364 miles long and wide. This covers an area in size equal to the western half of the United States.

The length, breadth and height of the city are equal so the height is also 1364 miles high. We are not told whether the city is constructed in the shape of a cube or is in the shape of a pyramid. Either shape is feasible. Since the rapture of the church the human body does not seem to be affected by the force of gravity and we are not told whether there will be a gravitational force on the new heaven and earth, so it may be possible for the believers to travel in a vertical motion as well as in a horizontal movement. If this is the case, then the streets may run vertical as well as horizontal.

And he measured the wall of it, an hundred and forty and four cubits, according to the measure of a man, that is, of the angel.

Rev. 21:17

The angel measures the wall surrounding the city and finds that it is one hundred and forty four cubits high. A cubit is the length between a man's finger tips and his elbow, or about 18 inches long. This would make the wall 216 feet tall. The measurement is performed by the angel, but he uses man's measurement as a basis to determine its length.

And the building of the wall of it was of jasper; and the city was pure gold, like clear glass.

Rev. 21:18

The wall is constructed of jasper or clear like a pure diamond. The city is constructed of pure gold, but transparent like clear glass. The beauty of God's glory shining through these materials will be beyond imagination.

> *And the foundations of the wall of the city were garnished with all manner of precious stones. The first foundation was jasper; the second, sapphire; the third, chalcedony; the fourth, emerald; The fifth, sardonyx; the sixth, sardius; the seventh, chrysolite; the eighth, beryl; the ninth, topaz; the tenth, chrysoprasus; the eleventh, jacinth; the twelfth, amethyst.*
>
> Rev. 21:19-20

The twelve foundations of the wall around the city are garnished (inlayed) with all manner of precious stones. God has an unlimited amount of wealth and precious stones at his disposal. It is 5456 miles around this foundation, and we do not know how tall it is, but just think of the vast amount of precious stones it will take to garnish this structure.

Each foundation is garnished with a different stone. The first is jasper or clear like a diamond. The second is sapphire, blue but clear like a diamond. The third is chalcedony, like an agate, sky-blue with other colors running through it. The fourth is emerald, a bright green color. The fifth is sardonyx, a red and white stone. The sixth is sardius, a reddish stone. The seventh is chrysolite, a golden transparent stone. The eighth is beryl, sea-green in color. The ninth is topaz, yellow-green and transparent. The tenth is chrysoprasus, another shade of green. The eleventh is jacinth, and is a brownish-yellow color. The twelfth is amethyst, or purple in color.

The glory of God shining through the city and walls, and reflecting upon all of these gorgeous precious stones, will be spectacular. We cannot begin to imagine what God has in store for his children in the New Jerusalem and for all eternity.

And the twelve gates were twelve pearls; every several gate was of one pearl; and the street of the city was pure gold, as it were, transparent glass.

Rev. 21:21

There are going to be twelve gates and each one is made from a single pearl. We often hear of meeting Saint Peter at the pearly gates; this is where that phrase originates. Those who are looking for Saint Peter will find his name inscribed in one of the foundations. There will be an angel standing at the gate guarding the Holiness of God and only allowing those who have been covered with the blood of the Lamb entrance into the city.

The street of the city will be pure gold of transparent glass. The street will reflect the glory of God and remind us of his eternal deity.

And I saw no temple in it; for the Lord God Almighty and the Lamb are the temple of it.

Rev. 21:22

There is no temple in the New Jerusalem because the earthly tabernacle and temple were only a shadow of things in heaven. The temple was where God dwelt among his people and revealed who he was. Everything in the temple was a picture of the Lord Jesus Christ. The gate indicated that there is only one way into the presence of God. The brazen alter represents Christ shedding his blood for the remission of sins. The laver shows that we must be cleansed by the washing of the word. Both our hands and feet, which represent our walk and service, must be clean in order to perform god's service. Jesus is our sustainer, as seen in the table of showbread. He is the illuminator and light of the world, as seen in the lamp stand. The altar of incense depicts Jesus as our intercessor. Inside the Holy Place was the mercy seat and Ark of the Covenant. Jesus is our propitiation as indicated in the mercy seat and the ark which held three articles of importance. The first were the tablets of stone providing God's standard of how we ought to live. The second was the bowl of manna that reminds us of God's provision, and the third is the rod that budded indicating that we too shall be resurrected.

Since the real temple, and the Lord God Almighty, and the Lamb are in the city, there is no more need of types and shadows.

> *And the city had no need for the sun, neither of the moon, to shine in it; for the glory of God did lighten it, and the Lamb is the light of it.*
>
> Rev. 21:23

The only light in the city will be provided by the glory of God and the light of the Lamb. There will be no further need of the light from the sun and moon.

> *And the nations of them who are saved shall walk in the light of it, and the kings of the earth do bring their glory and honor into it.*
>
> Rev. 21:24

All those who have been saved by the blood of the Lamb shall have access into the city and walk in the light of God's glory. The *nations* indicate that both Jew and Gentile will have access to the city. All of the kings who have been redeemed shall bring their glory and honor into the city. The only glory and honor that they have is what God has allowed them to have while they were here on the earth.

> *And the gates of it shall not be shut at all by day; for there shall be no night there.*
>
> Rev. 21:25

There shall never be any night there since the glory of God is eternal and it shall shine continually. There is no need to shut the gates because only the redeemed shall be in the new heaven and new earth. There will be no ungodly who will be restricted from entering the city.

And they shall bring the glory and honor of the nations into it.
Rev. 21:26

God has a place for the Gentiles, as well as for the Jews and the church. The Gentile nations shall bring anything that they have that will bring glory and honor to God and to the Lamb, and it shall be brought into the city,

And there shall in no way enter into it anything that defileth, neither he that worketh abomination, or maketh a lie, but they who are written in the Lamb's book of life.
Rev. 21:27

We have already seen that God has prepared a place for Satan and his angels, which is the lake of fire. All of the ungodly, who have chosen to follow Satan's pernicious ways, are already cast into the lake of fire along with their leader. These are the ones who have been defiled, work abominations, and make a lie. These people shall be in bondage for eternity and will never have access to the presence of God.

Only those who have received Jesus Christ as their Savior, and have their names written in the book of life, shall enter into the presence of Almighty God and the Lamb, and experience all of their glory and honor.

Don't wait until it is too late to trust Jesus as your Lord and Savior, and you too may share in his inheritance and enjoy the experience of sitting and walking in the light of his glory forever and ever.

CHAPTER 22

The Final State of Believers,
and Benediction

The Throne of God and the Lamb;
The River of Life; The Tree of Life

The first five verses of chapter 22 are a continuation of the description of the New Jerusalem and the blessings that shall flow from the throne of God for all eternity. The first blessing is the water of life and the second blessing is seen in the tree of life. God has declared that this world will pass away but His word will never pass away. There are two things that are essential for us to become a child of God and be declared worthy to enter into his presence in the new heaven, the new earth and especially into the New Jerusalem where his throne will exist for eternity.

The first thing is the word of God whereby we are convicted of our unrighteousness and led into the saving knowledge of the Son of God; without his word there is no knowledge of God. The second essential is the tree of life where our Savior bled and died for the sins of the world; without this act of sacrifice there would be no salvation for mankind and no one could enter into God's presence. These two things will be displayed in the New Jerusalem as a reminder of the grace of God and an evidence of his eternal love for his children forever and ever.

And he showed me a pure river of water of life, clear as crystal, proceeding out of the throne of God and of the Lamb.

Rev. 22:1

The angel shows John a pure river of water of life. Many times in the scriptures God's word is compared with some form of water and we should not look for any different meaning in this instance. Jesus declared himself to be the Word, and he also declared himself to be the living water. The word of God is the living water that can lead to eternal life. No wonder that it is declared to be *water of life*. This river is clear as crystal; it is not polluted in any way, but is the pure word of God.

The river of water of life is proceeding out of the throne of God and of the Lamb. This pure, crystal clear river will continue to flow from the presence of God and the Lamb as a continual reminder of the grace of God revealed in what he has done for us in the past, present, and future. We should never tire of hearing God's word declared in its purest form, straight from the throne of God and of the Lamb.

In the midst of the street of it, and on either side of the river, was there the tree of life, which bore twelve kinds of fruits, and yielded her fruit every month; and the leaves of the tree were for the healing of the nations.

Rev. 22:2

Try to picture this most spectacular scene described here. The street leading to the throne of God is gold, like transparent glass. There is a crystal clear stream flowing beside it and a huge tree planted in the midst of the street with its branches reaching across the stream. This tree is declared to be the tree of life. The beauty of the reflection of the tree upon the water and the golden street is beyond description.

God's plan of salvation and redemption of mankind was accomplished by having his Only Begotten Son die upon a tree, the cross of Calvary. The tree of life, in all of its glory, will be a constant reminder of this most solemn act of mercy and grace. We should never cease to be amazed at its simplicity and wonder.

The tree of life will bear twelve kinds of fruit. There will be a different fruit every month. This amazing wonder of God's grace will never become mundane or complacent as we shall be reminded by the fresh fruit being produced anew each month.

The leaves of the tree were for the healing of the nations. Nations speaks of Gentiles. The many Gentile nations that have been in existence throughout history could have been healed from their sin sickness if they would have availed themselves of God's grace by accepting his Son for the forgiveness of their sins. We can only imagine what a different world this could have been without the wars and divisions between the nations. The only hope for any form of peace in this world is to allow our Lord and Savior to have his way in the hearts and lives of the people of this world.

> *And there shall be no more curse, but the throne of God and of the Lamb shall be in it, and his servants shall serve him; And they shall see his face; and his name shall be in their foreheads.*
>
> Rev. 22:3, 4

This world was cursed when Adam sinned in the garden and man was separated from the face of God. This curse has been lifted and God will continually dwell with his children, and his throne and the throne of the Lamb will be in their midst. Those who have fallen in love with him will be his servants and they will serve him because of their love for him. There will never again be a time when we shall be separated from the face of our Savior, for we shall see him face to face. We shall not only see him but we will be identified as one of his by his name being placed in our foreheads. There has never been a time like this in human history and what a joy it will be to have such a relationship with our Lord.

And there shall be no night there; and they need no candle, neither light of the sun; for the Lord God giveth them light, and they shall reign forever and ever.

Rev. 22:5

It is hard to imagine a place where there is no night. There will be no need of a candle or artificial light. There will not even be any need for the sun during the day. How can this be? It can happen only because our God will be in our midst and he is light. His very presence and his eternal glory will provide all the light that we need. Not only will the eternal Godhead provide us with light but they will reign forever and ever.

This is the end of God's description of the New Jerusalem and his dwelling place for his children. There is much that is not told about the new earth or the new heaven that God has prepared for those that love him. The things that are told should be sufficient for us to get excited about being in his presence and seeing his glory.

THE BENEDICTION

And he said unto me, These sayings are faithful and true; and the Lord God of the holy prophets sent his angel to show unto his servants the things which must shortly be done.

Rev. 22:6

The angel that has been revealing the future events to John assures him that the things that he has seen are both faithful and true. They are true because the Lord God of the holy prophets of old is the one who has revealed them to him. An omniscient God desired to reveal to his servant (John) the things that will come to pass in a very short period of time at the time of the end of this age. When the things that John has seen begin to come to pass, they will all be completed before one generation passes away. A merciful God will not allow the suffering to continue any longer than is necessary for him to accomplish his judgment upon the nations of the world and see his people return unto him and to their promised land.

> *Behold, I come quickly. Blessed is he that keepeth the sayings of the prophecy of this book.*
>
> Rev. 22:7

When Jesus returns for his bride at the rapture he will come quickly. It will be in a moment, in the twinkling of an eye. When he comes back to set up his kingdom, at the end of the tribulation period, he will appear suddenly and every eye shall see him.

The book of Revelation begins with a blessing for those who read, and to those that hear the words of this prophecy, and keep those things which are written in it. The book concludes with a blessing to all those who keep the sayings of the prophecy of this book. This is the only book in the scriptures that promises a blessing to all those that read and hear and keep these prophecies, yet is the most ignored book of all.

> *And I, John, saw these things, and heard them. And when I had heard and seen, I fell down to worship before the feet of the angel who showed me these things.*
>
> Rev. 22:8

John is amazed that he has been allowed to see and hear the things that had been revealed to him. He must have been thoroughly filled with amazement, confused, and overwhelmed at the visions that God revealed unto him. He felt an urgent need to worship someone or something, and the only one around was the angel who had shown him these things so he fell at his feet and worshiped him.

> *Then saith he unto me, See thou do it not; for I am thy fellow servant, and of thy brethren, the prophets, and of them who keep the sayings of this book. Worship God.*
>
> Rev. 22:9

The angel will not allow John to worship him because he is only the messenger, and a fellow servant of the God of heaven who is the revealer of his secrets. The angel declares that he is no better than the prophets, and to those who keep the sayings of this book for they are all brethren and servants of the Living God.

God alone is worthy of any worship coming from John. We should all fall before an all-knowing God who knows the beginning to the end, and worship him for revealing the things that will happen in the future concerning this earth, the people of this earth, and his people.

> *And he saith unto me, Seal not the sayings of the prophecy of this book; for the time is at hand.*
>
> Rev. 22:10

John is told not to seal up the sayings and prophecy of this book for the time is at hand for the unveiling of Jesus Christ, The Son of God, and for his creation to understand what is in store for them in the near future. What a contrast to the instructions for Daniel to seal up the things that were revealed to him until the time of the end.

> *He that is unjust, let him be unjust still; and he that is filthy, let him be filthy still; and he that is righteous, let him be righteous still; and he that is holy, let him be holy still.*
>
> Rev. 22:11

It is decision time. The reading and understanding of this book should have an enormous effect upon the lives of all those who have studied the prophecies declared within its pages. The time is at hand for all who hear to make a decision on how the writings of this book will affect their lives. For those who do not believe, and take heed to God's word, there will be no blessing; the unjust will continue to be unjust, and the filthy will continue to be filthy. There is no hope for them in this world. On the contrary, those who do believe in God's only begotten Son will be made righteous because of their faith in their new-found Savior. Those who are righteous will continue to be righteous, and those who are holy (set apart to serve God) will continue to be holy.

And, behold, I come quickly, and my reward is with me, to give every man according as his work shall be.

Rev. 22:12

Again we are reminded that Jesus is coming quickly for his bride and she will be rewarded for her faithfulness to him. He is also coming quickly for the lost and they will be judged according to their works and then cast into the lake of fire.

I am Alpha and Omega, the beginning and the end, the first and the last.

Rev. 22:13

Jesus Christ is the eternal God who was with his Father in the beginning and will remain with him throughout eternity.

Blessed are they that do his commandments, that they may have right to the tree of life, and may enter in through the gates into the city.

Rev. 22:14

All of the blessings that are written in this book are afforded those who keep the commandments written in this book. Two of those blessings are recorded here. The tree of life which is in the midst of the New Jerusalem will be made available to the faithful. They will be granted entrance into the city through the pearly gates, walk the streets of gold, and dwell in the dwelling places prepared for them by their bridegroom. They shall be in the presence of their Lord and Savior forever and ever.

For without are dogs, and sorcerers, and whoremongers, and murderers, and idolaters, and whosoever loveth and maketh a lie.

Rev. 22:15

There will be no more filthy people to contend with, no more people who practice witchcraft, or sexually perverted people, or those who hate their brother and commit murder, or those who worship false gods and idols, or those who love to tell lies or practice to deceive. All of these will be banished from the presence of God and be cast into outer darkness.

> *I, Jesus, have sent mine angel to testify unto you these things in the churches. I am the root and the offspring of David, and the bright and morning star.*
>
> Rev. 22:16

Now Jesus comes forward unto John and declares that he is the one who has sent the angel to testify that these things are true. The message was to be delivered unto the church so it would not be without understanding of what is to take place in the near future, and until the time that it is in its eternal home in the new heaven. This is the first mention of the church since the close of chapter 3, which is a good indication that the church is in heaven during the events of chapter 4 until now. The credentials that Jesus uses to prove who he is are that he is the offspring of David, the promised messiah who is to appear on earth and set up his kingdom that shall remain forever and ever. He is also the bright and morning star that shall appear in the end time to lead his people (Israel) into their promised homeland where he will be King of kings and Lord of lords.

> *And the Spirit and the bride say, Come. And let him that heareth say, Come. And let him that is athirst, come. And whosoever will, let him take the water of life freely.*
>
> Rev. 22:17

Both the Holy Spirit and the bride (the church) are looking for his return and bid him come. Those who have read and heard and believed the message that is given in this book say, Come.

Anyone who is thirsting after righteousness says, Come. Jesus Christ is the living water and he will freely give eternal life to anyone that is anxiously looking for his return. *Whosoever* means you or anyone else who has the desire to know the One who has been unveiled in this book.

> *For I testify unto every man that heareth the words of the prophecy of this book, If any man shall add unto these things, God shall add unto him the plagues that are written in this book; And if any man shall take away from the words of the book of this prophecy, God shall take away his part out of the book of life, and out of the holy city, and from the things which are written in this book.*
>
> Rev. 22:18, 19

Warning—Warning

These two warnings are self explanatory. They are very severe because they are an indication of how precious and pure the word is to the God of heaven who declared his word to mankind. It must not be tampered with without tremendous consequences. Those who attempt to alter God's word are in danger of receiving the plagues that are written in this book, or be excluded from the presence of God in the eternal place that he has prepared for those who are obedient to his word and love him.

> *He who testifieth these things saith, Surely, I come quickly. Amen. Even so, come, Lord Jesus.*
>
> Rev. 22:20

Jesus Christ is the one who gave testimony to the words that John recorded for our edification. He is the one who says for sure I am coming quickly. Amen, so be it. All those who are looking for his return join in unison with the chorus, EVEN SO, COME, LORD JESUS.

His return for his bride is her hope. There is no greater hope for the church than to hear the shout and the sound of the trumpet and to be changed in a moment, in the twinkling of an eye and fly through the air and meet our Savior in the air and forever be with him.

The grace of our Lord Jesus Christ be with you all. Amen.

Rev. 22:21

Everything that God has for us in the future is given to us only because of the grace (unmerited favor) of our Lord Jesus Christ. May this grace be with us and sustain us until he comes. Amen.

CONCLUSION

God, who at sundry times and in divers manners spoke in time past unto the fathers by the prophets, Hath in these last days spoken unto us by his Son, whom he hath appointed heir of all things, by whom also he made the worlds…

Heb. 1:1, 2

God has revealed himself to the fathers in an orderly but progressive manner. He revealed himself to Abram as God, Almighty God, Lord, and his provider and sustainer of life. Each time God had an encounter with Abram he would reveal his character in a manner that fit the situation.

God met with Moses and gave him the law, which was God's standard by which man should conduct himself in every aspect of life. Man was unable to live up to God's standard; therefore, the law showed man that he was a transgressor and the law became a schoolmaster to lead him to Christ.

God revealed his character to his children through the prophets. Sometimes, such as in Daniel, the people could not understand what was being told them because God shut up the understanding until the time of the end. God finally revealed himself to the world through his Son and still he was rejected by many. In the last days, God will open the understanding of his word so believers need not be ignorant concerning the happenings during the end time.

Jesus declared the message of this book, through the aid of his messenger the angel, to John to be given to the seven churches of Asia. The message was not sent to the house of Israel. The message was to declare to the church how God was going to deal with the church and the Gentile nations until the time of the end.

If you want to know how God is going to deal with Israel during the tribulation period, and during the millennial kingdom, you must go to the Old Testament prophecies. In fact Israel is conspicuously absent in the book of Revelation.

The understanding of the true character of God has been slowly revealed to man. In like manner, the understanding of God's word is gradually revealed as God has seen fit. Early in the beginning of the church, the believers could not understand much of the teachings of eschatology.

After the awakening, during the reformation, the believers could not understand how the prophecies concerning the end time could be taken literally. During the eighteen hundreds and early nineteen hundreds the church was filled with great men of God and much was written about the book of Revelation and end time prophecies. Even at this time many writers could not see how the scriptures could be taken literally. From the writings of this age the traditional teachings of eschatology were derived. Since that time there has been very little change in the traditional teachings of end time events. The world has changed drastically during the past one hundred years and it only seems practical that our interpretation of the scriptures should also be reevaluated in light of the new developments on the world scene.

At the time of the establishment of the traditional teachings, the world was still in the horse and buggy days. If a man wanted to travel the world he would board a sailing ship and be at the mercy of the trade winds for his destination. Later the steam engine was invented and the ships could travel in a straight line much quicker to arrive at their destination. The only travel across our great land or any other place in the world was either on foot or on horseback. Then the steam engine was placed into a great machine and put upon rails to transport a man across the country in a few days.

Since the early nineteen hundreds there has been the invention of the automobile, airplane, spacecraft, telephone, computer, modern warfare, and many other modern conveniences. It is easy to see how the scriptures can be taken literally today in light of all the new technology.

The testimony of my own life and the life of most Christians should be an example of how God can gradually reveal the understanding of his word to those who have the desire to know the truth.

I accepted the Lord Jesus Christ as my personal savior in 1953 at the age of 17. I was intrigued with the teaching of the rapture and believed that it would be imminent. The teaching of end time events has always been an interest to me. At an early age in my Christian life I studied many books and charts concerning eschatology. After a few years, I began teaching Sunday school and eventually started teaching the book of Revelation and many other Old Testament prophecies.

My teaching was very much reliant upon the teachings of the many authors that I had studied. The traditional teachings were adhered to even though many times I did not see or understand how the author had arrived at his understanding of the subject. Some examples of my questions were; the rise of the antichrist upon the white horse in the sixth chapter, the antichrist and false prophet described in chapter 13 as the beast out of the sea and the beast out of the earth respectively, the tribulation following immediately after the rapture of the church, and who was the woman on the beast and the eighth head mentioned in chapter seventeen. If the beast out of the sea is the antichrist why does he have seven heads and ten horns, and which one of the seven heads is wounded to death? If the beast out of the earth is the false prophet why does he have two horns?

Even though I didn't completely understand I continued to teach what I had read from the writings that were written by great men of God during the turn of the twentieth century. After all they were learned men and someday I would also understand as they did.

During the time span of about thirty years of learning and listening to others, I learned about the plan to have a New World Order where all of the world would be joined together under the authority of one government. I also learned of The Club of Rome which was an organization established for the main purpose of deciding how to divide the entire world into ten regions.

They accomplished this task and printed a map of the world divided into ten regions. I thought that these two subjects were intriguing since the book of Daniel declares that there will be ten kings and that they will take control of the entire world until three of them are subdued by the antichrist. These ten kings will be in control of the entire world and they will relinquish their authority unto the antichrist until the time Christ comes to set up his kingdom. How does this information fit into the teaching of the book of Revelation?

During my studies I noticed two things about the teachers of eschatology. The first is that the subject of the ten horns of Daniel and Revelation is widely ignored mainly because no one understands the subject. The ten kings are generally declared to be ten countries in Europe that shall comprise the revised Roman Empire. The scriptures say that the ten kings have received no kingdom as yet and that they shall govern over the whole world, not just Europe. In some manner this kingdom will be the revised Roman Empire, but it will not be limited in size to the original Roman Empire.

The second thing that happens is that if an author does not understand a subject it is just ignored. It is my firm belief that God wants us to understand his word and that he will reveal it in his timing.

One Sunday afternoon early in the 1990's, after teaching a Sunday school class, my wife and I went on an afternoon drive. We were discussing the teaching and talking about current events.

The more we talked about what was going on in the world, the quieter I became and the more I began to realize that we may be looking at some of the things all wrong. I told my wife that it may be that we should reevaluate the way we look at the book of Revelation. She wanted to know what I was thinking but I said I cannot tell you yet until I go home and study the scriptures.

After reading through the entire book of Revelation I told her what I had been thinking. It dawned upon me that maybe the tribulation would not start until after chapter 10, and chapters 6 through 10 had to do with a period of time ruled by ten kings known as the New World Order. This all seemed to fit and was in total agreement, and dovetailed precisely with chapter 24 of Matthew.

When I looked at the book from this point of view I got excited because the world is ready to establish the New World Order and the goal of the UN is to reduce the population of the earth by fifty percent. This is exactly what will happen according to Matthew 24, and Revelation 6. This will create a period of time between the rapture and the tribulation of twenty-five to forty years, or one generation.

Pre-tribulation believers believe that the rapture must happen prior to the opening of the first seal. We must be logical and realize that there are many events that must happen before the tribulation starts. There must be a period when ten kings rule the entire world. Three of these kings must be subdued to allow the antichrist to be elevated into a place of authority. The antichrist must sign a peace treaty with Israel to initiate the start of the tribulation.

If we tie the rapture and the tribulation together, then we know that the rapture cannot occur for several years and it is not imminent. Why get excited about something that is not going to occur for several years? The rapture of the church is her blessed hope and is the one thing that keeps her living Godly realizing that the Lord could come back at any moment.

For the first time, some of my questions were beginning to be answered. Since that time I decided to teach my family and friends about what I believe and they have agreed that for the first time the book makes sense. This prompted me to write this book in hopes that others may get excited about the imminent return of our Lord and Savior.

The other questions that have been in the back of my mind for many years began to be answered and are discussed in the context of this book.

May the writing of this book be a blessing to all who read and love the word of God. May we all get excited about the soon rapture of the church. It is probably much closer than any of us realize.

Behold, I come quickly.
Even so, come, Lord Jesus.

www.ingramcontent.com/pod-product-compliance
Lightning Source LLC
Chambersburg PA
CBHW061817040426
42447CB00012B/2688